UNDER AGE
ANGEL

11TH AIRBORNE

The Angel Division

By James E. Richardson, M.S.
U.S. Army Retired

Limited Edition

_____ of _____

First edition

Library of Congress Catalog Card Number: 96-92041

ISBN: 0-942495-56-X

Published by
James E. Richardson
1611 Apple Street
Wisconsin Rapids, WI 54494

Printed by
Palmer Publications, Inc.
PO Box 296
Amherst, WI 54406

This book is dedicated to:

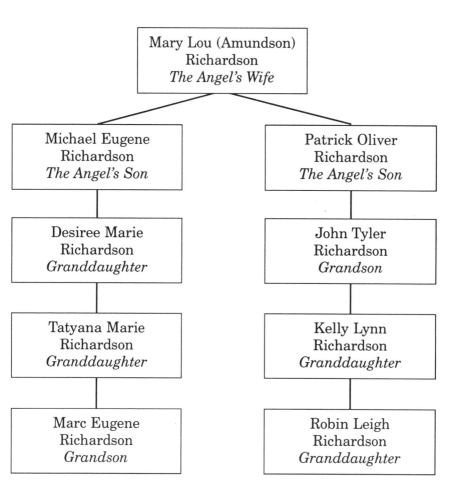

Mary Lou (Amundson) Richardson
The Angel's Wife

Michael Eugene Richardson
The Angel's Son

Patrick Oliver Richardson
The Angel's Son

Desiree Marie Richardson
Granddaughter

John Tyler Richardson
Grandson

Tatyana Marie Richardson
Granddaughter

Kelly Lynn Richardson
Granddaughter

Marc Eugene Richardson
Grandson

Robin Leigh Richardson
Granddaughter

By example, the author has instilled within his sons and grandchildren that they owe their allegiance to God, family and country.

It was with his wife, sons and grandchildren in mind (I love them) that motivated the author to attempt this autobiography of his life and to educate them on their heritage and love of country.

As author of this autobiography my thanks go out to my wife, Mary Lou Richardson.

She acted as my proofreader, typist and critic. Without her I am not sure if I could have sustained the motivation to complete this book. Let me say thanks, again.

THE BEGINNING

Hot, humid and hazy was the type of weather that existed in Pacific, Missouri, on August eighth in 1929. Earlier in the night heat lightning had been prevalent in all directions from the shotgun house that was rented by Herman and Florence Richardson.

Herman, who was also known as Slim, and Florence, also known as Flo, had moved to Pacific, Missouri, a short time ago in order for Slim to take a job with Pioneer Silica. They had been married in September of 1928. Flo was scheduled to have her first child August of 1929. Therefore, she had become very apprehensive as her due date drew near.

The shotgun house that Slim had rented was down by the railroad tracks and not far from the local tavern. On the night of August eighth, a bar room brawl had ensued and during the fight, a shot rang out—a man screamed, staggered up the street and fell in front of Slim and Flo's house, close to Doctor McNay's car. Doctor McNay was in the process of delivering the firstborn to Slim and Flo. At the exact time that the man on the street had died, an infant cry could be heard coming from the shotgun house.

The Underage Angel had just made his entrance into the world. Little did he know, at this time, the trials and tribulations that lay in front of him. They named this Angel James Eugene Richardson. The first name coming from a respected brother of Slim's and the middle name from Gene Tuney, a heavyweight champion boxer that Slim admired.

Slim had boxed Gene Tuney while he was in France. He, as the heavyweight champion of the 89th Division (Midwest Division) and Tuney, as champion of the AEF (American Expeditionary Force) and a Marine. To be sure, Slim was a fine figure of a man. He was five-feet eleven inches in height, weighed in at one-hundred-ninety pounds and Irish in appearance, that is dark wavy auburn hair and steel grey eyes. He had a gold tooth that shined when he smiled, which was often. In his community, he was highly respected by the majority of the people and feared by the rest. He was, by far, the best driller and powder monkey in any of the mines around Stanton, Missouri. To sum it up, Slim was a dandy of his time.

Flo, on the other hand, was an outstanding young lady who was not afraid of work. She was tall, six feet, and weighed about one-hundred-thirty pounds. She carried herself with poise and dignity. Flo was of German extraction—with a maiden name of Binsbacher, she had to be a German-American. When Slim announced he was going to marry the "Old German's" daughter, you knew it was going to happen, and it did.

After the marriage in Stanton, Missouri, they moved to Pacific, Missouri, where Slim worked in the Pioneer Silica mine and Flo was a housekeeper. After a few months, they moved to Cherry Valley, Missouri, to work in the iron mine. Then they moved to Stanton, Missouri, for employment in the Acid Mine, an iron mine, therefore, it was in Stanton, that the Underage Angel grew into boyhood.

Those who worked in the mine had a caste system among the workers. If you met on a path, the weaker had to get off the path and let the stronger go by. If you wanted to challenge, you stayed on the path. When that happened, the miners would wrestle to see who had the right of passage. Needless to say, Slim walked the paths without challenge. He was cock-of-the-walk.

Of course, being cock-of-the-walk would get Slim into trouble (on occasion), and he would be summoned into court. On this particular time, they were running late for court and Flo was driving from Stanton to Steelville, Missouri. Flo was a good but too-fast driver. While she was driving, she was also nursing the Underage Angel. In the back seat were Slim and a character witness for him. Flo's driving scared the character witness to the point of distraction. When they arrived at the courthouse in Steelville, the witness made the comment that was probably the fastest titty any youngster has ever had and lived. The court case did not amount to anything and was dismissed.

Slim and Flo, along with the Underage Angel, now resided with the "Old German" in a beautiful farm. The building was a two-story building with a wrap-a-round porch with beautiful columns all around. The farm had a two-acre vineyard, barn and thirty-eight acres of pasture and woods. The Underage Angel was now a toddler. He was fascinated by fire. He delighted striking kitchen matches and watching them burn. When he was told not to do this, he did it on the sly. On one occasion, he was in the outside toilet and, as he would watch the flame burn down, he would throw the match into the hole. This caused the paper in the hole to ignite, and the fire coming back through the hole scared the hell out of the Underage Angel. Needless to say, he burned the outhouse down. The "Old German," his grandpa, gave him one

2

hell of a spanking and that was the end of his playing with fire.

He was a very curious toddler and was aware of things around him. The Angel would watch as his dad drove the car. He figured he knew how to operate the auto. So, when Slim parked the car for the day, it was on a hill. The Underage Angel knew if he played with the gear shift and let the brake off, the car would roll. This he did and the car rolled down the hill completely out of control. At the bottom of the hill, it ran up and bent over a sapling and hung there. Flo was frantic, and Slim was proud of his son. He thought that a child doing this at two years old was a terrific thing and a good bragging point at the mine.

Slim could, at times, be an embarrassment to Flo. On one occasion, a carnival came to Sullivan, Missouri, at homecoming time. Slim had scored out early at the mine and had been drinking some that day. He was feeling so good that he did not shower after his shift. He came home as red as he could be from the iron ore dust. He told Flo that they were going to the homecoming carnival. He was a fastidious dresser; therefore, he dressed over the iron ore dust. At the carnival, the carnie wrestler challenged anyone from the audience to come forward. Slim took the challenge and climbed into the ring. He stripped down to his shorts and was standing in his corner of the ring as red as could be from the iron ore dust. The crowd broke up with laughter and Flo was completely embarrassed. The end result, however, was that Slim pinned the carnie wrestler in just a few seconds.

Slim liked to tell stories to the Underage Angel. One was the bear story. The bear story was as follows:

It starts off with Slim out doing road work to stay in shape. He is about six or seven miles into his run when he heard a noise behind him. On looking, he saw a very large bear coming out of the woods and running after him. At first, he tried to outrun the bear; however, the bear continued to gain on him. Finally, he thought why am I running when I can whip that bear. He then turned around and ran toward the bear. They were now running toward each other, both the bear and Slim growling. When they were very close, the bear stood up on its hind legs still growling. The bear's mouth was wide open when they made contact. At this point, Slim ran his hand and arm down the throat of the bear, took a hold of the bear's stomach and pulled. With a snap, he turned the bear inside out! Slim was great at telling stories and the Underage Angel would listen to them intently. Yes, he would believe them.

There was never a dull moment when Slim was around. He loved life and he lived it to the fullest. Slim enjoyed the movies and we went at least once a week. One week, we saw a very good western movie featuring Buck Jones. The day after the movie, I went to the barn with Slim to milk the cow. After milking, we let the cow out of the barn. Walking back to the house, we had to go by the cow. At this time Slim said, "Look at me. I'm Buck Jones," and he ran toward the cow and vaulted on its back. The cow then humped up vigorously and threw Slim rear end over appetite to the ground. Of course, he got up laughing and I thought it was the funniest thing I had ever seen. He made it fun to be alive.

Sundays we went to church and after church was visiting time. A friend of Slim's drove his team of mules out to our place and tied them up by the gate. Slim and this fellow were visiting and drinking moonshine and not paying attention to the mules. The Underage Angel slipped out of the group and went down to see the mules. He figured he would take them for a little ride. He had to work diligently to untie the reins from the gate post. When they were untied, he started to town with the mules and wagon. Bear in mind, that he was only four years old. Flo saw him going down the road with the mules and wagon and shouted the alarm. Slim, Flo, the visitor and the hired girl all ran to catch the Angel. When he looked back and saw them running to catch him, he whipped the mules with the end of the reins as hard as he could, but the mules would not run. The hired girl was the first to catch him. She drew in the reins to stop the wagon and the rest now caught up. Flo was very angry, but Slim got a kick out of the escapade.

Another event that happened that made Slim and Flo extremely happy was the birth of a daughter. This event happened on May 17, 1932. Everyone was extremely happy with the birth of Marcella Mae Richardson. The Underage Angel worshiped his sister.

We now moved from the farm into town. The move was made primarily to upgrade our standard of living, as this house was wired for and had electricity.

The extended family was now in the nadir of the great depression. The mines had closed and Slim had to take work where he could find it. He found work, but it was outside the country, to be specific, Chile, South America. We lived well, but we missed Slim. Sending money home was not like having Slim around stirring up things.

The depression, for me, was a time of learning. Stanton was situated on the Frisco Railroad the main migration route from St. Louis to San Francisco. Stanton was a coal and water stop and, therefore, had a rather large hobo jungle.

Entire families were on the move. People who possessed Ph.D. degrees were on the move. Therefore, I could take the leftovers from the evening meal, put them in a quart jar, go to the hobo jungle and bargain for stories. The stories were always outstanding.

At home, we always kept a pile of wood to be split. If a hobo came to the house for a meal, he would have to split wood for one hour for the meal. I must say that Grandma's meals were large. I found out that the difference between a bum and a hobo was a hobo would work, a bum would not.

The Angel at six months of age

*The Angel
First Grade*

The Angel Third Grade

*The Angel
Grade Five*

*The Angel
Eighth Grade
Graduation
1943*

Slim and Marcella
Richardson
1942

Slim and Marcella
Richardson
1947

John Binsbacher
(The Old German)
1942

Florence Binsbacher
Richardson (Flo)
1942

*The Angel's wife
and Mrs. John
1955*

*The Angel's—1944
Basic Training*

*Fred Terry and Slim
1942*

*Slim and two
unknown buddies
France 1918*

ELEMENTARY SCHOOL YEARS

The elementary school years were grades one through eight. My first year of school was not very exciting. The school was a mile out of town. Therefore, Flo hired a girl to pick me up, walk me to school and see that I got home in good order. I did learn that most of my fellow students had nicknames. My school chums were "Big Toe," "Six Fingers," "Buzzard," and "Tobacco Juice Buck." For some reason, I have never been able to figure out why the Angel did not have a nickname. He was just called "Gene" or "Jim" or "Rich." Of course, there had to be some reason for the nickname.

Big Toe received his nickname from the fact that he had hit his toe with a sledge hammer and his big toe never went back in shape. It was twice as large as his other big toe. Six Fingers had two thumbs on one hand. I would imagine that later in life he would have had one of them amputated. Buzzard had a nervous stomach and he had a tendency to vomit after he ate his lunch. Tobacco Juice Buck got his name from chewing tobacco to the point of it staining both sides of his mouth. Tobacco Juice Buck was in the first grade and had been there for three or four years. Therefore, he was much older and bigger than the rest of the first graders.

Because the Angel just thought it was an accepted name, he did not hesitate to call him Tobacco Juice Buck, little realizing that this would make him angry. After all, the big boys called him by his nickname, so the Angel did also. Bad choice of names, for he caught the Angel on the way home and beat the hell out of him. He sent the Angel home crying and bruised. When the Angel ran ahead and into the house, he told the hired girl what had happened. She, being about the same age and size of Tobacco Juice Buck, caught him on the way home and gave him a good beating. After he was beaten and down, she had the Angel stand over Tobacco Juice Buck and call him by his nickname ten times. Tobacco Juice never bothered the Angel again. In fact, later in life, they became good friends. Of course, by then the Angel was much bigger and stronger than Tobacco Juice Buck.

During the Angel's second year of school, the new schoolhouse was in operation. It was a very beautiful building. It had two rooms, with a folding partition between the rooms that could be opened to one large room. One room was grades one through four and the other room, grades five through eight. Each room had its own teacher. While the Angel appreciated going to the new school, he did not appreciate going to school. It was just hard to concentrate when the weather was good outside.

One of the teacher's eccentric methods of instruction and schoolroom order was to assign us fingers for requests. One finger in the air meant help was needed at the student's desk. Two fingers meant that the student wanted a drink of water. Three fingers was a request to go to the toilet. The most-used was three fingers. Since the toilet was outside, you could goof away fifteen minutes to a half hour before the teacher would send the big boys to bring you back to the room.

If you were fast-thinking, you had such a head start on the big boys that they could not catch you and bring you back to school. I also found out that if they were getting close to catching me, I would climb a tree. Being lighter than the big boys, I could climb higher on smaller limbs than they could. When they would see that they could not reach me in the tree, they would attempt to shake me out. The last resort, before they gave up on the Angel, was to rock me out of the tree. I could usually outlast the big boys. The Angel was also smart enough to select a tree within sight of a cousin's house. When he would see what was taking place, he would come out and run the big boys away.

By the time I was in the third grade, I had perfected my escape from school to a fine art. The third grade teacher had a particular method of discipline that hurt, but was funny at the same time. She would call you to the front of the room, place your left hand in her left hand, and using a switch (usually a peach limb), proceed to strike you across the back. This would make you go round and round in a circle. She used to say that this procedure would loosen your hide and make you grow.

The turnaround in education came to the Angel in the fourth grade. Education came easily to the Angel and his grades were always good; it was conduct that was the problem. A situation arose where the teacher and the Angel could not have a meeting of the minds. To establish rapport, the teacher would invite the student into the cloakroom where she kept the board of education. This was a paddle about two feet in length. She would bend you over a desk and administer the paddle to the gluteus maximus. The Angel had seen that happen to some of the other boys, so when he misbehaved and received his invitation to the cloakroom, he rebelled and the fight started. They fought tooth and nail through the cloakroom, classroom, down the steps to the basement, all the time hitting, scratching, biting and kicking. The fight went on and on. Finally, the Angel got a hold on the paddle and wrestled it from the teacher and threw it into the furnace. It had been a terrible fight. That night in bed, the Angel thought about the fight and the teacher, and it came to him that if she fought that hard to educate him, then there must be something good in education. While the Angel was still stubborn, he was now academically into education.

At the end of the fourth grade, the Angel was apprehensive about going into the so-called big room at school, primarily because the teacher in the big room was a man and had a reputation of being mean. The boys in the class all got together and brought excuse notes from home that would allow them to go the Veiled Prophet parade in St. Louis. The teacher would not give us an excused absence so we could go. This made us very angry and we went anyway. Of course, when we returned, the teacher gave us all a good spanking and threatened to keep us in our respective grade for two years. The latter did not materialize.

The boys got together and figured out how to even the score. The Halloween party was coming up and we made our plans around this day. During the week preceding Halloween, we took all the nuts from the bolts that held the outhouse on its foundation and set it directly behind the foundation and behind the cess pool. Then we made an abundance of noise. The teacher came running toward the outhouse to see what the trouble was. The flashlight that he had was used to scan the sweet clover field. He was so busy looking to see who was there that he did not focus his attention on the outhouse, but ran right at the door. He hit the cess pool with a splash. After pulling himself from the crap and goo, he continued to scan the area for one of the boys. He caught one of us climbing a tree. The next day school went as usual until the last hour of the day. He then put our names on the chalkboard for we boys to stay after school. We knew what was coming and it came. We had to wait in the little room until he called our name. The boy he caught climbing the tree was the first to be called into the big room. The teacher had him lay down across a desk and whipped him with a rubber hose. Each of us was then called, in turn, and received our punishment. Then, at the end, he called the boy who had been first and whipped him again for squealing on the rest of us. This was somewhat redeeming in our mind. He never brought the incident up again.

On another occasion, a minor thing happened. There were, in our school, two boys by the name of Gene, one in the fifth grade and one in the eighth grade. The one in the fifth was the Angel. At the end of recess, the teacher called out, "Gene, go ring the bell." Both of us took off to ring the bell, and arguing about which Gene he was talking about. Neither gave ground and both pulled mightily on the bell rope. We jerked it off the bell holder. Since the other Gene was the room teacher's pet, the Angel took the spanking. Just another in a long line of discipline measures that did not work.

Even with the things we had done to the teacher, and for some reason which the Angel does not know, he appointed the Angel to the "School Boy Patrol." The patrol consisted of a boy from the sixth grade, one from the seventh and one from the eighth. The boy from the sixth was the patrolman, the seventh was the patrol lieutenant and the boy from the eighth was the patrol captain. Our duty station was to see the other students across Highway 66, which was the main highway from St. Louis to San Francisco. We were issued a red cap, badge and white belt as our uniform. The patrolman would go west one-hundred yards from the crossings, the lieutenant would go the same distance east and the patrol captain would take charge of the crossing. Those on the outskirt patrol posts would place a school zone sign in the middle of the highway. On the Angel's duty station and just across the fence was a mean bull. The Angel could not resist teasing the bull until it would snort, paw the ground and charge. Of course, the fence would stop the bull. One day the Angel got to thinking and wondering about how much authority he had. He knew he had a badge and a belt which were symbols of authority. On this day, it was drizzling rain and ice was starting to form on the surface of the highway. The Angel decided to show his authority. A car-carrying tractor/trailer truck came down the highway. The Angel put his hand up in a stop configuration and the truck driver applied his brakes. When he did this, the trailer jack-knifed and came at the Angel. He had to run and climb the fence to get out of the way of the truck. What a dilemma—the truck on one side of the fence and the bull on the other. Fortunately, the driver of the truck got his rig under control, but in doing so, he had hit and destroyed the school zone sign. He shook his fist at me and continued down the road. I really did not care. At that time, it was just good to be alive. I reported the damage to the sign and was issued a new one. The other members of the patrol did not tell anyone about the incident.

About this time Slim came home from South America. It was now party time. The Irishman was on a roll. We traded the 1933 Chevy on a new deluxe model. It had all the gimmicks a car could have at that time: knee action, free wheel, cigar lighter, etc. The Angel was showing the cigar lighter to his cousin one day. We were watching the red and green lights on the cigar lighter when it was pushed in to make contact. My cousin inquired about the coil on the inside of the lighter. He wanted to know if it was still hot when the red went away. The Angel said, "Stick your finger in and find out." He did and found out. He still has a perfectly concentric fingerprint on the finger he used to test the heat of the cigar lighter.

Of course, I took advantage of Slim's homecoming to ask for a bicycle. No problem. He bought me the best one in town—a Goodrich knee action.

Flo figured that Slim's fun and games would slow down in time; they did not. The old cliche that absence makes the heart grow fonder did not work in this case. Flo said that she could not live with chicken one day and feathers the next. Therefore, a separation was inevitable. They agreed to separate and not to divorce at that time. The Angel and his sister would stay with the "Old German" (the grandfather). Staying with the grandparents was not a situation that created trauma. The Angel and his sister had always maintained an extended family relationship with their grandparents. We loved them. It was a pleasure in the evenings to hear the "Old German" play the French harp and my Irish and Cherokee grandmother teach us how to dance.

Moving into the seventh grade was smooth. By now, he had a tremendous appetite for education. This was coupled with the fact that we now had a different and extremely great teacher. She was an older lady who had been in the teaching game for quite a while. She would use the students' interest to build on in all directions. For instance, my area of interest happened to be military history. Using my interest, she would locate material for me such as Gunga Din (fine arts), moving armies from one area to another (logistics and geography) etc. She was, by far, the best teacher I had ever had. However, even our enjoying her method of instruction would not keep us in school on a good weather day.

Each boy in school always carried a fishing line and hook in his pocket. One very nice day, two of my friends and I decided to go fishing. So, we took off at first recess for The Frisco Pond. We had a great days fishing and started home from the pond. In the distance, we could see a large column of smoke. When we got closer to the fire, we could see that it was Lockhart's store burning. On arrival at the fire, we were told that a gentlemen had burned up in the fire. The gentlemen was elderly and had lived in a room over the store.

The old gentleman was known for making a superb horseradish dressing. Of course, he ate his own product. When they dragged his body out of the embers of the fire, it burst open. There was the stench of horseradish around the area, that if I think about it, I can still smell to this day.

When we returned to school the next day, the teacher talked to us individually and I know it made me feel bad for playing hooky on the preceding day.

With Slim being back in the country, I was enjoying the stories he told me. One of the stories was about hunting turkeys and it went as follows:

Slim would always start by telling the Angel the equipment he would need to take along for the hunt. You would need a hatchet, a fifty-foot length of rope, some matches, a gunny sack and of course, your rifle and one bullet.

The hatchet was needed to notch the tree, should the game go into a hole in a hollow tree. The notch would be at the bottom of the tree so you could rake leaves into the notch. The matches were used to light the leaves so you would smoke the game out of the tree. The gunny sack was to carry the game. The rope was needed to let yourself out of a tree or over a bluff. Being allowed one bullet made you a better shot.

Slim said that in going through the woods he came upon a flock of turkeys setting on a hickory tree limb. There was 11 hen turkeys and one old tom turkey. A hickory tree limb will crack if hit just right and then the crack will immediately go back together. Slim's dilemma was how to get the most turkeys with one shot. If he fired from the front he would get one turkey. If he fired from the side, he would only get two or three at the most. This is where being a powder monkey and knowing geometry came into play. If he figured right and his bullet would strike the hickory limb just right, it would crack; when it cracked the toes of the turkeys

14

would fall into the crack and the crack would immediately close, catching all twelve of the turkeys by their toes. He aimed carefully at the base of the limb and fired. It happened. He caught all twelve, now what? It was more than he could carry. Always on top of any situation, he climbed the tree, tied a rope around the base of the limb and around the outer area of the same limb. He then used the hatchet to chop the limb containing the turkeys from the tree. When the turkeys hit the ground they all started flapping their wings and lifted from the ground. Slim, not wanting to lose his catch, sat in the loop of the rope below the turkeys. Low and behold, they lifted off the ground with Slim in the sling. In the air he found that he could guide them by leaning left or right. In this manner he could guide his flight. Keeping them headed in the direction of home, he brought them into the yard. Of course, his father-in-law was very happy and they dined on turkey for some time to come.

When the Angel was small he honestly believed this story by Slim, but as each year passed the doubt become greater. However, the Angel still looks on this as a great story and one he would pass on to his youngsters later on down the road.

It was in the seventh grade that the Angel became completely enamored with the opposite sex. Yes, he had found girls. Oh, there had been times of experimenting during hide and seek play in the tie yard, but this was puppy love. In our school we had double desks, two students to a desk. If a boy was caught talking during class the teacher would make the boy set with a girl. Well, the Angel was caught and put with, what he considered, the best looking girl in the class. Of course, he proceeded to sweet talk her and he finally convinced her to meet him in the coal bin at recess. She did, and the Angel and the girl were so busy they did not hear the recess recall bell ring. After a while we realized that we had been making out too long so we concocted a story to tell the teacher. We tried our concocted story out, but it did not fly. After all, we were standing before the teacher and the class and both of us were covered with coal dust. How embarrassed we were.

By the time the seventh grade rolled around, the Angel had gone through a fast growth period. In the preceding year, the Angel had gone from 80 pounds to 160 pounds and had grown six inches or more in height. He looked like a man, even if he was only twelve. On Saturday night the Angel and some of his friends would go to the movie and later to a dance. The movie was in

Sullivan, Missouri, six miles from Stanton. It cost 15 cents to ride the bus, so we usually hitchhiked a ride by using our thumb. This one Saturday night was a little different; the Angel was alone. Low and behold a car stopped to pick him up. It was a 1939 Buick coupe. When the Angel opened the door he found an absolutely stunning girl around 25 years old. She gave him a ride and asked how far it was to the river. The Angel told her. She asked if he would like to ride to the Merrimack River with her. The Angel felt like shouting "Yes! Yes! Yes!," but he kept his composure and merely said "Yes." They drove down to the foot of Sand Ford mountain, where the girl came on to the Angel. Yes, the Angel found sex that night. For the next six or eight Saturday nights after the movie the Angel would be out on Highway 66 hoping against hope that this girl would come by again. There was absolutely no thought of being molested. Yes, the Angel had matured, but he never saw her again.

While in the seventh grade, the Angel's allowance was 25 cents per week. It sounds small now, but it was a sufficient amount then. A large hamburger was five cents, a malt was five cents, the movie was five cents, popcorn was five cents and for five cents you could have a cherry coke and read comic books in Shorty's Drug Store all afternoon. It was enough, but the Angel always wanted more. Therefore, Slim devised a way for the Angel to increase his allowance. The community hall was about 200 yards from the Old German's house. Slim would give me one shot a day with the rifle at the pulley on top of the flag pole. You would know when you hit it, because it would turn on its pivoting movement. If I hit, Slim would give me an extra nickel. I did not know it then, but this practice made an expert rifleman out of the Angel.

By this time World War II had begun with the Japanese attack on Pearl Harbor. That was on a Sunday, December 7, 1941. The next morning Slim was one of the first in line to try to enlist. He was definitely an adventurer. However, his enlistment was not to be. Slim had been gassed in World War I, and he only had one operating lung. Being physically rejected was a heavy blow to his pride. Therefore, he did the next thing he could do to help the war effort, he signed on to work in the shipyards in California. In the shipyards he worked as a chipper.

Flo also was active in the war effort for she worked in the small arms plant in St. Louis.

For the Angel it was a bad time; he wanted to enlist in the worst way, but was too young. He was big enough and mature enough that people would mistake him for 18 or more years old. In fact, people would stop him on the street or in a public building and ask him why he was not in the service; after all their boys were. This was very embarrassing to the Angel because when he would try to explain that he was only 12, they would not believe him.

At this time the pulse of the nation was rapidly beating toward a maximum output of war material. The railroads of the nation were running at full capacity. War material and troop trains ran by the hour instead of by the day. The railroad bulls made it very hard on a hobo or bum getting a free ride on a freight train. On the Frisco railroad, the one with the meanest reputation was Frisco Red. It was said that he would throw a hobo off a train while it was traveling at full speed. Riding freight trains had a calling for the Angel.

Because Stanton was a coal and water stop and train traffic was heavy, it usually happened that trains would pass each other in Stanton by way of a side track. That is, the east bound train would occupy the side track while the west bound train went by. When the west bound was clear, the east bound would pull out. The boys in town would catch a ride and go for about a mile until the train had to slow down for the breakie to throw the switch and catch his train. At that time the boys would jump off the train. It was dangerous, but fun.

One day without our knowing it, the breakie had asked the depot operator to throw the switch for him. This meant that the train did not have to slow down for the breakie to get back aboard. Well, the Angel and one other boy happened to be on that train. When the train did not slow down, the Angel and the other boy could not get off. It was a hot shot train and ran straight through to the Linden Wood Yards in St. Louis. The Angel and the other boy did not know it, but back in Stanton there was turmoil in the air. The father of the other boy contacted the railroad bulls in St. Louis to pick up the Angel and his boy who had been lured away by the Angel. Of course, he failed to mention that his boy was 17, six feet two inches tall and that the Angel was only 12 years old. The railroad bulls did not catch the Angel and the other boy, but they, on their own, kept building the quandary like a snowball, for the train they caught to take them back to Stanton was a train that went down the Mississippi River line toward Memphis, Tennessee.

When the other boy saw that we had caught the wrong freight train, it was moving too fast to get off. However, the other boy was about to try jumping off. The Angel talked him out of this foolish act. The train was a hot-shot and did not stop until it reached Chaffee, Missouri. This was a division point halfway between St. Louis and Memphis. This railroad yard was infested with very mean railroad bulls. They watched us very closely and we knew they were looking for us. It turned into a game, the bulls trying to catch us, and we trying to outsmart the bulls, which was not hard to do. The bulls constant surveillance did keep us from catching a north bound train.

By this time we were very hungry and extremely dirty from the coal smoke from the train engine. We had not eaten in at least 48 hours; therefore, eating was first priority. That night we got into some gardens. We ate green tomatoes, seed potatoes and anything else we could find. Between us we figured we were not going to catch a train out of the Chaffee train yard. What to do? We had noticed that a Missouri Pacific railroad crossing was about a mile north of the Frisco yard.

I told the other boy that I knew that the Missouri Pacific line ran through Pacific, Missouri, and that Pacific was only thirty miles from Stanton. I did not know that the Missouri Pacific out of Chaffee was a branch line. Well, we caught a west bound Missouri Pacific train. About midnight the train went into a side track at Dexter, Missouri. There it stayed through the dark hours of early morning, through dawn and into the early morning hours. Our box car was setting in a railroad cut and on top of this cut was a farm house.

We were again hungry as hell! I learned a lesson here. The Angel found out that he was not now, or never would be, a bum. We could smell the bacon frying. We could smell the hot biscuits coming from the farm house and we were starving. The other boy and the Angel drew straws to see who would go to the farm house and ask for something to eat. The Angel lost on the draw. The Angel dutifully set out for the farm house, dirty and hungry. He approached the back of the house and knocked on the screen door. A lady came to the door and the Angel tried to ask for something to eat, but he could not do it. He did ask for a glass of water. He knew now beyond a doubt that he was not a bum. About this time

18

the train blew its whistle and started to move onto the main line. The Angel thanked the lady and ran to catch the train. The Angel and the other boy thought they were on their way to Pacific, Missouri. However, in truth they were headed for Poplar Bluff, Missouri.

As the freight train pulled into the Poplar Bluff train yard the Angel and the other boy jumped off the train. Again, they were dirty and hungry. Where they left the train there was a bridge across the Black River. They went under the bridge to get away from any bulls that might be in the area. Once under the bridge they decided to clean up as well as they could. Therefore, they undressed and bathed in the river. They also washed their clothing as good as they could without soap. After skinny dipping and clothes washing, they laid on some warm rocks, heated by the sun until their clothes were dry. How good it felt! Now we were relatively clean and the hunger pangs began. Down the tracks about a quarter of a mile there was a railroad section crew working, aligning track. They had their section car off the tracks and standing close to the bridge. We knew there was ice water on the section car, so we decided to quench our thirst. When we got to the section car we saw their lunch boxes setting all in a row. We could not make ourselves take their lunch, but we did decide to take one item out of each lunch box and arrange what was left in the box in a good and orderly fashion. I sincerely hope it worked and that none of their wives got into trouble for short changing their lunch.

We now realized that we were hopelessly lost. The only way we were ever going to get back to Stanton was to backtrack. Therefore, we caught the next Missouri Pacific train back to Chaffee, Missouri. No trouble back to Chaffee, but we ran into trouble in the Chaffee yard.

The railroad dicks were still trying to get hold of us. But they were unsuccessful. They were middle aged and we were young and more agile than they were. The first night back in the Chaffee train yards, they thought they had the Angel and the other boy. They caught a glance of us with their flashlights. They were so busy trying to catch us that they were not looking where they were running. We led them over by the rip-track. This is a track on the side of the train yard where debris is taken from the box car. When they clean the cars out a pile of material is left beside the track. With them chasing us we ran around the piles of debris, when they hit them running full tilt they would lose their footing and fall. When this happened their cussing would call on God to send evil or injury down on us.

The next day they checked the outgoing trains very closely and we could not catch one. We layed low all that day. That night we found a good place to sleep. It was in a box car that was used for hauling watermelons. There were no melons in the box car, but it did have good clean straw. Evidently, I slept very soundly for I awoke to a loud noise; after shaking the sleep from my eyes, I saw the other boy running along-side the box car and shouting for me to get out of the box car, as it had been hooked on a train that was headed for Memphis. I immediately jumped out of the moving box car and landed on a cinder pile. Nothing broken, just a few scratches and some ripped clothing. We made up our minds then that no matter how many bulls were looking for us, we were going to catch the next north bound train out of there.

The next day we watched, out of the railroad right-of-way where the bulls could not catch us, as they made up a train that would be north bound. The only trouble was that it was a local and would stop at every whistle stop between Chaffee and St. Louis. We knew that we were going to catch that train, local or not. What we would have to do was jump from the train before it stopped in each town. We would have to run off of the right-of-way. Then when the train pulled out, we would run and catch it again. It was a slow process, getting back to Linden Wood Train Yards in St. Louis. Some depot operator along the route evidently had called ahead and notified the St. Louis train yard that the local coming in from Chaffee, Missouri, had a couple of non-paying riders aboard. When the train pulled into the yard a number of railroad bulls checked the train in detail.

The Angel and the other boy were caught. We just knew that we were going to be worked over by the bulls. While taking us to the holding shed, the bull began to talk to us. When he found out the truth about our odyssey he became more tolerant toward us. In fact, he became downright friendly. Yes, we were a mess. Tired, hungry and dirty by reason of being covered with coal soot. He asked us a few questions about Stanton, Missouri, and we answered him truthfully. After he satisfied himself that we really were just trying to get back home, his mood changed to that of a benevolent gentleman. He showed us where they were making up a train that would go out on the Frisco main line to Stanton. He also took us to a restaurant just outside the train yard and bought us a dinner. How good it tasted! After eating he took us to the area where they were making up the train. He opened a box car and had us get in. He then told us that the first stop the train would make for coal and water would be Stanton. When we arrived it was two or three o'clock in the morning.

It was about a quarter of a mile to the Old German's house. When I knocked on the door and they opened it, they were indeed very happy. What a trial the Angel had put them through. Mrs. John fixed a big meal. Water was drawn and heated so I could bathe. Clean clothes were provided. Clean sleeping undergarments were provided, and above all no punishment was given because they were happy to see the Angel alive. After eating, the Angel went to bed and slept for 48 hours. How good it was to be home! However, adventure was still in the spirit of the Angel.

After being back from the trip, the Angel was back in the social flow of the town. The boys in the town never tired of hearing about the escapades of the other boy and the Angel. Yes, they envied us. It was still summer and we drifted into the routine of things boys do to kill time. One of the things we would do is to see who could dive the deepest. We did this in the Frisco Railroad's water tank. The tank was about 40 or 50 feet high and 25 or 30 feet across. The water in the tank ran from ground level to the top of the tank. On top of the tank there was a flange about four to six inches wide. The tank had a ladder going up the side of the tank. There was also a gauge on the tank to show the water level inside the tank. A float on the inside of the water tank would go up or down to display the water level. This float was attached to an inside cable.

The boys in the town who were not considered a sissy would take a clothespin that they had painted and we would climb to the top of the water tank and work ourselves around the top flange. Then one at a time, we would dive. When we had reached our individual depth for the dive, we would attach our clothespin to the cable and take the pin from the preceding boy's dive back to the surface. Therefore, there was no doubt about who could dive the deepest. We had one little fellow who could usually outdo the rest of us. That was his claim to fame. In the water either at the Merrimack River or at the Frisco water tank, he would excel.

A regular morning ritual for most of the boys of Stanton was to meet at Hammer's Store and decide what they were going to do for the day. This particular morning Mrs. John (my Grandma) gave me a quarter and asked me to bring back a quarter's worth of sugar when I came home. I now had money in my pocket that I could not spend.

Upon arrival at Hammer's Store I found Tobacco Juice Buck in the group on the bench at the store. He had been back in town for four or five days, but this was the first time he had been at the store. He had just returned from Arizona via freight train. He was telling his story of how he had been hired as a cowboy while in Arizona. We were all ears. In fact, he made it sound so good that another boy and the Angel said that they would go back with him if he would go along. Tobacco Juice Buck, never to be outdone, said that he would be happy to go along. We counted our money, including that quarter that Mrs. John had given the Angel. Between the three of us we had a dollar and a nickel. So it was decided to go. We had visions of owning our own horse, our own pistol and of riding the range like in the movies.

We agreed to catch the first train that came in heading west. Within an hour a west bound was on the side track waiting for the east bound to pass. The east bound had right-of-way because it was a troop train. This gave us time to find an empty box car, and to talk to the breakie. He informed us to be careful because Frisco Red, the mean bull, was at the Newburg train yard that week and that he was meaner than ever, because some hobo by the nickname of Alabama had worked him over during the past week. However, this did not change our minds; after all we were going to be cowboys!

About this time a girl whom we all knew came along the track with a sack full of groceries. She was curious as to what we were doing in the box car and where we were going. When we told her Arizona to become cowboys, she gave us the sack full of groceries saying that we needed them worse than her family did. I've often wondered what her mother said when she got home. Finally the east bound passed and the west bound pulled out of the side track, we were on our way to Arizona and fame.

About two hours later we were in the Newburg train yards. The engine went to the round house to be turned and a different engine was hooked on to our train. The breakies walked the train looking for hot boxes. We made up our minds to jump Frisco Red if he stuck his head in our box car. Thank goodness, this never came about. In about three hours we were on our way to Springfield, Missouri. We could breathe easy for awhile now. It was fun going through the small towns and waving at the boys and girls our own age and seeing the envy in their eyes. They would have liked to break loose, but did not have the guts to go. Everything was going great, but it would change drastically within the next few hours.

It was dark when we arrived in Springfield, Missouri. It was strange territory for the three of us. Here one must understand the times. We were at war. The railroad bulls, who were not too bright anyway, had been told to be on the lookout for possible or potential saboteurs. After all, the trains were carrying large amounts of war material. The hobo jungle had pretty much gone by the way, as work was plentiful. This allowed more time for the bulls to give to the surveillance of each incoming train. The train we came in on had at least four bulls checking it out. Well, they caught the three of us and two more that had been on the train.

They took us into a small building for interrogation. This was both physical and mental. After being slapped around and kicked, we were marched to a place under a viaduct and made to lean spread-eagle against the viaduct buttress. We were blindfolded. They told us that we had been identified as being engaged in espionage. They had the Angel, and I suppose the others, scared to death. Then they hit us on the side of the trunk of the body with a night stick and fired a round from a pistol into the viaduct buttress by our head. One of the two who had been picked up with us wet his pants. They now gave us directions on how to get to Highway 66 and suggested we hitchhike back to Stanton. We did not follow their instructions. Instead, we circled around the yard, careful not to be caught, to a place where they were making up a train. We caught it on the run. The two whom we did not know caught it first, then the other boy from our town, then Tobacco Juice Buck and finally the Angel. By this time the train was rolling fast, it felt like it tore the arms from their sockets when the Angel caught the train. However, it did not, and they were off for Tulsa, Oklahoma.

It was early morning when we arrived in Tulsa. Our sack of groceries had been taken from us in Springfield, we still had some cash from the dollar and a nickel that we had started with. We bought a can of pork and beans and a loaf of day old bread. That was breakfast for the three of us. How good it tasted! We were careful not to show ourselves before the imminent departure of the train that was being made up in the train yard. When it started to roll, we caught it. Now we were safely on and headed for Oklahoma City. We arrived in Oklahoma City around noon and started looking for a store to buy something to eat. We bought pork and beans and day old bread again. It still tasted good, but not as good as before. In a discussion with the store owner, he said that if we were going west, we had better find us a container for water to drink so we would not become dehydrated. In fact, in talking further, he said he would look in the back of the store to see if he could find some containers. He found some and gave them to us to use. I love Okies; they are great and generous people. After all, they had just come through very hard times themselves.

The Angel, Tobacco Juice Buck and the other boy managed to catch a west bound train going into New Mexico with no trouble. We were dirty from coal soot but happy that we were getting close to becoming cowboys. At this time we were highly motivated. However, before we got to New Mexico we had Amarillo, Texas, to contend with. One of the other hobos on the train said that Amarillo was a chain-gang town and that, if we were caught, it would mean 30 to 90 days on the chain-gang. Now our motivation was dulled somewhat. We decided to get off the train as soon as we individually thought it was safe. When the train slowed Tobacco Juice Buck was first off and running to get off of the right-of-way. The other boy exited the box car and, when he hit the ground, went face first into the chat and cinder track ballast. Now the Angel jumped; he hit running. As soon as he was stabilized he ran back to help the other boys. The other boy was scratched badly, his clothes were torn. Fortunately, nothing was broken but his pride. We laid low the rest of the day and used up the last of our dollar and a nickel for food. That night we slipped through the town and came to the railroad on the other side of Amarillo.

By this time we were hungry again, and now we were broke. This is where the past experience of Tobacco Juice Buck came into play. He told us to follow him and to do what he did. Well, he would follow the milk delivery wagon and when the man set the milk, butter, etc. off at each house, Tobacco Juice Buck would kneel, drink the quart of milk, eat some of the butter and go on to the next house and repeat. The other boy and I were now in a dilemma; Tobacco Juice Buck would not share and the other boy and I left Amarillo very hungry and Tobacco Juice Buck was well fed and happy. Now it was on west, on to New Mexico.

Other than our extreme hunger, the trip was uneventful. We arrived in Albuquerque in good order and on west to Arizona almost immediately. We knew that we were now in cowboy country. We passed through the Petrified Forest, on through Holbrook and Winslow and now the lay of the land started to change. We were going higher and it was getting cooler; therefore, we decided that the next large town we came to, we would get off and look for work. We would do anything to get rid of the pangs of hunger we now felt. We did not know that the next town of any size would be Flagstaff, Arizona. We dismounted from the train, now what? We got our heads together and decided to go to the local police and ask for help in finding work.

We must have been a sorry looking group of individuals to the policeman. I am sure the town didn't have over one or two law officers. When we posed our request for work to him, he burst out laughing. After the outburst of hilarity died down, he said that he would do anything to get us out of town. He also said that we would have to clean up before he would see what could be done with us. He drove us outside of town, gave all three of us one bar of soap and told us to get into the animal watering tank and wash our bodies and our clothes. After washing he took us to what I believe was their police station and put us in a holding room. Why, I don't know, but he called the Angel out first. Scared to death, I stood before him. He asked a number of questions—Where had I come from? Why I had left there? How old I was? I told him the truth, except for the age. I boosted it five years to seventeen.

He told us to go out and get into his car and he would see what he could do about finding work for us. The policeman drove me out into the country about 20 or 25 miles. Finally, we came to a covered wagon and off away from the wagon was a herd of sheep being tended by a couple of dogs. By the wagon was a tripod set up and under the tripod in an iron kettle was a stew of some kind simmering. It was tended by a grizzly looking old man who looked and sounded like he had just come to this country from Bohemia. He did not acknowledge me, but instead addressed the policeman. The policeman said that he had brought him a helper. The old man now asked if I could shoot a rifle.

I told him that if he would give me three rounds to zero in the rifle I would show him. He walked out about 200 yards and placed a tin can. He came back and handed me the rifle and gave me three bullets. I took my time and adjusted the sights for windage and elevation after each shot. I adjusted by the puff of dust that I could see when the bullet hit the ground in the vicinity of the can.

He then handed me three additional rounds and the policeman now told me to fire for effect. This is where Slim's training would come in handy. The Angel hit the can all three times. It was not luck, just good training. The old man told me to hang on to the rifle for it was mine as long as I stayed with him. The policeman and the old man talked a while and the policeman left.

The old man dipped into the stew pot and filled his tin plate. He then called in the dogs and fed them, not until both dogs had eaten did he offer me a tin plate of mutton stew. I was so hungry that anything would have tasted good.

The old man gave me my duties. I was to stay up nights and kill any varmint that tried to kill his sheep. I could sleep through the day in the wagon, but I had to prepare the daily meals. What could I say but okay. But I knew that I would be heading back to Stanton, Missouri, at my first possible chance. I wondered what had happened to Tobacco Juice Buck and the other boy.

The first night it was very cold for I only had a short-sleeved shirt. However, I did manage to kill a coyote that was trying to get into the sheep. This made the old man happy. So happy, in fact, that he cut a hole in a blanket and gave it to the Angel to wear as a cape. It sure helped.

The old man was not mean, he was just withdrawn and quiet. He would talk to the dogs, and to Molly and Jewell, his mules, but he rarely talked to me. He always fed himself and his animals before the Angel. It was a good and yet a terrible time for the Angel. My stomach was full, but I did not know where I was. Oh I knew directions and that was about all.

After about two weeks, we came to a place called Navajo Ord Depot; there was a railroad running through this place. The place was on an upgrade that would slow down all east bound traffic. I watched one train go through; I saw how slow it moved, perhaps 15 to 20 miles per hour. I knew I could have caught it. It was daylight, and I was supposed to be sleeping in the wagon. I had no money and knew I would never be paid anything other than what I ate. So I did not feel bad when I filled a sack with dried mutton, potatoes, carrots and raisins. I left a note for the old man; however, it probably did no good for I do not believe he could read. When the next train came through, I ran for it carrying my sack of staples. The train was moving faster than the Angel thought, but the Angel said a prayer, grabbed hold of a box car and held on. I was on my way back home to Stanton.

The first town we came to was Flagstaff. I hid in the corner of the box car and prayed that the policeman would not check it. He did not and I was on my way east with a sack of groceries. Times were good. However, it was lonesome traveling alone. What had happened to my two comrades?

I got through Albuquerque in good order, no trouble. It took longer than expected to get around Amarillo, because the fear of a chain gang made the Angel more careful than usual. But I finally got out of there with no trouble. My groceries were holding out because I used a consumption discipline. I would eat just a given amount each day. Oklahoma City was no problem as everything went well there. Then the Angel got careless coming into Tulsa, Oklahoma.

Things had just been going too good to continue. I was carried away with the goodness of the Okies heart when I ran across a truly bad one. While trying to catch a freight train out of Tulsa bound for Springfield, Missouri, my luck ran out. The Angel was apprehended by a railroad bull. He took away what was left of my groceries. He checked to see if I had any money, which he was going to take. He said for five dollars he would let me catch the train. He threatened to put me on the pea farms hoeing peanuts for 90 days. Please understand that the train was moving and gaining speed all the time that he was talking to me. Finally, he said for me to catch the train if I did not want to go to the pea farms. The train was really moving now. I took off after the train and caught the first ladder on a box car. The movement of the train slapped me up against the side of the box car, but I held on for dear life. Finally I settled out and crossed over to the train car in front of me, which was a gondola car. I shook for awhile from the surge of adrenaline. Finally I settled down for the trip to Springfield. I sure did not want to get caught in the train yards there.

I was extremely cautious in Springfield and detrained before the train got all the way into the train yard. The Angel walked very carefully around the yard. In walking around the yard, I came across a fellow dressed like a train crewman: his overalls, white cap and lunch box gave him away. I asked him where and on what track they were making up an east bound train. He told me, but he also said to be extra careful as the bulls would be checking it good. I thanked him and moved out to place myself in a position to catch the train. When it started to roll, I waited until it picked up some speed, then I darted out and caught it. I was now on my way to Newburg, and to Stanton. I cannot say I was not happy, but I did wonder what had become of Tobacco Juice Buck and the other boy. Huddled in the end of a coal car, I was on my way back home. I just knew that the "Old German" and "Mrs. John" would welcome me home.

Now all I had to worry about was getting through the train yard at Newburg and not getting caught by Frisco Red. I was lucky; no problem in Newburg. I grabbed the first east bound out of the yard and now I was rolling through the night and only 45 miles from home. The Angel could not help but shout "I'm Back" as the train ran through Sullivan, six miles from home. I was hungry, but extremely happy. The Old German and Mrs. John were very happy to see me well but thinner than I had been. They gave me clean clothes, a tub bath and plenty of good food to eat. Then it was to my room and to bed. I told them I would tell them about the trip the next day, and I did. The Old German was all ears as he had never been more than 50 miles from where he was born. As I told him about my odyssey, he lived the adventure with and through me.

Well, my summer was rapidly coming to an end. I would soon be back in school in the eighth grade with a teacher I truly enjoyed. However, that did not mean our fun and games had to end. In fact, we boys would get together at Hammer's Store each day and discuss what we would do during the coming year.

About a week after I returned from Arizona, the other boy that was with the Angel showed up in Stanton. He too had returned on a freight train. We were the focus of attention as we told of our adventures to the other boys in town. Both of us had lost about 20 pounds on our odyssey. However, it did not take long to gain it back and to gain beyond the weight we were at when we started the trip. Then about a week or ten days later Tobacco Juice Buck came wandering back. He had actually gained weight on the trip. He was a natural bum. Their stories were about the same as the Angel's from the time they were split up by the policeman in Flagstaff, Arizona.

Incidentally, that would be the last long trip by freight train, that the Angel would take. Oh, we would on occasion or on impulse grab a handful of box cars and ride into St. Louis or ride from St. Louis back to Stanton, but the long trips on freight trains had come to an end for the other boy and the Angel. For Tobacco Juice Buck it was just the beginning.

Before school started, the Angel did try one more thing. He tried to join the United States Civilian Conservation Corps, in short the CCC, or as we used to call them affectionately, "Brush Apes." They paid $30 a month and you had to send $22 home and you kept $8. That was big money for the Angel. The Angel approached the officer in charge of Company 2728 in Merrimack State Park and inquired about enlisting. It was too close to home; while the Angel would pass for 18, he was too well known by the officer in charge who had a good chuckle and then denied him enlistment. After all, it would be an embarrassment to the officer in charge to allow a 13 year old young man into the three C's! He told the Angel to grow up and then to come back and see him. Shortly after this the three C's ceased to exist due to most of the men going into the military service of their country.

Finally Labor Day came and the next day it was off to school. When we told of our adventures over the summer, some of the other students just classified it as hyperbole. Of course, the town boys knew better and convinced the rest of the class of the truth of our story. We were the top dogs of the class! Tobacco Juice Buck did not start school. I guess he was old enough to quit school. He went back to Arizona and sheep herding.

At recess we boys would get together and think of things we would do for the coming Halloween. It was a real brain storming session and we came up with some outstanding things to do. Of course there was the usual; you know, turning over the outhouses, etc. But we also had some tricks that were extremely creative. We just had to wait until Halloween to pull them off. What to do until then—there was always hunting.

One morning as we all gathered at Hammer's Store the decision was made to go rabbit hunting. We had already had our first frost, so the rabbits would be good to eat. The first frost tended to kill any worms that may be in the rabbit carcass. One of the boys present was "Hause." He claimed that he had the best rabbit dog in the country. He bragged that all we had to do was go to the woods and that his dog would bring the rabbits around to us. Of course, this was more brag than fact. We went home and got our rifles and had agreed to meet behind the cemetery to start the hunt. After hunting awhile around the edge of a field where the field blended in with the larger timbers, we had a couple of rabbits through no credit to Hause's magnificent rabbit dog. The dog finally did jump a rabbit, but instead of bringing the rabbit around, the dog chased the rabbit into a briar patch. The dog went into the briar patch after the rabbit. We posted ourselves around the briar patch and waited for the dog to bring the rabbit out. Finally Hause shouted, "I see him", "I see him," and he shot. However, what he thought was the rabbit was actually the dog. The dog came out of the briar patch yipping in pain. As far as I know that was the last time that dog ever chased a rabbit. Poor Hause, he never lived the incident down.

A good hunting dog is particular about who they hunt with. The Angel had one of the best squirrel dogs in the country. The dog truly enjoyed hunting! When you went to the woods with him he would almost always bark treed within 15 minutes. The dog never lied. However, if you did not bring the squirrel down when you shot, the dog would give you a pitiful look and then he would go home. You had to be a good shot for the dog to accept you as a hunting partner.

On one occasion some of the Angel's city cousins were visiting with the Old German and Mrs. John. The Angel asked the boys if they would like to go squirrel hunting. They said that they would, so the Angel scrounged up some weapons from the Old German and from some of the other boys in Stanton and took the city cousins hunting. They were unfamiliar with the woods and not very good hunters. The Angel should have known this, for the good squirrel dog refused to go with them. The Angel was bragging about being a great white hunter when a squirrel appeared on the trunk of an oak tree. The Angel got a good sight picture, took a deep breath and squeezed the trigger. The squirrel remained on the oak tree trunk after the shot. The Angel, being fast on the up take told his cousins that he only meant to knock the squirrel out. Low and behold, when they got up to the tree the Angel looked the squirrel over and found that he had just grazed the squirrel's head and indeed had just knocked him out. What luck! Now it was brag time for the Angel. To this day those city cousins believe that the Angel was that good with a rifle. He was good, but not that good!

On occasion the boys of Stanton would decide to go frog gigging. This was particularly interesting as a sport and for good eating. Who doesn't like frog legs? Each of us had our own gig and gig pole. We usually frogged down on the Merrimack River or on Wenzel Creek. Wenzel Creek was the most fun, as the farmer who owned the property would try to keep us out. It never worked as we would get in somehow. All we needed to frog was a gig, a gig pole, a gunny sack and a good flashlight. We would wade down the creek, which was about waist deep, and with the flashlight look for their shining eyes. Once you saw the eyes shining you would go in over the light with your gig and stab the frog with a short fast thrust. This was not a sport for a squeamish person.

To go frogging of a day we would take a piece of bright colored cloth and put it on a fish hook. Then we would dangle it over the river or pond bank. The frog would be attracted to the bright color and jump for the cloth. Of course, he would be hooked. Yes, life was fun in a small town.

Labor Day weekend was finally upon us. It had been some time since I had seen Flo, so I decided to grab me a handful of box cars and go to St. Louis one more time before school started. Thursday evening I caught an east bound freight and was in St. Louis in a couple of hours. I really had not paid a lot of attention on the type of train I caught. This was during World War II and I had caught a train carrying priority war material. It would be scrutinized very carefully when coming into the train yard in St. Louis. I was caught as I got off the train.

The railroad bull was walking me over to a shed in the train yard. I felt that he was a sadistic type of person. He had me lace my fingers together and place my hands on the back of my head and as we walked he would hit me in the ribs with his truncheon. I made up my mind that if the chance ever presented itself, I would kill the sadistic, cruel son-of-a-gun. The area he was taking me to was known as the interrogation shed where I would be worked over by two or three bulls. However, to get to the shed we had to cross an area where a switch engine was putting together a train. This was my chance. I crossed the tracks in front of the switch engine and very quickly turned and pushed the bull as hard as I could push. The bull caught the back of his shoe on the rail and fell backwards into the path of the switch engine. The Angel took off running as fast as he could. The bull recovered before the switch engine hit him and shouted for the Angel to halt or be fired on. The Angel kept running. The bull fired six rounds either in the air or at the Angel. The Angel ran across the train yard and down into the River DePere, an open sewer. After about two blocks the Angel came out of the sewer and walked south on Manchester Road to Kings Highway, then north on Kings Highway to Flo's place of business. The Angel never told Flo or anyone else about the incident. On Monday the Angel decided to hitchhike back to Stanton so he caught a city bus and rode it to the end of the line on Chippewa Avenue and from this point thumbed his way back. For the Angel it was time to start school on Tuesday. He was ready, in fact he was extremely happy, to be going back to school. The education bug had bitten him.

Being in the eighth grade had its privileges. For instance, the Angel was now the captain of the school patrol. One point of interest that happened between the start of school and Halloween was that someone had broken into the school and stolen the accumulated lunch money. The teacher was at herself with dismay. It was reported to the Franklin County Sheriff and he sent an officer out to investigate. It was a superficial investigation. He dismissed the girls from the class and then had the boys stand and empty out their pockets. Then he shook us down to see if we had displayed everything in our packets. Because he was embarrassed, one boy had not displayed his billfold. When he turned it over to the investigator he found a condom in the billfold. The police officer went into great detail asking the boy what he had, and what it was used for, etc. I felt badly for the young man. The policeman really made a fool out of him. The next day two other boys in the school owned up to taking the money. One of the boys was from a foster home and the other had just moved to Stanton from St. Louis. They were shunned the rest of that year by the remainder of the class and they both moved away before the year was out.

During the period between the start of school and Halloween there were a couple of incidents that happened that were rather amusing.

Some of the older men in Stanton were setting on the rails of the railroad talking and in general socializing. They were smoking their RJR (Run John Run) or Bull Durham, or if they had the money, their Marvel cigarettes. If they were really lucky, they would have a bottle of Muscatel (a cheap wine). On this day they were feeling no pain. As a train came down the track upon them, they all moved except one fellow. He was still setting on the rail when the train hit him. He was hit by the cow catcher on the front of the engine and tossed down over a cinder fill. When the train had stopped and a statement was taken from the man, he complained about his left arm and his torn clothing. The next day the Frisco Railroad sent a claims agent out to settle with him. When the man came to town to talk to the claims agent, he had on his torn shirt and now he had his right arm in a sling. When the claims agent indicated this discrepancy the man said, "Buy me a new shirt and a pint of whiskey and we'll call it even." The other men in the town never let the poor guy forget his situation.

Another situation took place in Stanton that I do not believe has ever been solved. The Angel and some other boys were in the town's 3.2 beer tavern shooting pool. We noticed a young lady from the town walking west on the shoulder of the highway across from the Rock House, a tavern. All of a sudden she ran backwards screaming. We immediately ran up the road to see what had caused her to scream. We found a dead man in the ditch; some weeds had been pulled and placed over him and pennies had been strewn around him. He was well clothed, but he had on two shirts. We called the county law, and after a brief examination of the area, the funeral director was called. The man had been dead long enough for rigor mortis to set in. One of the boys carrying him to the funeral coach pushed his arm under the cover and the arm flew back at him. He dropped the stretcher and took off running. Of course, he took a lot of razzing from the others in town. He never lived it down.

By this time, many of the Angel's friends had enlisted or been drafted into the armed forces. The Angel truly wanted to go, but he was only 13. He was big enough, but not old enough. After all, he was only in the eighth grade. The general feeling of the men in Stanton was to look on the military as an adventure. They were anxious to do their duty. At this time the draft board was taking men from 18 to 45. To be classified as 4-F was a stigma no one wanted. 4-F was considered not fit for the military—what a blow to one's self-esteem. Some of the men who had correctable physical problems had them taken care of on their own so they could qualify for military service.

This was also a time for rationing. Just about everything was rationed: gas, tires, shoes, sugar just to name a few. It was a time to be creative. An "A" sticker for your car only allowed you four gallons of gas per week. Many of the fellows around Stanton would find them a farmer's daughter to date. The farmer had almost an unlimited amount of gas. If the daughter of the farmer could get the gas stamps, the date was on. If she could not, she was dropped. Of course, there was also the black market, but this meant buying at a high price and, of course, it was not patriotic to patronize a dealer in the black market. It just was not right.

The school year of 1942-1943 moved along in good order for the Angel. However, it pained him to see his buddies go off to war without the Angel going along. Of the three who had gone to Arizona to become cowboys, Tobacco Juice Buck was now in the army and the other boy was just about to turn 17 and was chomping at the bit to go. The Angel also was anxious to go, but he was way too young.

As soon as he turned 17 the other boy asked some of us to go with him to St. Louis so he could enlist, hopefully into the US Navy. Sure we agreed to accompany him. How to get into St. Louis? Why, catch a freight train, of course. With an excused absence, the Angel would go with him. The Angel, the other boy and some others caught a freight around four o'clock in the morning. It was about two hours to the train yard in St. Louis. Therefore, we arrived there about six o'clock. This gave us time to walk down to 12th and Market Street, the location of the US Navy Recruiting Station. The other boy filled out his papers and took his physical exam. He passed, no problem at all. He now had to get his parents to sign, as he was only 17. On the spur of the moment the Angel asked for parent consent papers also, and was given them with no questions asked. We returned to the train yard and caught an outgoing freight. The only rail car we could catch was an open gondola. In the meantime, the weather had turned colder than a well diggers butt. By the time we got to St. Clair, Missouri, we were almost frozen. It was about two o'clock in the morning and we could not catch a bus to Stanton until six o'clock. Nothing was open in the town, so we had to huddle together for warmth. Finally the produce delivery man came along, and when we told him our situation, he gave us a ride to Stanton in his produce truck. It was only about ten miles.

I still had the parent consent papers and I would see both Flo and Slim that weekend. I knew that Slim would be going back to California on Monday. I would have to work fast if I expected to get their signatures on the parent consent forms before Slim left for California. Therefore, I broached the subject to them over the weekend. They both laughed and said they would be more than happy to sign when I turned 17. Oh well, live and learn, and that is what the Angel was doing. In his mind he knew if there is a will there is a way. The other boy's parents signed the consent forms and he was off to the Naval Training Station in Farragut, Idaho, before the week was out. Oh, how the Angel did admire him! Now two out of the three that went to Arizona were in service to their country.

As the men from Stanton entered the military one by one, or en mass, it left a void for the Angel. He looked 18, he acted 18. What for him was to be done. He would either have to run with other 13 year olds, who seemed immature to him, or hang out with the older men of the town. The Angel chose the older generation as his social circle of friends.

There was one man in this group that the Angel liked very much. He was the type of man that other men enjoy, but not necessarily a good family man. In his mind booze and a good time came before family. Although, I must say his wife and children admired him.

Ole Joe had been in World War I. In fact, he was in the same division as Slim. The 89th Infantry Division. At this time, it was not difficult to find a job, due to the war. Ole Joe procured a job as a pumper for the Frisco Railroad in Pacific, Missouri. A pumper was responsible for keeping plenty of water on hand for the steam engines. Each day he would ride one of the freight trains to work (it was 30 miles from Stanton). Ole Joe would ride in the caboose of the train. If the Angel had a free day he would go with Ole Joe to Pacific just to keep him awake on his shift. The Angel could not ride in the caboose, but he would catch one of the other train cars, knowing it would stop in Pacific. Then the next morning he would catch a train back to Stanton with Ole Joe.

When Ole Joe started his shift, he was usually at least half drunk and likely as not fully drunk. To start the pump engine you had to exert a back pressure on the fly wheel and then when the engine started, you had to very quickly get off of the fly wheel. The fly wheel was about six feet in diameter and would produce a lot of back pressure. It was hard enough to get off the fly wheel in normal conditions, and extremely difficult if you were drinking. On many occasions, I have seen the fly wheel throw Ole Joe for 20 feet through the air and across the pump house. On many occasions, the Angel would start the pump for Ole Joe if he was drinking too much. Later we would work on another job together and room together in St. Louis. There was never a dull minute with Ole Joe around.

With the draft age men gone, there was definitely a shortage of men around. The Angel, being mature looking, was a willing subject for the girls to teach what men were for. The Angel was a very willing student for this type of eduction. In fact, he was a very rapid learner in the area of female anatomy. At the dances on Saturday night the young ladies would line up to get a dance with the Angel. On one occasion Mrs. John had to run a couple of girls away with a broom stick saying in a loud, angry manner, "You girls get out of here and let that boy alone, he needs his rest."

The Angel was constantly trying to figure a way to get into the military. The self motivation was there, the age was not. However, he thought one little thing like being 13 should not keep him out; there must be a way around the age thing. He promised himself that he would keep trying until he found the answer.

Eighth grade graduation was drawing near and the Angel set his goal on being in the military before the coming fall. He would keep searching until he found a way. In the meantime, life went on for the Angel.

One of the things that happened before the end of school in 1943 was an incident at the Sullivan theater. The manager of the theater was a small man, and as a small man he made it very difficult for youngsters at his theater. For the least little thing he would eject a child from the show, but would not return the money the youngster had spent to get into the movie house. He was disliked by all the school-age kids. On one occasion, upon exiting the movie theater the Angel noted the manager man handling a boy from the town. It was more than he could stand, so he came to the aid of the kid. At first he just asked the manager to let the boy go and not to hurt him. When the manager told the Angel to mind his own business and to get out of the theater, it was more than the Angel could take. At this point, the Angel remembered what Slim had taught him. Slim had taught him that if you used a right cross you should land it at the butt of the ear and carry the punch on through the head. He had also said to let the power generate through the body. The Angel did this to the manager of the movie and just like Slim said, it worked; the manager was down and out. The Angel told the other boy to go home and tell his parents about the incident. The boy took off running, and the Angel walked up to Highway 66 and started to hitchhike to Stanton.

That was when the local police came and took the Angel to jail for disorderly conduct. The next morning the Angel was released. On getting back to Stanton, The Angel asked Mrs. John what she would have done if someone had told her I was in jail, and she said that she would have told them that if I got in there, I would just have to get out on my own.

One morning, while still in bed, the thought came to me. EUREKA! I have found it, a way, to get into the military service under age and not require parents' consent. What if I just signed up for the draft as 18? Those being drafted did not have to show a birth certificate nor did they have to have the consent of the parents. After all, most thought that a draftee did not want to go anyway. Sure, that was it, the Angel could pull it off. As soon as school was out he would try it. After all, it was now 1943 and the Angel just knew that the war could not end without him. The Angel could not visualize the war ending before he had a chance to do his duty behind a rifle. His father had served underage in World War I, and his grandfather had served underage during the Civil War. Surely the Angel could not break the chain. The Angel did not mention his plan to anyone, not even his best buddies knew what he was going to do. For the next week or so, the Angel went over and over in his mind the new birth date that he would use when he registered for the draft. He did not want a sloppy flow of detail while registering the facts and answers to the draft board clerk's questions must flow smoothly. He decided not to use the draft board in Franklin County where Stanton was located, but to use the one in St. Louis County because there was less chance that he would be recognized in St. Louis County. He was now extremely anxious for school to end for 1943. In addition to becoming comfortable with the questions the clerk of the draft board might ask, the Angel had to somehow make his disappearance from the home of the Old German look natural.

The Angel wrote to Slim in California and asked him for money to come live with him over the summer. Slim immediately sent the money. The Angel then told Flo that he would be with Slim, he also told the Old German that he would be with Slim. He then wrote to Slim and informed him that he had a job and would not be coming to California as planned. Now it was set. As far as he knew all angles had been covered. The Angel could now put things together to get the ball rolling toward entry into the military. He had planned his work, now he had to work his plan.

On graduation day from the eighth grade, Flo threw a party for the entire class. It was a great party and everyone enjoyed it to the fullest. In fact, it is still talked about today when old classmates accidently get together. The Angel returned to St. Louis with Flo, so he could look for work. The first day in St. Louis he registered for the draft; everything went well.

The Angel then asked the clerk of the draft board to place him at the top of the list for the next call. This the clerk was extremely happy to do, for it helped her fill her quota for the next call. Now it was just a waiting game for the Angel.

In the meantime, the Angel heard that Ole Joe had lost his job as a pumper in Pacific, Missouri. He had lost it for being drunk on the job. The Angel liked Ole Joe, so he gave him a call and had him come to St. Louis so they could look for work together. He came, and the next day he and the Angel started looking for work. We found work at the St. Louis Shipbuilding and Steel Company at the foot of Arlee Street in Lemay, Missouri, a suburban area to the south of St. Louis. The Angel's job was as a shipfitter helper, and Ole Joe as a chipper. We rented a room close by and started to work. This was big money at the time, 85 cents per hour and all the overtime you wanted at time and a half. The Angel was 13 and dragging in the money.

When you make the kind of money I was making, a young man starts thinking of a car. The automobile bug had bitten the Angel. The Angel and Ole Joe started frequenting the used car lots on Kings highway. We became very friendly with some of the used car lot owners. The Angel found an automobile he liked very much, but he informed the lot owner that he would be getting called into the service very shortly. The lot owner said that he would let the Angel have the car for $20 a week and when I was called into the service, I could just return the auto to him. It was a good deal and the Angel now had wheels at 13 years of age. The car was a 1936 DeSoto coupe in perfect condition, good tires and all. How proud the Angel was; he could really show off around Stanton on weekends now!

At the shipyard, the Angel was introduced to the game of chance called "shooting craps." There was always a game in progress in the bath house. After losing some money, the Angel figured out that the percentage of the game was not with the player; therefore, he did not become a regular of the game. What he would do was get in and get out of the game. He would lay a ten spot down and if he made his point he would pick up the twenty and get out of the game. If he did not make his point, it was only a ten dollar loss and he could stand that. The Angel had only been working about a month when he received his induction notice. You know how it read: "Greetings! Your friends and neighbors have selected you," and gave the date you were to report for induction into the service.

Reporting to the Armed Forces Examining and Entrance Station at Jefferson Barracks, Missouri was a true adventure. The Angel reported in on the date that his greetings had indicated. He was given a fast orientation as to procedure and expectations for the day. After the orientation we were moved inside and told to strip. We were each given a cloth bag for our valuables. This we would put around our neck. On the floor were white painted squares exactly 36 inches apart. As our name was called we took our place on the square that was behind the person who had been called just before. When the white squares were full the line started to move. We were completely naked except for the cloth bag around our neck. I asked the man in front of me why the white squares were an equal distance apart. The Angel was surprised at his answer. He said that some of the men present did not want to serve their country and that they would do anything to be rejected. They would even go so far as to try to show that they were perverted and try to bump against the fellow in line that was just ahead of them. The Angel immediately checked the fellow behind him, and just to keep it straight, he informed the guy that if he so much as touched him, that he would break his scrawny neck. The Angel could get away talking this way because he was now 5'10" tall and his weight was now 186 pounds. The fellow behind him in line assured the Angel that he would keep his distance.

The Angel may have been only 13, but he was built like a man. Because of Slim training him during his early years, he had outstanding upper body strength.

The line proceeded through the various stations and the medical form was stamped either accepted or rejected at each station. The last station in line was an interview with a psychiatrist. The Angel wondered why in the hell they were asking him such questions, like did he like girls, etc. Hell yes he did, why even ask that question of a man? Then it dawned on him that they were just trying to ferret out those funny type people. I'm sure they probably found some. As was said before, some would try anything to get out of doing their duty to their country. The Angel was rapidly becoming aware that there were weird people in this world and it was better to stay away from them. Finally, my medical form was stamped acceptable military service, Army, Navy or Marine Corps. Oh happy day!

Now it was time for my final interview. I sat across the table from the interviewer and he asked for my preference of service. When I told him Marine Corps, he studied a note that had just been given to him. He studied for awhile, then said "Sorry," the Marine Corps quota for the day has just been filled. He said that I could go on a list to be called, or I could do the following: The Angel could go Navy, put in for Pharmacist Mate School, and serve as a medical aid man with a Marine unit. That way there would be no wait. I could return the next day for induction. Being underage the Angel figured the longer it took the more chance of being caught for being underage, so he said "Make it Navy." The Angel did not know until boot camp that the interviewer had fed him a line. The situation he had layed out for him could happen but the percentages were against it.

During the physical exam a couple of older men from Stanton were also being inducted. They knew that the Angel was 13, but they did not squeal on him. In fact, they went Navy also.

At the end of the day we had our swearing in ceremony. Those who lived close by could go home, but they had to report back the next day at 08:00 hours.

*The Angel
immediately after
his release for being
underage.
1944   Age 14*

*The Angel, age 14
April 1944*

*John Binsbacher
(The Old German)
Evelina Binsbacher
(Mrs. John)
1944*

*The Angel as a member
of the 187 P/G RCT
Boxing Team
1946*

*Left to Right–
The Angel;
Lt. Olinski, OIC;
Phillips, 187 P/G RCT ,
11th Airborne Division
1946*

Members of the boxing team, seated, Gomez; standing, left to right–Price; unknown; Vargas, Hartman, London, Richardson (The Angel)

The Angels patrol-Driver, unknown; Kamura, Japanese-American; and Japanese native

The Angel as an escort for WWII deceased, 1948-49

November 1945
Returning to the states for reenlistment leave
Left to right–Soldier from Iowa, name forgotten; Straight Leg
Trooper, name forgotten; The Angel; Roberts from Illinois

1945-46
Chitose, Hokkaido, Japan (A pay jump)
The Angel was stationed at Sapporo with Company "G", 187
Para/glider Regimental Combat Team, 11th Airborne Division

44

Andong Korea
1950-51

Andong Korea
1950-51

Andong Korea
1950-51

Tanyang Pass, Korea
1950-51

*Conditioning march
1950*

*The Angel,
77th Special Forces Airborne
(Green Beret) 1955*

*The Angel with his two sons
Mike and Pat
1952*

*The Angel's sister, Marcella
and his father (Slim)*

46

THE MILITARY YEARS 1943-1967

The Angel was convinced that he had cleared all the hurdles for entry into the Navy—he was outstandingly happy. They had given us a list of things to take along—you know, toilet articles, etc. That evening Ole Joe, the Angel and Gramma (the landlady) had a going away party. Gramma sent the Angel to the local tavern for a bucket of beer. During the party, Ole Joe said that he would feel honored if I would wear a particular shirt of his that the Angel was fond of. In fact, he wanted to give it to the Angel as a present. What could the Angel say but yes! The Angel was extremely happy.

By 08:00 hours the following day, the Angel reported to the designated area at Jefferson Barracks that he had been ordered to the previous day. It was now a series of hurry up and wait, a procedure that the Angel was to get used to. The rat race continued until about noon. Some of the older men were griping about the rat race, but not the Angel—to him it was fun and games. About noon, we boarded three passenger train cars but were not told our destination. Most of us figured it would be Great Lakes Naval Training Station. Those that thought this way were in for a surprise. About two hours after leaving Jefferson Barracks, we were told we were headed for Farragut Naval Training Station, Farragut, Idaho. I will say one thing, it was much better riding the cushions of a passenger train than it had been riding freight trains. However, not necessarily safer. When our passenger train was passing through Moberly, Missouri, the last three cars of the train jumped the track. It was absolute pandemonium in those three cars after they jumped the track and before the forward motion stopped. When it stopped, the passenger cars were leaning at about a forty-five-degree angle. This added to the scared attitude of the passengers. We cleared the train cars as rapidly as possible. One fellow who had been on the toilet when the train jumped the track, came off the train with his pants down and without cleaning himself. Needless to say, he took a razzing from then until he finished boot camp. We had to wait several hours until the railroad wrecker came to lift the cars back on the track. The remainder of the trip was more or less uneventful and friendships began. We joked about the antique passenger cars we had been assigned. For instance, one fellow said he found a sign that read "Do not shoot buffalo while train is in motion." Of course, we did not believe him. Finally after about four days of travel, we reached our destination. What a rude awakening we were in for. It was off the train on the double and stand at attention while some Chief Petty Officer berated us as the sorriest scum of the earth and how did the Navy think we could win the war with scum like us being sent to Farragut for training. He ended his long tirade by saying he would either make sailors out of us or kill us trying. We had a tendency to believe him. To us, he looked and sounded like God himself.

First item of business on the in-processing agenda was a hair cut. It all came off and as we left the barber shop, a sailor printed a number on our bald head with methylate (a colored disinfectant). In the next station, we completely undressed and filled out a card regarding who to ship our civilian clothes to or we could put them in a charity box. From there we entered a large gymnasium. However, we had to wait until our name and number were called to enter the gym. In the top of this gym was a large basket-type thing and in it was the Chief Petty Officer that had greeted us as we detrained. He now had a bull horn. In physically processing through the many stations in the gym, the Chief would observe from his high position, and if you got out of line, his tirade would embarrass we poor, insignificant globs of flesh until we found our proper place in line. I am sure he enjoyed his job to engulf us with his profane vocabulary and create total embarrassment within us. If that was his mission, then he succeeded. The people on the floor treated us as humans, but the Chief in the crow's nest treated us as the scum of the low-life.

The last thing to accomplish during in-processing was the issue of clothing and equipment. The Angel was disappointed when it came to the issue of shoes. His size had all been issued, which meant that he had to wear brown civilian wing tip shoes half way through boot camp. To look like you do not belong makes it easy to assign details. It was easy to say, "You, in the brown shoes—you are on this or that detail."

Upon completion of clothing issue, we boarded a bus, still in numerical sequence, and were driven to Camp Ward, one of the six camps at Farragut. Here, we were met by the Chief that would be our Company Commander. This Chief was a good and honorable man who had been a teacher prior to coming into the Navy. He proceeded to orient our group on his expectations of what he demanded from us. We were now informed that we were in

Company 568-43 and that we belonged to the Chief for the next eight weeks. He informed us that we could give our soul to God because our ass belonged to him for eight weeks.

With the end of the orientation, our training regimen began. There were many rules and regulations to remember. These came easy for the Angel. The Angel enjoyed very much the physical training that was given on a daily basis. He enjoyed the marching, the learning of knots; after all he had been a Boy Scout and knew the knots without the classroom exercise to learn them. He liked the bugle calls, etc. Most of all, he enjoyed the rowing of a whale boat on Lake Ponduray. The area was absolutely beautiful. The Angel felt blessed that he had been assigned to Farragut for training. The Angel only saw the two other men from Stanton when the smoking lamp was lit, which was in the evening after training. The Angel did not smoke, but the smoking area was about the only place that one could socialize with the other boots (trainees).

During our eight weeks of boot camp, we were allowed two liberties to town. Of course, to get the liberties one had to have no demerits. The Angel met the requirement of no demerits, so he had one liberty to Sandpoint, Idaho, and one to Coeur D'Alene, Idaho. The liberties were a pleasant break from the training routine.

One of the scheduled events in our training was an afternoon of boxing. It was a challenge situation and one of the trainees challenged the Angel. What this trainee did not know was that the Angel had never been taught to lose. The Angel accepted the challenge and went forward into the ring. The challenger looked to be about twenty-five or thirty years old and was very well built. What he did not know was that Slim had taught the Angel the finer art of boxing when he was back in grade school. Slim used to tell the Angel that if you were fighting a man that did not tuck his chin behind his shoulder, then his neck was probably exposed, and to take a neck shot if you got the opportunity. The first round would probably be rated a draw by the cadre who had been assigned to judge the fight. Between the first and second round, the Angel's corner man told the Angel, "We have a turkey." Also, to take a neck shot if I got the chance. The chance presented itself in the second round and the Angel caught his opponent with a straight right to the neck. The opponent fell to the canvas immediately and started gasping for air. The blow had inverted the trachea, that part which conveys air from the larynx to the bronchi and the challenger could not get his breath. It scared the devil out of the Angel as he thought he might have killed the man. During these boxing matches, a doctor had to be at ring side for just such a situation. The doctor came into the ring, stuck a tongue depressor down his throat, gave it a twist and the challenger started to breathe. The Angel was happy to see him come around.

This event boosted the self-image of the Angel because now he knew that if he stayed cool, he would come out on top. The remainder of Company 568-43 were happy to see a braggart and bully put in his place. The two men in the Company from Stanton saw what a thirteen-year-old could do. However, they remained quiet about the age of the Angel.

By now, the Angel had his full issue of equipment and was no longer referred to as, "Hey, you in the brown shoes." It was now Seaman and the proper last name, even by the Chief-in-Command.

Along about the fourth week of training, those of us in 568-43 filled out what was referred to as our wish list for training after boot camp. After giving it considerable thought, the Angel selected aviation radioman, gunner as first choice. For second choice, he selected gunner's mate and for third choice, cook and baker school. To this day, the Angel does not know why he selected the third choice. My original thought of becoming a medic in the Marine Corps had now passed.

During the sixth week of training in boot camp, I was ordered to report to sick bay for a physical exam to see if I qualified for aviation radioman gunner on a Grumman Avenger type of aircraft. At the end of the mental and physical exam, the Angel was informed that he did not meet the criteria for the school because the Angel was too big. The Angel was 5'11" and weighted 180 pounds. For the school as an aviation radioman gunner you had to be 5'8" or smaller and under 165 pounds. The Angel felt badly about not being selected. However, there was still the second and third choices. Surely one of those would come through.

In the meantime bootcamp continued and finally the eighth week of training rolled around and graduation from boot camp was upon those of us in Company 568-43.

After the graduation ceremony we were moved to the OGU (outgoing unit) at Farragut and received our orders for a ten-day leave. This meant three days by train to get back to Missouri, about three days there and three days to return to the outgoing unit at Farragut, Idaho. The extra day the Angel allowed as a day of grace just to be sure he was back on time. The problem facing the Angel was how to spend three days around Stanton or Sullivan, Missouri, without Slim, Flo or the Old German finding out he was in the Navy. One way to do this was to stay with a friend in Leasburg, Missouri, and only make night runs to Sullivan. It worked, and the Angel had three days of fun and games. Yet, one thing happened during those three days that was almost too much for the Underage Angel to fathom.

On the first night he was home on leave he met and dated a very pretty and nice young lady. He had known this young lady for some time, but never had a date with her until the first night of the leave. When he took the young lady home that night he made a date with her for the next evening and night. He kissed her goodnight at the door and left. The next evening at the specified time for the date, the Angel showed up at her home. The Angel was greeted by the girl's mother, who stated that her daughter was not at home right now, but the Angel could come in, which he did. The mother had a housecoat on. She asked the Angel if he would like a tour of the house. The Angel being polite said "Sure." She indicated that she had just redecorated her bedroom and we would start there. The Angel followed her into the bedroom and to be polite was glancing around the walls. When his gaze returned to the woman, she had dropped the housecoat and was standing there as naked as a jaybird. She did look fine! However, it was just too much for the Angel. It scared the hell out of him, when she turned down the bed and invited the Angel to lay with her. The Angel, being very polite, said that he had a dozen things to do and exited the house as fast as possible. He ran all the way to the "Eagles Nest," a hang out for high school age youngsters. There he ran into the daughter of the woman, the girl he had the date with. The Angel did not tell her of the incident at her home but, did ask why she was not there when he had called. She said that her mother had told her I had called and was to meet her at the "Eagles Nest." The Mom was just too mature for the Angel.

After three glorious days around Sullivan, Bourbon and Leasburg and spending the three days almost constantly with the young lady, it was time to return to Farragut, Idaho. With one last big party, the Angel's friends drove him to St. Louis to catch the train. It was hard to part with the young lady, but duty called.

I arrived in Idaho on the ninth day of my leave. I knew that if I reported in early, it would just be another day of details. Therefore, the Angel spent the day in Coeur d'Alene enjoying himself immensely. It was just a low-key wind down from the leave. On the proper date, the Angel reported into the OGU (outgoing unit) at Farragut. Here it was pulling details and waiting for your name to appear on an assignment or school draft. By the end of the week most of those who had been in 568-43 had departed either to a school or reported to a new construction ship. The Angel could not understand why his assignment did not come through. Many thoughts ran through his head. Had they found out his true age? Finally his name did appear on a draft for signal school at Farragut. The Angel was pissed! He definitely did not want to be a flag waver. What to do? He approached a Chief that he had an acquaintance with and he inquired about getting off of the draft. The Chief asked him what he wanted for an assignment and the Angel said he wanted to go to sea. The Chief laughed and said that if that was all I wanted, that it would be easy. He said "When they call your draft just don't go." The Angel followed his instruction and after the signal school draft had left he reported to the OIC (Officer in Charge) of the OGU and informed him that he had missed his draft and that he wanted to go to sea. The Officer stated that he should bring me up before a Captain's Mass for discipline, but since my desire was to go to sea, then that is where I would go.

The next day, the Angel came out on a draft to the Naval Base at Pleasington, California. The Angel was ready and anxious to go on this draft. At Pleasington Naval Base, it was again pure details and wait. After about a week the Angel came out on a draft to the USS Deede, DE263. His draft boarded the ship at Treasure Island in San Francisco Bay. There was about 20 of us that went aboard that day. The Angel was now fourteen and chomping at the bit for action. The ship looked great! It looked sleek, fast and deadly. After all for a boy from the Midwest it was the first real ship he had ever seen. The bad part of the assignment was that the ship was now over-crewed and some of the draft from Pleasington would have to sleep in our hammock. That meant lashing up your gear anytime you were not in it. When our draft reported to the ship, the ship was taking on stores and preparing to go to sea. Then the Captain came on the squawk box and informed the crew that our destination was Pearl Harbor. The Angel was assigned as lookout on the bridge for regular duty and loader on the forward, port side, 20 MM for a battle station. In addition to this he was assigned to the second division for ship maintenance. This left very little time for sleep; perhaps four hours per day. It was about seven days to Pearl Harbor and this time was used for gun drill, general quarters, battle stations and more gun drill until we could do our assigned duty with our eyes closed. I was also to find out that the ship was not as sleek and fast as it first appeared.

The first sight the Angel saw coming into Hawaii and Pearl Harbor was Diamond Head, a beautiful sight. However, on entry into Pearl Harbor one could see some of the damage that had taken place on December 7, 1941. The USS Arizona was down and still is. The USS Oklahoma was down, and the USS Utah was down. After all, it had only been about a year and a half, give or take a month or two, since the Japanese attack on Pearl Harbor. The Captain docked the Deede at the Destroyer Escort dock near a hospital. Seeing some of the patient casualties brought the war very close at hand.

During our all too short stay in Pearl we took on stores and ammo. We were also allowed liberty to go into Honolulu. Liberty was granted on a port or starboard situation depending on your General Quarters battle station. You could only go into Honolulu on a daylight basis, which meant that an enlisted man had to be back aboard his ship at least one hour before sunset. You had to be on your battle station one half hour before sunset until one half hour after sunset. However, it was a break just to be off the ship for a time.

A number of friends of the Angel asked him to go on liberty with them. They said that a sailor was not a sailor until he had liberty in Honolulu and had been stewed, screwed and tattooed on Hotel Street. The first thing one noticed on Hotel Street was that you had to stand in line for everything. You could not get an alcoholic drink unless you could get a place to sit. You could not fornicate with a whore unless you stood in line for a city block or more. The whorehouses were condoned by the government and most of the whores had been procured from the United States. You even had to stand in line to be tattooed! When the Angel and his shipmates got to the tattoo parlor, the wait caused them to think smaller and smaller about the tattoo they were going to get.

Initially, the Angel said that he was going to get a chest

spread. That was a picture of a ship coming out of his chest with US Navy over the top of it, as he waited and became more sober and saw how the tattoo was applied, he decided on a right forearm tattoo of a rough facsimile of the USS Deede. By this time it was time to return to Pearl for evening battle stations. We were all now sailors, we had been stewed, screwed and tattooed. Our liberty into Honolulu provided conversation for a long time.

The next day, hung over and all, the Angel had a gun watch on the forward, port side, twenty MM. To kill the time and to keep occupied, the Angel thought he would get in a little practice on the forward, three-inch fifty by tracking some of the incoming and outgoing ships. The gun was manually operated and the Angel was busy as could be in tracking when the gunnery officer shouted from the bridge for me to report to him immediately, if not sooner. I reported to him as soon as possible and got one of the worst ass chewings I had ever received. It seems that it was against regulations to track another ship even if the gun was empty. The Angel was no dummy and he was a fast learner. He would never do that again!

Finally, the day came when there was no liberty. All stores had been loaded and locked down and the ship was ordered to sea. We, the deck hands, just figured we were out on another training run. Oh, how wrong we were! Shortly after exiting Pearl Harbor we picked up two APA's (attack transports); I believe it was the USS Titon and the USS Typhoon. They were loaded with marines and we were on our way to the Gilbert Islands, more specifically Tarawa and Makin. The Deede had screened for the two APA's all the way.

Somewhere between Baker Island and Tarawa we crossed and recrossed the equator. This was the occasion for a shellback celebration. Not many on the ship were shellbacks; however, those few, perhaps a half dozen, gave us polliwogs a good initiation into the domain of King Neptune. It was not good to be in the back of the line of candidates for becoming a shellback because as you were accepted into the realm of King Neptune, you became a part of the celebration and assisted in the initiation for the remainder of the polliwogs. I guess the officers of the ship considered themselves above the celebration for they did not participate in becoming a shellback. In fact, the officers of the ship kept themselves aloof from the crew. Looking back I think this was a mistake on their part.

After delivering the USS Titon and the USS Typhoon to the Commander of the Gilbert Island operation, the Deede was assigned a submarine station and also a pickup station for downed airmen. For awhile the Tarawa operation was in doubt. Those aboard the Deede who did not have a priority battle station were issued marine gear and assembled on the fantail ready to go ashore, if needed. Thank the good Lord, they were not needed. The Angel would not have gone ashore because he had a priority battle station on a twenty MM gun. About the time that Tarawa was secure, the Deede was ordered to Makin Island for submarine patrol. The USS Biscombe Bay had been torpedoed and sunk with a great loss of life.

During the time between being on station off Tarawa and being on station off Makin, a Japanese Betty (aircraft) made a run on our ship. Of course, fire control kept those of us on gun stations aware of the bandits even coming in, that is, how far out the bandits were, what direction they were coming from—all the information they could give us. Finally, the Betty was right upon us and we received the order from the bridge to open fire. We did, with everything we had. The Betty was so close to us on the starboard side that you could see the pilot very clearly. However, I don't think we touched the Betty with one round of ammo. Our weapons were on manual control and the Betty was so close that we just could not track the Betty fast enough. Of course, after the cease fire and secure from battle stations, the head (toilet) was the busiest place on the ship. The adrenaline was running and there was a lot of talk, mostly about one of our officers who could not hold his water during the Betty's run on our ship and had pissed all over himself. He just happened to be the most disrespected officer aboard. Enlisted men take their victories where they find them.

A DE is a rough ride even in a calm sea. Usually, if the sea is rough the DE would go over one wave and under the following wave. When you plunged into the following wave, it would on occasion be with enough force to pop light bulbs out of their socket. If the sea was very rough we had to string lines on the main deck so you would not be washed overboard. On occasion, the sea was so rough that we could not stand gun watch on the forward three-inch fifties, nor the forward twenty MM. The gun crews would have to stand the watch in the forward clipping room (ammo storage and preparation room). In the clipping room there was a bucket for anyone who became seasick. This included some of the old salts. If you were not seasick and the bucket came around in the circle you were sitting, a glance into the bucket would certainly bring anything in your stomach up. In the crew's quarters one of the signalmen told us of a message he had received from the USS Tennessee, and the message stated that the USS Tennessee would try to get a message to the USS Deede, DE 263 between submergings. It was a joke by the crew that a DE sailor should get half of flight pay, and half of submarine pay, as we were under the sea and in the air all the time. Of course, when the ship plowed into and under a wave the screw of the ship would come out of the water and shake the ship unmercifully. The ship would shudder from bow to stern. Yes, it could be a rough ride. However, a tin can sailor is a proud individual and in general would rather serve on a destroyer than on a battle wagon.

In general, the Deede was a good ship, but it did have some problems. The majority of the crew was outstanding; however, the Deede was also a stealing ship. When the ship was docked in Pearl Harbor the Angel had purchased several pairs of dungarees (work uniforms) at the ship store. Your name was stenciled on the back of the shirt and the hip of the pants. If you used the ships laundry the seaman in charge would throw the entire wash on the fantail of the ship to be picked up by the owner. Sounds simple, doesn't it? The system would have worked well if everyone would have been honest. The Angel noticed that his laundry was not coming back to the fantail of the ship. He also noticed that a couple of individuals had dungarees with patches where names had been stenciled. When the Angel brought this to the attention of the division officer he was ignored completely. The Angel learned not to use the ship laundry, but to tie his dungarees on a line and drop the dungarees into the wake of the ship and let the gyration of the water wash them.

As indicated previously, the division officer did not enjoy the respect of the crew. There was another individual who also lacked the respect of the deck hands. The man was extremely dumb and how he made his rate is beyond me. Of course, this was the Boatswain Mate Second Class. Yes, he was as dumb as a box of rocks.

The evaporation equipment on the ship could not make enough fresh water for the crew to have fresh water baths. Those who have taken a salt water (sea water) bath know that sea water will leave you feeling very sticky. Therefore, it was a luxury when we tied up alongside of an LST (landing ship tank) and were allowed to go aboard the LST for showers and on occasion they would have ice cream on board that they would share. What a treat that was!

From the ship's arrival at the Gilbert Islands on or about the 20th of November 1943 until we departed for Pearl Harbor was about a month or so as the Angel remembers it. It was a happy crew that started our return to Pearl, at the time our home port. During our tour of the Gilberts, Tarawa had been secured, Makin had been taken and we were on the offensive in the Pacific Theater of Operations.

Back in Pearl Harbor, the crew looked forward to port and starboard liberty again, and of course getting back to Hotel Street. However, this time the Skipper was very stingy with liberty and most of our time was taken up loading stores, painting the ship and dyeing anything white to a blue-grey color. We even dyed our white hats this blue-grey color.

We also were ordered out to meet and convoy ships coming from the states. In addition to this we had what seemed constant gun drill. Finally, the ship was ordered out to escort the invasion group headed for the Marshall Islands. It was now January of 1944. In the Marshalls we did very much as we had in the Gilberts. The ship assisted in the landings, then we were assigned a station to patrol for submarines and/or aircraft, and if needed, to pick up downed airmen. After the Marshalls were secure it was back to Pearl for the ship. Again, we tied up at the Destroyer Escort Docks, and again took on stores and ammo so we would be combat ready ASAP (as soon as possible). Shortly after docking, the Angel was ordered to lash-up his gear; he was being transferred to the Receiving Ship at Pearl.

The Angel was sure he was being sent back to the states for new construction, or being transferred to another ship at Pearl, because the Deede was presently over-crewed. At the Receiving Ship the Angel was a mess cook while awaiting orders. The duty was hard with long hours, but it was not unpleasant. On your free days, you could have liberty into Honolulu. On one occasion a sailor who was restricted to quarters asked the Angel to bring him a pint of whiskey when he returned from liberty. The Angel said that he would as a favor to the man. However, on returning to Pearl from Honolulu the Angel had to pass through the gate being guarded by marines. Of course, it is well known that sailors and marines are friendly enemies. The marine guard on duty when the Angel passed through the gate, I guess, just wanted to be a mean son-of-a-gun. He evidently saw the bulge around the waist of the Angel and he hit it a very hard blow with his night-stick. The blow broke the pint of whiskey and left the Angel in a terrible mess. The Angel's white uniform was drenched with whiskey and broken glass. Deep down, I guess, the marine did have a conscious for he told the Angel to move on through the gate and that he was not going to put the Angel on report. As rapidly as the Angel could, he returned to the Receiving Ship for he stank to the high heaven. He suffered a few small cuts from the broken whiskey bottle. The sailor that the Angel was getting the whiskey for had the gall to ask for his money back. In good navy vocabulary, the Angel told him to climb on it and pivot. He was not getting the money back. The Angel also told him that if he wanted the money bad enough, he could try to take it out of his hide. After looking at the Angel's size, the sailor decided not to push the issue.

After a week or so, the Angel's name and serial number came out on a draft back to the states. He was going as a working passenger on the USS Tulagi, a Kaiser flat top. His orders were to report to Treasure Island, San Francisco, but the Tulagi was destined for San Diego. It was a pleasant trip, the passengers slept on the hanger deck and were only responsible for the cleanliness of their living area on the ship. This allowed time for poker and if you were broke, hearts. After docking in San Diego and reporting to the Receiving Ship, the Angel was told that he would receive tickets to San Francisco the next day. With just a one day stay in San Diego, the Angel took liberty into town and the very next day he was on his way to Treasure Island and San Francisco. The Angel still believed he was on his way to a new construction assignment. He hoped that it would be another (destroyer) with an honest crew and somewhat better officer personnel.

Upon arrival at Treasure Island, the Angel reported to the incoming office on the base. He was given his billeting assignment, which was a large open bay type of billet that had been built for the 1940 World's Fair. The Angel now settled down with detail assignments and watching the bulletin board for his new assignment. Many of the friends the Angel had made were shipping out regularly for new construction. Finally, the entire group with the exception of the Angel had moved on. The Angel reported to the OIC (Officer in Charge) to inquire about his name not appearing on a draft for new construction. The OIC stated that he would look into the situation. This he did and the Angel came out on a draft a couple of days later. However, it was not one for assignment to new construction. The Angel's assignment was to the Naval Annex, 571 Market St., San Francisco for duty with Headquarters, 12th Naval District. What a plush assignment it was! My duty was in the message center as a courier. That is the Angel hand-carried all classified material from the code room to the Admiral or to any other designated officer, procured their signature and returned for filing in the classified document room. The Angel has given a lot of thought to this duty in later years. Here was a 14-year-old sailor who knew every ship incoming and outgoing from San Francisco and its load contents and destination. Of course, the OIC of the message center did not know the Angel was 14.

The message center had two couriers. The Angel and a very pretty WAVE. I suppose she was perhaps 21. We were both seamen and had identical duty except the Angel had been in a couple of campaigns. The Angel and the WAVE got along extremely well, and in fact dated for about a month. We hung out at the El Patio on Market Street and our money was usually no good as the drinks seemed to flow toward us from the bar's clientele. Evidently, we made a good-looking couple. It was fun! We would occasionally have dinner at Fisherman's Wharf, or take in China Town, or ride the cable cars. It was a time of feeling free. However, all good things must come to an end and about the first of April the Angel was ordered back to Treasure Island. He was informed that his age had been uncovered and that he would be processed out of the navy.

It was with a sinking heart that the Angel spent the next six days out processing. During the processing procedure, the navy ran into a real problem. Regulations covered a discharge for 14-year-olds who had entered the navy, but not for 13-year-old sailors. Therefore, Treasure Island had to contact BUPERS (Bureau of Personnel) to find out how to handle my case. It was decided to take the easy way and just void my enlistment. On April 6, 1944, I departed Treasure Island with a letter of honorable release from the navy. I knew I would not be out very long for when there is a will, there is a way. Therefore, I bought a bus ticket and headed back to St. Louis and Stanton, Missouri.

This bus trip turned into one of the exciting times of the Angel's life. The bus was completely filled and there was not a sore head in the bunch. The party was on before the bus left the station. As we headed north into northern California it started to snow when we hit the higher elevations. The more it snowed the more boisterous the riders became. They were boisterous in a friendly manner. In the party the booze flowed like water and everyone aboard shared. When you became tired you took a cat nap. Upon awakening you would continue with the party. Girls, boys, men and women, service members, non-service members— it made no difference, everyone had a great time. The bus was an express bus so we kept the same people on the bus. When the bus arrived in Cheyenne, we lost a few people, but those that came aboard were happy to fit right in and continue the party. The late spring storm had now increased in its fury, but we continued the trip and headed for Denver. Once in awhile we would hit a snow drift that the bus could not break through, then everyone would pile off and push the bus through the snow drift. We did make it to Denver, late but happy. Still snowing, we left Denver headed east. The road became more and more impassable as we neared the Kansas line. Finally, by pushing the bus through snow drifts we arrived in Goodland, Kansas. The driver of the bus decided we could go no further and the Greyhound Bus Company put all the passengers up in a hotel at the company's expense. This just made the party grow and a great time was had by all. When seen the next morning, all the passengers had a large smile on their face. By morning the roads had been cleared and we continued on our way. Finally, the Angel arrived in St. Louis, tired but happy. When he walked into Flo's place of business her face lit up and The Angel had to put up with a series of hugs from those he knew. He found out that he was fairly well known for the STAR TIMES and the GLOBE DEMOCRAT newspapers had each written an article on the Fourteen Year Old Battling Youth of the South Pacific.

The Angel told Flo that he was not home to stay, but would be going back into the military as soon as possible. Flo did not like this. Finally she gave in and said she would not sign my papers to help me get into the military, but if I returned to the military, she would do nothing to get me out.

In my partying around St. Louis for the next few days I met a buddy. He was a happy-go-lucky type of individual. He was 4F because his eyes would not focus properly. The cause of this was an automobile accident that Tiger had been involved in. He had merchant marine papers and had made the Murmanck Convoy to Russia and returned. Tig was not anxious to sign on for that run again; at least half of the ships he had started with on the Murmanck Convoy did not make it to Russia. If your ship was hit, life expectancy in the frigid water was about 15 to 20 minutes. Tiger also had papers for the merchant marine inland waterways and had in the past worked the Mississippi River from St. Louis to New Orleans. He knew that because of my age, the Angel would have trouble signing on for the Federal Barge Lines. He also knew the SOCONY (Standard Oil Company of New York) was at the time under manned and also non-union. He figured we could be hired for a deckhand by SOCONY. He was right, and we were hired for the lower Mississippi River run.

The lower Mississippi run was a milk run indeed. It was enjoyable and interesting. Moving the tow through the locks required attention to detail. Usually, we had to break the tow in half to get it through the locks. On occasion we would release the first half of the tow and then pick it up on the run. This was a dangerous practice for to pull it off, the deckhand had to be nimble indeed. One missed step and the deckhand would be crushed between the barge tow sections. My navy experience helped me, and Tiger had been down the river before.

The Angel and Tiger worked 12 hours on and 12 hours off. This was more time off than I had in the navy aboard the USS Deede, DE 263. The First Mate on this tow was a fine man and took time to explain the lock procedure and our general duties. As we passed through or between Memphis, Tennessee, and West Memphis, Arkansas, the mate informed us that the regular crew would be back from vacation and would come aboard in New Orleans. Therefore, we would be paid off in New Orleans. He also stated that he would give us a letter of introduction and that if he could find a vacancy on another tow we undoubtedly would be rehired, as we were outstanding hands.

This was great for the two of us because Tiger had a date for a boxing match back at one of the athletic clubs in St. Louis. Therefore, when we reached New Orleans and had secured the barge tow, we were paid off. After a night on Bourbon Street we headed north by hitchhiking up Highway 51. We caught a ride into Memphis and spent a night on Biel Street. Then it was hitchhiking again on Highway 51 into St. Louis. We made it in time for Tiger to meet his obligation for his place on the boxing card as a middle weight. Tiger won the fight by a close decision. The day after the boxing match we were down on the Mississippi River looking for a berth on another SOCONY tow. We found the tug and went aboard and presented our letters and were hired immediately for another down river run.

The second run down river was not as pleasant as the first one had been because the First Mate was a crazy individual. He would stand in front of the pilot house and harangue the two of us unmercifully with a bull horn. He would stand there shaking his private part at us and shout that he had more know how in the head of his private part than the two of us had together. He was just mean and ornery. Yes, he had an ugly disposition. Tiger and I started to plan on how we could get back at this sorry individual. Finally, we worked out a plan.

We knew we would be leaving the boat in New Orleans. We also noted that the Mate's quarters were right by the gang plank. When the tow had been secured in New Orleans and Tiger and I had been paid off and when leaving the boat for the last time, we noticed that the mate was in his quarters getting ready to go ashore. At this time we turned the fire hose on the no good son-of-a-gun. He could not fight the force of the water, and we blasted his sorry butt real good. Then we grabbed our sea bags and left the boat. Fourteen-year-olds will have their revenge. I will bet he gave better treatment to the next deckhands he had on the boat. Tiger and the Angel headed north to St. Louis with a very large smile on their faces.

Upon arrival in St. Louis, Tiger reported in to the athletic club to assure them he would be present for the coming fight card. The Angel headed for Stanton to spend the weekend with the Old German and Mrs. John. The Angel also found out that Slim had returned from California and was now working for St. Louis Ship Building and Steel Company. He also found out that Slim and Old Joe were rooming together and that they would be in Stanton over the weekend. The Angel was happy to get back together with them.

Between the two of these old World War I types, they harangued the Angel unmercifully about him becoming a sailor. They jokingly teased him and indicated that he was not man enough for the infantry and that was the reason he had gone into the navy. Slim indicated that the Angel had broken the family tradition by not serving his time behind the rifle. At about this point the Angel decided to show them he could and perhaps go a step further. After all, he had made it into the navy, why not try it again? Only this time stay away from the US Navy. On Monday, the Angel was present at the draft board in Union (Franklin County), Missouri, to register for the draft. After all, it had worked before. Again he asked for a speedy call.

By Tuesday, he was back in St. Louis and he and Tiger were looking for some adventure. They went downtown to the unemployment office and registered for work. Several job openings were available, but the one that looked the most exciting was working on an extra gang for the Union Pacific Railroad in Nebraska. We were given transportation and told to report to the extra gang now located in Kearney, Nebraska. Our intention was to work until the first pay day and then to return to St. Louis.

The extra gang was quartered in converted box cars. Some were bunk cars and we also had a cook car. The extra gang was replacing ties and rail in certain sections of the railroad. We also learned that an extra gang worker was called a "Gandy Dancer." We were called gandy dancers because in placing new ties the railroad ballast had to be tamped under the tie with a shovel. When you cover an area of about a half mile to a mile of extra gang workers all bobbing up and down with one foot on the shovel it gives the impression of dancing. Therefore, we were now gandy dancers. Tiger and the Angel gandy danced for two weeks and then it was pay day. Then it was back to St. Louis by thumb. We estimated that we had each moved a train load of chat (pea gravel) under the ties while we were with the extra gang. Now it was back to St. Louis and the unemployment office again.

There were plenty of jobs available so there was no use worrying about getting work. In fact, some places would give you a bonus just for signing on with them.

Tiger and the Angel signed on with the Bridge and Building Section of the Missouri Pacific Railroad, one of the companies that gave an increased hourly wage. The Bridge and Building section was responsible for the painting and maintenance of the railroad bridge across the Mississippi River. To do this we had to work high on rigged scaffolding. We would work up to 200 feet over the river. It was an absolutely grand view of St. Louis.

The work was going well and we were in about our third or

fourth week of work when a piece of scaffolding fell and landed across Tiger's back. The foreman of the crew had the Angel take Tiger to the Missouri Pacific Hospital to be checked out for possible injury. The hospital sent Tiger home for the remainder of the day. The next day Tiger did not show up for work. The foreman asked the Angel if he would go to Tiger's apartment and check to see if he was well. The Angel found Tiger at home and drinking. After killing half of a day, Tiger said that he was ready to return to work. At work we were painting on the high scaffold, when the foreman in a very decisive manner started to question Tiger regarding his not reporting for work that morning. The fact was, the foreman was trying to cover his back side, because he had not made out an accident report after sending Tiger to the hospital. The words back and forth became more angry between the two of them and finally Tiger hit the foreman and the fight was on. The Angel was hanging onto the swinging scaffold for dear life. It's no place for a fight-200 feet up and on a swinging scaffold. Finally, they both came to their senses, shook hands and went back to work. The Angel had his close call for the day. Both Tiger and the foreman now had more respect for each other.

After about a month on the MoPac bridge and building crew, the Angel received a long distance phone call from Mrs. John. She said that a government envelope had arrived at her house addressed for the Angel. She said that it looked important. The Angel stated that he would open it then. He was fairly sure he knew what it was. He figured it was his draft notice and he was ready to get back into the service, because, people were still stopping him on the street and asking him why he was not in service. It was the same as before he had entered the US Navy. Perhaps it was even greater now, as he was now 14 years old. He just hoped against hope that he would not be recognized as he processed through Jefferson Barracks the second time. Sure enough, it was his official greetings from friends and neighbors.

On the date specified, the Angel reported to the processing station at Jefferson Barracks, Missouri. There he ran across three other men from Sullivan, Missouri. We greeted each other. However, the Angel knew that they all were aware that the Angel was underage for the military. Since he knew the three personally, he asked them not to spill the beans on him and they assured him they would not.

The fear that the Angel had that some of the processing personnel would remember that he had processed through there over a year ago was truly unfounded. Thousands of men had processed through Jefferson Barracks since he had. Also, many of the processing personnel had been transferred to other posts, camps or stations and replacements for them were now on the processing line.

The Angel from Stanton and the three from Sullivan decided to try to remain together, if at all possible. Upon completion of the in-processing, the four of us had our paperwork stamped acceptable for army, navy or marines. The three from Sullivan were interviewed before the Angel and they came out of the interview accepted for the US Army. During the Angel's interview, the psychologist doing the interview stamped the Angel's paperwork as acceptable for the US Navy. The Angel knew this would not work. The probability of him being caught going into the same branch of service he had been in before was extremely high. The Angel had to talk himself out of this dilemma. He told the psychologist that the four of them would like to remain together. The psychologist was not moved by this argument. The Angel insisted that there had to be a way. The psychologist still was not moved, but to get us out of his hair he sent the four of us to see the head of his section. The section leader looked over physical exam papers and stated that he may have a way that we could remain together. He stated that all four of us had passed the physical well enough to volunteer for the Paratroops. This we did right then and there and departed his interview cubicle extremely happy. After the exam, we were taken to the area for the swearing-in ceremony and to our assigned quarters. We were now soldiers of the United States Army.

The next day, while going through the clothing issue line, the Angel was issued a set of old blue denim fatigues. The Angel, remembering the brown shoe situation during navy boot camp, did not want anything that would make him stand out from the rest of those present. The Angel's argument, to replace the old pre-war fatigues with some olive-drab fatigues, fell on deaf ears. All the Angel heard was a sorry, shut-up and move along! Do not hold up the line! Well, you win some and you lose some—the Angel continued to move along. He was happy, at 14, to have pulled it off again.

After clothing issue, we were fed and then taken to the assembly area to catch the train that would take us to basic training.

When we boarded the train, all of the window shades were closed and we were admonished to keep them closed. Shortly after leaving Jefferson Barracks, the porter made-up our pullman beds and we had to occupy them. Again, it was great to be riding the cushions. It was more comfortable than a boxcar or a gondola. The Angel knew that parachute training was conducted at Fort Benning, Georgia, so he just figured that was our destination. The next morning, at full light, the train was on a side track, so the Angel figured he would sneak a peek to ascertain our location. When he peeked around the window shade, he saw the sign in the depot and it read Atlanta. This reinforced his thinking about Fort Benning being our destination. The Angel could not have been more wrong. The Atlanta we were in was Atlanta, Texas. Finally, we moved west through Dallas and Fort Worth—always continuing west. The train finally stopped in a town named Mineral Wells, Texas. Here we waited for about an hour before military cattle-like trucks pulled up along side the train, one truck for each train car. Then each train car had a soldier board who, shouting in a boisterous manner, told us to pick up our duffel bag and load onto the truck outside when he called our name. This we did as rapidly as possible.

When all the trucks were loaded, they moved out in convoy order. A few miles out of town we entered a gate that read Camp Wolters, Texas-IRTC. As soon as the trucks were on the parade field, we unloaded while being shouted at and called all kinds of low-life. As soon as possible, the Angel asked one of the cademen what the IRTC meant that I had seen while coming through the gate. He very roughly informed me that IRTC meant Infantry Replacement Training Center, and that we would be trained to fill a position that someone had been shot out of providing, of course, that they could make soldiers out of such a sorry group as we were. We were placed in platoons in alphabetical order. The three from Sullivan and the Angel from Stanton, Missouri, were now split up in different platoons, but we were still in the same company.

The Field First Sergeant had us gather around and informed us that our training would begin the following Monday. He also stated that we would be pulling details until then. He then turned us over to our respective Platoon Sergeant for some very basic training, such as how to make a bunk so the blanket would be so tight that it would flip a quarter if one were to be dropped on the bunk. He then taught us how to make a combat pack and a full field pack. Of course, there was close order drill, how to maintain a footlocker, etc. During all this, we would have rat races just to keep us mentally alert. The Angel actually enjoyed this—some others did not have the same mind set the Angel had. The training was very good; it instilled in us what we could do, and more importantly, what we could not do.

The Angel well remembers the detail he was ordered to do the second day in Camp Wolters. The Platoon Sergeant ordered the Angel to get a bucket and some rags from the supply room and to report to the First Sergeant in the orderly room to wash the windows of the supply and orderly rooms. Since I had been ordered to do this I did not think the sign on the orderly room door pertained to me. Therefore, I just walked in and said to the First Sergeant, "Where are those frigging windows you want me to wash, Mac?" He looked at me for a good minute without speaking, as if he could not understand what I had just done. Then he spoke in a soft voice and said, "What did the sign on the orderly room door say?" The Angel said, "It said knock before entering." The First Sergeant said, "Well, do it now recruit!"

The Angel did and the First Sergeant let him stand for a good ten minutes before he said to come in. He then put the Angel at a brace (rigid attention) and let the Angel stand there for a very long time. The First Sergeant then pointed to his insignia of rank on his arm and informed the Angel in no uncertain words that he was to be addressed by his rank and last name. Then he told me that I could proceed with the windows and just to be sure I did not forget what he had told me, I was to report to the Mess Sergeant after I had completed the windows, for a week of KP (kitchen police).

The Mess Sergeant was a tough son-of-a-gun. In fact, he was Camp Wolter's heavyweight champ in boxing. He was not a person to argue with and the Angel did not attempt to argue with him. The First Sergeant had told the Mess Sergeant why I was to report to him and why he had ordered me to. Therefore, I was given the hardest detail on KP. The Angel was assigned to pots and pans. The Angel had to keep the water in the sink at 160 degrees or hotter. He kept a thermometer in the water and was constantly checking it to be sure the water remained at 160 degrees or better. Over a period of time, this hot water will start to cook your arms. At the end of each day, the Angel's arms would be blistered to the level of water in the sink. As each day ended, the Angel would have to report to the dispensary to have his arms medicated and wrapped. This cycle continued for a full week. Yes, the Angel had learned and he now addressed cadremen by their rank and name.

Our Platoon Sergeant was an outstanding, non-commissioned officer. He had seen combat, been wounded and returned to the states. The First Sergeant and the Field First Sergeant had not been baptized by fire. Therefore, we tended to listen more to the Platoon Sergeant, even though he was out-ranked by the First Sergeant and the Field First. I guess the Platoon Sergeant was just more knowledgeable about what we would be getting into when we were finished with our 17 weeks of light weapons infantry training.

Since it was the policy of the training company to have only one cadreman, a Platoon Sergeant, assigned to each platoon, he needed to assign acting squad leaders and assistant squad leaders from the trainees. The acting position gave more responsibility to the trainee, but no more money. The trainee having these positions were referred to as acting sergeant or acting corporal. Along the way, some had to be replaced because they just could not handle the job.

About the third week of training and after a particularly difficult day, we all made for the shower as soon as it was possible, including the Platoon Sergeant. During the shower the Platoon Sergeant noticed the tattoo on the Angel's right forearm. He asked the Angel about the tattoo. Things like what was a ship named the USS Deede doing on my arm. It was the tattoo that the Angel had gotten in Honolulu, Hawaii while in the navy. A light flashed in the mind of the Angel. Was the Platoon Sergeant on to my age or prior service? Was his question a catch trial? The Angel immediately became defensive and mentally alert. However, he did answer the Platoon Sergeant's inquiry. He said, "Platoon Sergeant there are some things that are better not asked or answered."

This answer seemed to satisfy the Platoon Sergeant's curiosity, and he did not pursue the subject any further, although he did say that the Angel seemed to be more knowledgeable regarding military subjects than the other trainees. He also said that one of his acting sergeants was not capable of holding down the position of acting sergeant and would the Angel assume the position. The

Angel said sure, he would be happy to give it a try for the experience. At the next formation, the change was announced and the Angel took over one of the squads in the platoon. He was now an acting gadget at the age of 14. Of course, only three others who came into the service with the Angel, the three from Sullivan, Missouri, knew his age. At least he hoped that was the case.

About two months later the training schedule called for their company to be on the KD (known distance) rifle range. It was fun and the Angel took to it like a fish takes to water. This is where the training Slim had given him in the past paid off. The Angel fired expert and was top scorer in the company. His squad was top squad on the KD range that week.

The weekend after the rifle range, the Angel's squad was granted a pass to go into Mineral Wells. It was just a typical western town inflated due to its proximity to Camp Wolters. The soldier the Angel went to town with was a man in his squad we all called, in a respectful manner, Fat. Fat was from Marked Tree, Arkansas. He was not fat, just big. At the bus station to catch the bus back to Camp Wolters, we noticed a fight taking place. This was not a one on one fair fight but a gang beating up on one soldier. Fat waded into that gang like a bulldozer gone wild. The gang was going down left and right. Of course, the Angel was doing his part also. Finally, the gang broke and ran. We took the soldier they were beating on back to camp and to the dispensary for treatment. The Angel gained a lot of respect for Fat that night.

Things were moving along in extremely good order. On the daily barracks inspection by the Field First Sergeant, our barracks was usually designated the outstanding barracks. The acting gadgets got along extremely well with the troops. The training was going like clockwork.

Then about the seventh week of training, the Platoon Sergeant noticed that the Angel did not look well. He ordered him to go on sick call. To go on sick call, you had to turn in all your equipment just in case you were hospitalized. The Angel did not want to go on sick call, primarily because his gear was immaculate and you did not get the same gear back when you returned from sick call or the hospital. This turn-in of equipment was primarily to make going on sick call difficult so that it would not be used just to goldbrick. However, an order is an order and the Platoon Sergeant had said go on sick call, so I went. The doctor at the dispensary checked the Angel out and had him admitted to the Post Hospital for the Angel had the mumps. This meant that after his illness the Angel would be reassigned to another training battalion. Needless to say, the Angel was not a happy trooper.

Upon returning to the hospital for admittance, the Angel had to turn into storage his uniform and was issued hospital garb. He was told what ward to report to. He was given a bed and told that he was not to get out of the bed for any reason. This included going to the bathroom. After a couple of hours, nature started to push him. After another hour, it felt like he was going to burst wide open. The Angel asked the soldier in the bed next to him what to do, after all he had been told not to get out of the bed for any reason. The soldier told him to call the nurse and to ask for a duck. The nurse was a captain and a complete grouch, but she did bring the duck. However, it was smaller than the Angel figured it would be. Therefore, he told the nurse she had better bring two ducks. The nurse, in an extremely haughty manner, informed the Angel that one duck would be sufficient. She said that if I could fill more than one just to finish on the floor. She said that no one had ever filled more than one duck. The Angel took her at her word. He urinated in one until it was completely full and he still had to go, so he did what he had been told to do—he urinated on the floor. This made the nurse extremely angry. The Angel tried to tell her it was what she had told him to do. The remainder of the hospital time passed more smoothly.

After ten days, the Angel was sent to the rehabilitation center. This was a great place to be. We had no reveille formation. Breakfast was served from six to eight in the morning. First call was at eight o'clock. Then we were given an hour to clean our barracks. From nine o'clock until eleven-thirty, we had physical training. In the afternoon we participated in sports, usually baseball. At five o'clock we had post privilege. On each Friday we had a track and field meet and the top three places were granted a weekend pass from Friday afternoon until Monday morning. To the Angel, this place was a little bit of heaven. The men who had mumps were only supposed to stay in rehab for one week. The Angel was wishing he could stay there forever. One morning, very much out of the ordinary, a detail was selected to clean the record center for an upcoming inspection. The Angel volunteered for the detail.

When they arrived at the record center they were given cleaning material and put to work. The soldier in charge then left the building and told us he would be back to check our work in an hour or so. It is human nature to want to know what is in your medical record, so we all pulled our record from the file cabinet and read it. The other soldier on the detail then put their records back into the file cabinet. The Angel just dropped his medical record between the wall and the cabinet.

After about eight weeks, the Angel was called to the orderly room and was informed that his records had been misplaced and had now been found. They also said I would be returning to duty the following Monday. Oh well, all good things must come to an end. It had been great, a weekend pass every weekend and sports every day. The Angel was in top shape physically. This would get him into trouble with his new Platoon Sergeant.

The Angel was assigned to a training battalion that was in the same week of training that his old battalion had been when he had to go to the hospital. The company and platoon that he was assigned to had as cadre a platoon sergeant and a corporal. Neither of these soldiers had any combat experience. Both were all go and no show type of cadremen. They were loud and boisterous in their treatment of the trainees. The Platoon Sergeant thought he was an outstanding physical specimen. As he had been doing in the past, he would challenge individual trainees to try to work him down in physical training. When he worked the trainee down, he would belittle the trainee in front of his peers for being so weak. He was just downright nasty.

When the Angel reported to him and informed him that he had been assigned to his platoon, he spent some time belittling the Angel. The Angel did not respond to the profane tirade but maintained his brace of attention. However, in the Angel's mind, he knew the opportunity would come for him to belittle this extreme egotist. The time came sooner than expected.

During the first physical training exercise that the Angel participated in with the new platoon the Platoon Sergeant asked if anyone thought they could outdo him in sit-ups. The Angel politely said that he could. He then walked to the center of the platoon formation and took his place by the Platoon Sergeant. With other members of the platoon holding our ankles, we started to exercise. With the other trainees of the platoon giving the Angel vocal encouragement, the challenge was met. The Platoon Sergeant finally could go no more. The Angel, just to rub salt into the mental wound of the cadreman, added another 50 sit-ups before he terminated the exercise.

The Platoon Sergeant never went back to his old tactic of challenging the trainees to try to work him down. His ego balloon had been deflated. However, with his type of personality, he would try to make it rough on the Angel. On our hikes, if there was a mortar base plate or a machine gun to carry in addition to our full field gear, it was always given to the strong boy from Missouri. Yes, he was a sore loser.

The company the Angel had been assigned to was about one-half Japanese-American. Many of them had volunteered right from the concentration camps they had been assigned to at the start of the war. There were camps in Utah, Montana, etc. They were outstanding soldiers for they had something to prove.

Just as the Angel had entered the service under age, one of these Japanese-Americans had entered the service over age. He was in his early sixties. The training was very hard on him, but he would not accept help on the hikes or any other light weapons infantry training. On the hikes, he would sometimes have to fall back, but he would never fall out. When the Angel would offer to carry some of his equipment, he would smile and politely say no. The Angel admired this man for the backbone he showed.

As the training progressed, the Angel enjoyed it more and more. It was exciting and created a self-assurance within the Angel. A can-do attitude.

About the tenth week of the training cycle, the training schedule called for a 15-mile forced march of a night. As it was a night problem, contact had to be maintained between the platoons. The Angel and two other trainees were posted between their platoon and the platoon in front of them. The term for this was to be the "connecting file." The trainees had no prior knowledge of the route of march. It was an extremely dark night and for some reason, the Angel lost contact with the platoon in front of him. When he came to a fork in the road, it was a toss-up as to which trail to take. The Angel decided to take the trail most-used. It was a wrong guess and the Angel lead them on into an unknown situation. The cadreman who would have put us on the correct trail did not correct the error in judgement by the Angel. The error in judgement cost the platoon an extra five miles of forced march. This made it a 20-mile forced march with full field pack and weapon. Needless to say, some within the platoon were not happy with the Angel. It was a nadir in the training cycle for the Angel.

The Corporal that had been assigned to our platoon as a

cadreman was not mentally the swiftest man on earth. He was loud and that was it. One Sunday we had headed off for church and care and cleaning of our equipment. That afternoon two of us had our equipment checked and were released for the remainder of the day. We decided to go to the beer garden and down a few. As it turned out, we had more than a few. We returned to the barracks about 9:30 p.m. We were happy and singing. Surely, we were making more noise than we should have been making. It was enough noise to bring the Corporal out of his cadre room and to put the two of us at a brace. He was extremely angry and was verbally berating the two of us, one at a time. After he finished with the Angel, he started on the other trainee. At this point, the Angel unbuttoned his fly and while still at attention, pissed down the Corporal's leg. The Corporal shouted, "What the hell do you think you're doing?" He jumped back in his cadre room and slammed the door shut. The Angel figured he would be called on the carpet the next morning, but nothing happened. It is almost as bad to believe something is going to happen and be waiting for it to happen as it would be to get it over with. The Angel was on pins and needles for the next week or so.

The training cycle continued to move along in good order with the Angel carrying more than his load. He was learning the ways of the Army and becoming an outstanding soldier. One of the lessons he learned was when to take things easy and when not to take things easy. One weekend we could have a pass to Mineral Wells, Texas. However, to get the pass we had to pass a rifle inspection. Our Platoon Sergeant was a CQ (Charge of Quarters) and he was the one giving out the passes to town. The Angel worked on his rifle until it was perfect. He then took it to the orderly room for the CQ to inspect it and to grant his pass. The CQ said it was dirty and needed more attention to detail. The Angel took it back to the barracks, placed it in the rifle rack and took a nap. In about an hour, he woke up, took his rifle from the rack and took it to the orderly room. The CQ now stated that the rifle was perfect and the pass was granted. He was still angry that the Angel had worked him down in sit-ups.

The Angel was really aggravated that his pass had been held up for he had promised a friend of his that he would go home with him over the weekend. Playing games with the pass had caused the friend and his family precious pass time. After all, the pass was only good for Saturday afternoon and Sunday. We had to be back to Camp Wolters by reveille on Monday morning. He and his family were still waiting when the Angel received his pass. Fortunately, they did not have far to drive. Just to Weatherford, Texas.

It was a beautiful weekend with the friend and his family. The friend had a sister that was outstandingly beautiful. It was a pleasure to be seen with her. It was a party on Saturday night and church on Sunday with the family always present. Absolutely no hanky panky took place. I sincerely hope the friend made it through the war.

By now we were getting well into our training cycle. About the twelfth week, the company was marched to the local post theater for a presentation on the Airborne. Two of the sharpest looking soldiers I had ever seen gave the presentation. They were both qualified paratroopers. They stated that they were there to recruit for the Airborne and that at any time during their pre-sentation if you felt that you were not man enough for the Airborne to please get up and leave quietly. About a fourth of the audience left the theater. When they stated that Airborne train-ing would be at lease twice as hard as the infantry training at Camp Wolters, we lost another fourth of the audience. When they stated that during Airborne training one did not walk, but ran, from reveille until taps, another fourth left the theater. During the presentation others filed out regularly until just a few remained. Our names were taken and after we returned to our company area we were told to report to the hospital the next day for our Airborne physical. Here we lost a few more. Finally we were told that those of us who remained would indeed be ordered to Airborne training on completion of our 17 weeks of training at Camp Wolters. Yes, we were very proud at this time. Not only was the Angel fully Airborne training qualified, but he was just 15 years old. Those of us who were Airborne volunteers were harassed considerably until our infantry training cycle ended. The Angel figured that the straight leg platoon sergeant just was not man enough for the Airborne.

By now the Angel had qualified with all the weapons that a light weapons infantryman would use. For the last three weeks of training we would put into practice what we had learned. We would live in the field and practice shooting, moving and commu-nicating. We would work with squad problems, platoon problems and company problems. We would practice field sanitation. We would practice scouting and patrolling. It was a time to learn and for some it would only be perhaps six weeks before they would receive their baptism to fire. They would see combat close up. They would realize that the mission of the infantry is to close with and destroy the enemy.

Just prior to going into the field for the last three weeks of training, the Angel's company had to go through the water expedient course. We had to swim 200 yards fully dressed. We had to jump off the 10-meter platform, undress, tie our fatigue pants legs in knots, catch air in the pant legs and float, we learned to swim through fire. However, the most difficult part was a 100-yard swim fully dressed and carrying a full field pack.

To do this, a raft had been anchored in Lake Mineral Wells 100 yards from shore. We were to swim out to the raft and then be brought back to shore by assault boat. The Angel was never a strong swimmer, but he figured he would have no trouble with this phase of training. The pack and the fatigues he was given to complete the exercise had been used before and therefore were completely water logged. The Angel should say here that the water expedient course was strictly on a volunteer basis. The Angel was the last to leave the shore for the raft. The fatigues he was wearing were split down the pant legs and this acted almost like an anchor. About two-thirds of the way to the raft the Angel ran out of steam and slipped beneath the water. It felt like he was suspended about a foot below the surface of the water. He tried to swim up, no luck. He tried to swim down and push off the bottom of the lake, no luck. Now he had held his breath as long as he could. He had to breathe and he did. The water felt cool and pleasant in his lungs. The Angel figured it was the end of the line for him, but he kept trying to break the surface, no luck. In the company was a young soldier from Hawaii and he was an outstanding swimmer. He saw the Angel's plight and came to the Angel's aid. When he pulled the Angel back to the surface of the lake and air started going into the Angel's lungs that was the first time the Angel had strangled. How good the air felt. Oh well, from there it had to be onward and upward. The Angel thanked the soldier from Hawaii profusely. The Angel also wondered if the platoon sergeant was mean enough to save the waterlogged pack and the torn fatigue pants just for him, surely not.

On Monday morning after the water expedient course we set out for the field and the last three weeks of our infantry training.

Our spirits were high and we were a motivated group of ground pounders.

It was about 10 miles out of our first bivouac area called "Pinto Ridge." About eight or nine miles into the hike was a place they called Separation Hill. It was supposed to separate the men from the boys. It was so steep that traction strips had to be put into the road for military vehicles to negotiate the gradient of the hill. The men of the company used to jokingly say that the hill was so steep that it would skin your nose going up and drag your ass going down.

At Pinto Ridge we were assigned a buddy to pitch our shelter half with. The Platoon Sergeant assigned a Portuguese fellow from Southern California for the Angel to buddy with. He had worked on the fishing boats around Monterey Bay, California, prior to coming into the service. He was a dirty, lazy type of person who used people. He would fall out on hikes so the Platoon Sergeant would redistribute his load to others in the company; usually the Angel would get a good part of his load. At the end of the hike he would be the first at the Service Club, jitterbugging all over the place. Well, no way out; the Angel had to share his shelter half with this person. Toward the end of the week at Pinto Ridge the Angel noticed some itching and patchy spots in his pubic hair.

The Angel decided to see the medic who had been assigned to stay with us in the field. He was a grizzled old prewar regular soldier and his rank was only buck sergeant. When the Angel approached him, he asked what the problem was. The Angel told him he thought he might be infected with crab lice. The old medic laughed and asked how I knew and the Angel told him of the itching, etc. The medic stated that it could be heat rash, but if the Angel thought it was crab lice to go pull one off and bring it to him. The Angel did and the old medic laughed and said "You sure have a dose of crabs young soldier." The Angel asked him how he was going to get rid of them. The old medic said to make up a solution of whiskey and sand and use it around his groin area. He said that the crabs would get drunk and throw rocks at each other. Then he laughed hysterically. He then gave me a can of DDT powder and said, "You use it and have that lazy son of a gun you share a shelter half with use it also." It was that no good bastard that gave them to me. The DDT took care of the crab lice situation.

We spent the week at Pinto Ridge setting up a perimeter defense, reconnaissance patrolling, combat patrolling and other military subjects that would help keep us alive later on.

At the end of the week we moved from Pinto Ridge to Baker's Valley. This was a distance of over 30 miles, 30 hard gruelling miles with full field equipment. Many of the old 1918 haversack packs had slipped down during the hike and would hit you in the butt each step you took. Some could not make it and had to fall out. The Angel wound up carrying his full field pack, his rifle and the rifle of two of his friends. He offered to carry the rifle of the old Japanese gentleman, but he said no thanks, that he could make it. He might be late, but he would complete the hike.

During the hike we passed through a little built-up area of perhaps a dozen houses, certainly no more than a dozen. Many in the march had drank their allotted canteen of water. One fellow in the little town who was watering his garden as we passed through, hung his watering hose through the fence so the soldiers could fill their canteens. The cadreman that was with us made all of those he caught pour the water out. The Angel was lucky again; he had refilled his canteen and not been caught. Could he have a guardian angel looking after him?

It seemed that they would never get to Baker's Valley bivouac area. After getting there we would have to assault a mock village as a problem in combat in cities, before we could set up our bivouac perimeter. The week at Baker's Valley moved along and we had problem after problem based on combat in cities. By the end of the second week in the field with little sleep we were all dog tired. However, we still had another week of bivouac at Hell's Bottom. The march to Hell's Bottom was about 15 miles. Of course, it was with full field equipment. Of course, the Platoon Sergeant had the Angel carry a mortar base plate in addition to his regular gear. The hike went as if it was an everyday stroll. By the end of the march, the Angel was carrying three rifles, a mortar base place and his regular gear.

In Hell's Bottom we set up our perimeter defense for the night and prepared to assault a hill the next morning. The problem was to assault a position using overhead artillery and a walking barrage. At about two o'clock in the morning we moved from the perimeter to the assembly area; then from the assembly area, we formed into a scrimmage line and moved toward the objective. We crossed the IP at the correct time and the artillery came in about

100 yards ahead of us. It was the first time we had worked with artillery that close. It was a sight to behold!

During the week at Hell's Bottom we had other assault problems. One of which was a great learning problem for the Angel.

The company had been given an objective to assault. The objective was a high ground area, but at the foot of the high ground was a muddy slow-moving creek. For this mission, the Angel had been assigned a BAR (Browning Automatic Rifle). At the proper time and on the proper signal (green smoke) we headed for the objective on a run. The Angel noticed that some trees had fallen across the creek. He immediately made up his mind to use one of the trees to cross the creek. He hit the downed tree at a dead run. He then slipped on the tree and fell into the creek. The Angel came out of the creek sputtering and muddy. The cadreman that was in charge of the problem asked the Angel where his BAR was. The Angel said that it was in the creek. The cadreman ordered him to go back into the creek and to retrieve the BAR. This was no easy task as the Angel had to repeatedly dive to the bottom of the creek and feel in the mud and slime for the BAR. The cadreman then ordered the Angel to clean the weapon and to bring it to him for inspection every hour on the hour for the next 24 hours. No sleep that night!

On Friday of that week we had a forced march of 15 miles back to our battalion area at Camp Wolters. It was the last item of our infantry training. The next day we would have graduation ceremony and receive our orders. It was during this last forced march that the Platoon Sergeant would get his last shot at breaking the Angel. He loaded the Angel up with his regular gear, including the ever-present mortar base plate. After about five miles or one hour, into the forced march, the Platoon Sergeant asked, "How are you going, strong boy from Missouri?" The Angel told him that he would still be there after the Sergeant had fallen out. Of course, the Sergeant, who was carrying no equipment, laughed hilariously and moved on along the route of march. In a few minutes, he came back with a medics first aid packet and gave it to the Angel. The Angel then threw the first aid packet as far as he could off the road. The Platoon Sergeant shouted, "Angel, you've had it when we get back to Camp Wolters." The Angel said nothing, he just continued to march. On arrival back in the Battalion area, we had to clean and turn in our gear. After this had been completed, the squawk box in the barracks barked out that the Angel was to report to the orderly room ASAP, if not sooner. The Angel reported using his best military bearing. He was shown a pack with a sandbag in it that weighed 90 pounds. The pack had a sign on it that said "I disobeyed orders". The Platoon Sergeant and the First Sergeant had decided that because I had thrown the first aid packet into the ditch that I would have to carry this pack around the parade field until reveille the next morning and that I would have to sign in at the orderly room every 10 minutes. The Platoon Sergeant was taking his last shot at the Angel.

During our training, the entire Battalion had run the expert infantryman's course for the award of the Expert Infantry Badge. This badge, if awarded, increased our pay by five dollars per month. The next day, the day of graduation, we would know who had won the coveted award. The next day when we fell out for the graduation ceremony and parade, the Angel was almost unable to keep his eyes open. When the formation was in line, the Adjutant shouted, "ATTENTION TO ORDERS" and read the names of those who had been awarded the EXPERT INFANTRY BADGE.

The Angel could not believe his ears for his was one of the names the Adjutant had read. Only eight men from the Battalion had made the award, only two from the Angel's Company. We, the awardees, were called front and center and presented with the award and orders for the award. Then we were invited to the reviewing stand to review the troops as they passed. When the band played "ROGER YOUNG," the tears crept out of my eyes and slid down my cheeks. Was I proud? You bet I was! The Angel was dog tired and extremely proud. After the parade and back in the company area, the troops were all shaking my hand and congratulating the Angel. However, the Platoon Sergeant was not man enough to shake my hand. In the Angel's mind, he made him stronger for he could not break the Angel. The Angel had worked him down in physical training and he knew that the Angel was the better man. The Angel could stand tall.

The last formation that our training company had at Camp Wolters was to give us our orders. Most of the trainees had a 10-day delay in route to visit their home and then report to their Port of Embarkation on either the West Coast or the East Coast. They would go to the Pacific Theater of Operations or the European Theater of Operations as replacements. The only soldiers in the Company who did not receive a 10-day leave were those of us who had volunteered for the paratroops. Our orders had us reporting to Fort Benning, Georgia, for Airborne training. About 10 of 12 of us from the training battalion would be going to Fort Benning.

One of those going was a cadre Staff Sergeant from one of the other companies who had volunteered for the paratroops. He turned out to be an outstanding and motivated noncommissioned officer. The Angel figured he had just grown tired of running cycle after cycle through their infantry training. The Sergeant was put in charge of our group and was given our train and meal tickets and we were on our way. The trip was uneventful and we detrained in Columbus, Georgia. It was early in the morning and the Sergeant took us to a restaurant for breakfast.

When breakfast was served it was a man's meal. However, it had some white grainy stuff on the plate that the Angel took to be cream-of-wheat. He therefore proceeded to put milk and sugar on the stuff. He noticed the waitress looking at him kind of funny and smiling big. When he tried some of it he knew he had never tasted it before. He asked a friend of his in the group what the hell it was. The soldier friend was from Alabama, and he told the Angel that what he was eating was grits. The Angels next question was, how do you eat them? The Alabama soldier said that you put eggs on top of the grits along with a pat of butter and then cut the eggs into little pieces and let the egg yolk drain down through the grits. The Angel followed his instruction and immediately became a confirmed southerner. It sure as the devil beat cream-of-wheat. After breakfast we caught a bus to Fort Benning, which was just a little ways out of town.

The ride out to Fort Benning was a pleasant one. It went through a pine forest. The trees had been tapped and the smell of turpentine was the aroma that filled the air. The bus stopped and we off-loaded our gear. We were met by a couple of outstanding looking noncommissioned officers. They had us shoulder our duffel bags and follow them.

They informed us that this was the last time we would walk for the next four weeks. They smiled and said to take advantage of this walk. They took us to our billets, which were just on the hill from Lawson Field. We found out later that we were lucky, we could have been billeted in the frying pan area.

Our first chore was to clean the barracks. They looked clean to the Angel, but what the hell, don't make waves. Here the knowledge of the NCO that had come with us from Camp Wolters came into play. He had us move our gear, our bunks and everything outside, and using a hose, we washed the entire inside of the barracks down and scrubbed it until there was not a speck of dust anywhere. After the inside had dried, we moved our gear back inside and reported to the CQ (Charge of Quarters) that we were ready for inspection.

On a Sunday afternoon we received our orientation regarding what would be expected of us while in the Parachute School. In our formation, we were told to look to the left and to the right and informed that one of the people we just looked at would not be there at the end of the school.

This situation made me happy that I had told no one that I knew back at Stanton, Sullivan or St.Clair, Missouri, that I was going to Parachute School. This was just in case I would be one of those who did not make it.

The instructor told us that the school was broken down into four stages: A,B,C and D. "A" stage would be physical training and parachute landing falls, "B" stage would be the swing landing training and the 34 fast towers. "C" stage was the 250 feet towers. "D" stage was the jump stage and we would make five jumps from an airplane in flight during that stage. It sounded simple, but there was a lot more to it than the Angel figured on. We were told that we would, in training, respond to a whistle blown by one of the instructors. On one whistle we would fall in at ease, and button the top on our fatigues. On a second whistle we would come to parade rest. On the third whistle we would come to attention and be ready to engage in the training. Every move we made would be at double time. Any infraction of the rules would bring on push-ups.

I knew that it was going to be a tough school when a Lieutenant Colonel in our jump class spit in the sawdust pit where we were doing calisthenics and the instructor made him pick the spit back up in his mouth and crawl to the side of the pit and get rid of the spit. When the officer tried to argue with the instructor, the instructor stated that he could either do as he was told or sign a quit slip and get the hell out of the way of those who were motivated to become paratroopers. The Lieutenant Colonel apologized to the instructor and to the class and returned to the exercise pit. At the end of "A" stage the class had a cross country run and anyone who fell behind the last instructor had his name taken and had to repeat "A" stage. The class had several who had to quit or repeat, however, the Angel was not one of them.

During "A" stage, the Angel had gone through sheer misery for he had developed a boil on his gluteus and during parachute landing fall training the gluteus was a point of contact with the ground. The Angel took the pain instead of going on sick call because he did not want to be washed back in training. At one point, later in the week, he felt the core of the boil burst when he hit the ground. It was all the Angel could do to keep from screaming out, but he held it in and finished the day with the matter in the boil running down his leg. The Angel hoped his instructor would not notice or smell it; he did not. On a Saturday morning after a week in "A" stage the class had a cross country run. One of the instructors trailed the formation and if a runner fell back to the position of the instructor he would check your name on the class roster and that person would have to take "A" stage over again. When the Angel would catch himself falling back toward the training instructor, he would find the energy somewhere to stay with the group. After four hours, the run terminated at the post swimming pool. There we had to swim 50 yards. With the swim complete, the trailing instructor read from the roster the names of those who would have to quit or repeat "A" stage. When we returned to our living area, the instructor had those of us who made "A" stage wait until the quitters or the washouts packed their gear and left the area. Some I saw in the class behind us, and some I never saw again. The Angel was one fourth of the way to graduation.

Monday the Angel started "B" stage. This stage was lots of physical training. It was also the swing landing training and the 34-foot towers. The instructor said that if you could make it out of the 34-foot towers you could make it out of a C47 aircraft. This was not exactly true. Every day of the week we had to make three qualifying jumps from the tower. The Angel concentrated and made his three qualifying jumps easily. However, his friend from Oklahoma was not so lucky. He had to make 10 to 20 jumps from the tower every day to get three that would qualify him. The three qualifying jumps were more or less gifts of the instructor, for poor old Okie would be all bruised and beat to hell at the end of the day. He just could not keep his feet together or maintain a good body position out of the door of the tower. "B" stage moved right along and before you knew it, the week was over and we were closer to the actual jump stage.

The third week was "C" stage. We laughingly called this the carnival stage for this was the 250-foot towers. The parachute would be fastened inside a hoop and then you would be hoisted the 250 feet, held for awhile and then released while the instructor berated you with a bull horn. The tower had four arms for chute release, but you could only use three of the arms, because the wind would always cause one arm to be dirty. Here again, the Angel paid attention to detail and got his qualifying jumps in early. Poor old Okie was still having problems; on his first jump from the tower, he did not listen to the instructor and slipped his chute the wrong way. This caused his chute to get tangled up in the tower structure and there was old Okie, hung up in the tower structure and dangling in the breeze. The instructors had to go up the tower and bring old Okie down. Even when slapped in the face with a quit slip Okie would not quit.

It was during "C" stage that the Angel found out that being tall was not always an asset. In rigging the parachute to the hoop the tallest person in the squad was the pole man. This was the person that pushed the apex of the chute up and into the release mechanism. The remainder of the squad would snap the skirt of the chute to the hoop. The slow arm in rigging always had to do 25 push-ups. If the pole man missed on the first try, it was almost always true that they would be the slow arm. By the end of the day, the pole man, usually the Angel, was beat. Of course, the squad was on the pole man's back if he missed on the first try.

Finally, the class was in "D" stage. This was the week we had been waiting for. This was the week we made five parachute jumps from a C47 aircraft. This was also the week that we had to pack the parachute that we jumped. This was also the week that would be the crux of four weeks of training. After packing the chute and placing it on a shelf with our name on it, we received a lecture on how safe the transportation from plane to ground by parachute really was.

On Monday afternoon we withdrew our chutes from the shelf and put them on. Then we were taken into the sweat shed to wait for our airplane. While in the sweat shed they played "Sentimental Journey" over and over on the public address system as you worked your way into the plane loading area. Finally, it was our time to board the aircraft. The flight to the drop zone was a study in human nature. Some tried to cover their nervousness with bravado statements or jokes. Some said silent prayers.

Some looked straight ahead. For many, including the Angel, this was the first time in an aircraft. Old Okie, who had so much trouble getting through "B" and "C" stage was seated to the right of the Angel.

The C47 taxied down to the end of the runway and revved up the engines. The plane vibrated and the engine power was reduced. The engines revved again and we were rolling down the runway. We were off! Some in the aircraft let out a breath of air that they did not realize they were holding.

After a short flight, the jump master gave us the jump commands after telling us to remember that the main factor in a parachute jump was mental alertness. After a few minutes, the jump master shouted over the noise of the aircraft, "Stand Up,'"Hook Up," "Check your equipment," "Sound off for equipment check." On this command the stick of jumpers shouted from 10 okay (the last man in the stick to all okay for the first man in the stick). The jump master now knew we were ready. His command was "Stand in the door". We shuffled forward to keep the stick closed up. The next command from the jump master would separate the men from the boys. The command was, "Ready Go." As the stick of jumpers moved forward, it reminded the Angel of meat going through a meat slicer. Within seconds Okie was in the door, but he would not jump. The jump master tried shoving and kicking but Okie held on to the anchor line cable. Finally, the jump mater pushed Okie on toward the rear end of the plane. Then the Angel was in the door and out. The Angel counted, 1,000, 2,000, 3,000, the chute popped open with a sound like a shot gun. The Angel checked his chute. It was a beautiful sight.

The Angel never saw Okie again. By the time we had gathered our chute on the drop zone, turned it in, double timed back to Lawson Field and packed our parachute for the next jump, Okie and some others who would not jump had been transferred out of our class. They were gone; we never saw them again.

The jump stage proceeded and along the way we had several that had to be dropped from the class. They were good men. They just were not cut out to be paratroopers. The class finished the week with two non equipment jumps, two equipment jumps and a night jump. The Angel did not know about the others, but for him the third jump was the most difficult to make. For the first jump, the adrenaline was running. The Angel was out the door before he knew it and there was no going back. On the second jump the Angel had a very hard opening shock. It was one that left strawberry bruises on top of each shoulder. For the third jump the Angel had to force himself to exit the aircraft. The body position was great on the third jump and the Angel now had all the confidence in the world about the safety of jumping. Jumps four and five were routine exercise. "D" stage was now complete and those of us left could call ourselves paratroopers.

Saturday morning was the graduation ceremony and the awarding of our jump wings along with the certificate of completion of the Parachute School.

On Saturday afternoon the class was moved to the Alabama area of Fort Benning. What a letdown this was, for we were billeted in tarpaper hutments. Each hutment had a pot bellied coal stove for heat. The walls had openings for the windows. These openings had wooden flaps that could be closed to try to hold in the heat. The good part was that we would only be here for two weeks of advanced training. Some of us, including the Angel, were selected for three additional weeks of demolition training. Some things like getting a pass to go to Columbus, Georgia, or to Phoenix City, Alabama, which made the Alabama area somewhat more enjoyable. We would make one parachute jump while in our two weeks of advanced training. This jump would allow us to wear our branch background under our jump wings. Infantry backgrounds were blue and artillery or engineer backgrounds were red.

We were constantly reminded that one paratrooper was as good as five regular soldiers. Not only were we constantly told this, we really believed it. After all we had done things we did not think were possible in a short time. There was a certain bounce to our step and don't-give-a-shit gleam in our eye. We were the top of the heap, the military elite. Of course, this brain washing was to get us ready to close with and destroy the enemy.

The jump we made while in the Alabama area turned into a real debacle. We were to jump, regroup and follow through with an assault problem. The VIP (very important person) stand was completely full to observe the jump. The rumor was that the President Roosevelt was in the viewing stands. That day the ground wind was far too high for a parachute jump. A jump should be called off when ground winds exceed 12 knots per hour. That day, the day of the jump, the ground winds were about 35 knots per hour. With the President in the stands, they were not going to call off the jump. When the jump master said go, we went. The drop zone was an old mortar range impact area, so we knew it would be a rough parachute landing fall. The Angel knew that he was oscillating very badly and he could see that he was going to hit the drop zone on a down swing and on his right side. This was the side his rifle was on. He knew that if he came in on the right side, it would probably break a leg. Therefore, he picked his legs up and hit like a sack of crap on his right, on his coccyx. The sensation was like a million needles pricking him over his entire body. The chute was dragging him across the drop zone at a very rapid rate. One of the men in our class got hold of the apex of the chute and ran around dumping the air from the canopy. The Angel tried very hard, but he could not move his arms or legs. The Angel figured this was what it was like to be dead. He was waiting for his soul to leave his body and wondering what it would be like. The Angel's Platoon Leader came running by, he stopped and asked the Angel if he was alright. The Angel said "No". Because he could talk, the Angel now knew that he was not dead. The Lieutenant called for the medics and the Angel was carried from the drop zone and taken to the hospital. Here he was observed for 24 hours and then returned to his unit. Back at the unit, he found out that he was one of the lucky ones; he only had a sore tail bone. About half of the class were in the hospital with broken bones. Whoever made the decision to jump in that high ground wind made a very poor decision Oh well, c'est la guerre.

While in the Alabama area it was not all work and no play. We were granted passes to go into town anytime that we were off duty. My favorite pass town of all time was Phoenix City, Alabama. In Phoenix City you could get anything you were looking for. If you were looking for a good time, you could find it in Phoenix City. If you were looking for alcoholic drinks, you could get it in Phoenix City. If you were looking for a girl, you could find her in Phoenix City. If you were looking for trouble, you definitely could find it in Phoenix City! It was truly a paratroopers kind of town. The Angel has many pleasant memories of Phoenix City, and some that are not so pleasant!

One of the memories that was not so pleasant was a run-in the Angel had with the Army riot squad. The situation started out easy enough. There was a place just across the bridge from Columbus, Georgia, on the right side of the street where a riot squad was quartered until they were called on to do their duty.

The Angel was in town alone and walking by the building where the riot squad stayed. As the Angel walked by, one of the members of the riot squad stopped him and made a big issue out of the fact that the Angel did not have buttons under his tie, the top button on his shirt was unbuttoned. The Angel buttoned his button, but the member of the riot squad just kept ranting and raving on and on.

Finally, the Angel took all he could take. The Angel informed the soldier that no paratrooper had to take crap from a straight leg soldier and that he had better back off while he still was able. When the soldier of the riot squad did not stop the haranguing the Angel hit him and knocked him back into the riot squad building and out like a light. However, the other 11 members of the riot squad came at the Angel. He took off running as fast as he could, but they caught him at the next intersection. The Angel felt the night sticks hit his head and it felt as if each one that hit him would buckle his knees another inch. Finally they beat the Angel all the way down. Yes, down, but not out. They wrote up a DR (Delinquency Report) on the Angel and had the post military police take him back to his unit. The next morning, just after reveille, the Angel was told to report to the orderly room. The First Sergeant read the DR and shook his head and smiled. He informed the Angel that he would have to see the Company Commander and took him into the CO's office. The CO read the report and also shook his head. The CO asked the Angel if it was true that he took on the entire riot squad. The Angel replied, yes, he had and he could tell it this morning by the way his head felt. The CO then stated that the Angel was the type of man that made an outstanding paratrooper. He also said he had to RBI (Reply by Indorsement) as to the action taken on the DR. Therefore, the Angel was restricted to the post for two days, but if I really wanted to go to town to see him, he would grant me a pass. Other than having a very sore head, the Angel had gotten away clean. In fact, the First Sergeant told the Angel that he was very proud of the Angel's run in with that no good, straight leg, riot squad.

The next pass to town the Angel definitely did not go to Phoenix City. He just did not want to take the chance of a run-in again with the riot squad. Therefore, he made up his mind to go to Opelika, Alabama. It was a nice town and the Angel was enjoying the visit to town very much. However, he wanted to find the place that had the most action. A fellow in the pool hall told the Angel that a honky-tonk between Opelika and Auburn was the place with the most action around there. In fact, he told the Angel that they were having girl's mud wrestling that very evening. This sounded like fun to the Angel, so he placed it on his mental agenda for things to do that night. The Angel put in the remainder of the afternoon shooting pool; he even made a few bucks. About eight o'clock that evening he caught a taxi to the mud wrestling honky-tonk. The dance floor had been converted to a wrestling ring by placing some six by six timbers in a square about 20 feet on a side. A plastic sheet had been put down on the timbers, this had been filled about half-way with water. Then red colored dirt, had been put into the water and mixed to the consistency of slimy gooey mud. The four contestants were introduced to the crowd and the referee explained the rules. The idea was for all four girls to go into the mud ring at the same time and the last one in the ring was the winner. It was an outstanding free-for-all fight. The champion of the evening was a very good looking, rather muscular, tall lady of about 20 to 25 years of age. In short, after she cleaned up she was a real knock-out in looks. Her fee for winning that evening was $25. After cleaning up and returning to the honky-tonk she started buying drinks for the Angel. After a couple of drinks she said that if the Angel would like to go home with her that they would have to catch a bus at 12:20 to her home town. Her home town was LaGrange, Georgia. It turned out to be an extremely great weekend spent with a very beautiful and exceptionally nice girl. That weekend pass sure was better than the one to Phoenix City.

The Angel had one more weekend pass before shipping out as an overseas replacement. This weekend he wound up in Newnan, Georgia. Again, a very nice town. Slim had always told the Angel that if you wanted to know what was going on in a town, to ask the taxi driver. Newnan, at that time was a dry town. However, like most towns in a dry county there had to be a bootlegger around some place, and there was. The cab driver took the Angel and his friend a short distance out of town and told them to knock on a house that was there. We did, and a black man answered the door. When we told him that we wanted to purchase some "Shine", he asked us into the house so he could look us over in the light. We did and he looked us over. In the house with him was a black woman that must have weighed 300 pounds. She was sitting in an oversized rocking chair. The black man said to the black woman that we could not be law because our shoe soles were not thick enough for us to be law and that he would sell us the "Shine". The price was agreed on and he nodded to the woman, who rolled to the side and extracted a pint of "Shine" from a built in compartment under her seat. When the Angel asked him why the hidden compartment, he said that there was not a lawman born that could move the woman, so the "Shine" was safe under her.

After we left the bootlegger's place we asked the taxi driver where the action was. He told us where we could find a dance and we said for him to take us there, pronto. It was a great dance everyone was having fun. However, the Angel and his buddy, being paratroopers, got a little cocky during the evening. I'm happy to say the crowd kind of overlooked us and took our cocky attitude as youthful tomfoolery. Thank goodness they did. About 10:00 in the evening the temperature and humidity became almost unbearable and the people were sweating profusely. The gentlemen started taking their suit coats off and hanging them up. It was then that the Angel noticed that over half of the men were packing iron (a pistol)in their hip pocket. No wonder it was so peaceful there! The cockiness left the Angel and his buddy and they settled down to just having a very good time.

There is an end to all endeavors and good times. Therefore, the Angel's time in the Alabama area of Fort Benning was coming to an end. On the last Friday of our training we were on the machine gun range. In training on the machine gun, you are taught to fire in short bursts. This reduces the malfunctions of the gun and keeps you from burning out the barrel of the gun from overheating. The Angel knew that at the end of the day he would be picking up his orders and going home on a delay-in-route to the Port of Embarkation at Camp Stoneman, California. To say that the attitude of the Angel was a little cocky would be a true statement. After all he was a member of the elite, a paratrooper.

When the Angel was told to fire for effect he did but not in the precise manner that he had been taught. The Angel, "John Wayne'd" the machine gun and ran 250 rounds through it without a break in the firing. This made the OIC (Officer in Charge) extremely unhappy. The OIC rapped the Angel across the soles of his feet with his swagger stick and told the Angel that if he could not give him 75 perfect push-ups, he could be held over and take the training again. The Angel rolled over on his position on the range and started the push-ups. He had to do 100 push-ups before the OIC counted out 75 perfect ones. After the OIC left the area the Angel joked with his friend next to him that he should have asked the OIC which arm he wanted the 75 push-ups on.

At the end of the work day and after retreat on Friday, we could pick up our orders and sign out as of 08:00 hours the next day. This gave us some extra time at home on our delay-in-route. We had 10 days of leave and the allotted travel time to Camp Stoneman, California.

When the Angel had cleared supply after turning in his equipment, he went to the orderly room to pick up his orders. Then, he found a very pleasant surprise. He had been promoted to PFC (Private First Class). This made him feel more like a soldier and less like a recruit. After all, he was a paratrooper PFC at the age of 15. Only those men in the unit who had completed advanced Airborne training and demolition school were promoted.

The week before leaving the Alabama area of Fort Benning, the Angel had gone to the PX (Post Exchange) and purchased ten sets of parachute wings. These he intended to give to the girls he dated at home during leave. He also intended to present them as his original wings. No one back in Stanton or Sullivan, Missouri, knew that he was taking airborne training. Between knowing this and snowing the girls with the wings, he figured he would make out fine. The Angel knew that he was the only one from Stanton that was a paratrooper, and he only knew of one other in Sullivan and that was the man he had entered the service with.

Fort Benning was now behind the Angel and he was headed home on leave for 10 days. The Greyhound Bus Company had routed the Angel through Birmingham, Alabama, through Memphis, Tennessee, to St. Louis, Missouri. The Angel remembered the fuss he had on the bus trip from San Francisco to St. Louis when he was released from the navy. He was hoping this trip would be the same.

In Birmingham, he was sitting on the bus watching passengers come aboard and admiring a beautiful young lady who was going to board the bus. When she came aboard she walked up the aisle of the bus until she came to the seat the Angel was in. She then stopped and very politely asked if the seat by him was taken. What luck! Of course, the Angel said no. He also said that he would like her company. As the bus pulled out for Memphis, the two of them entered into conversation. They were feeling each other out. To help in the conversation, a gentlemen in the seat in front of them asked if we would care for a drink. The gentlemen had a quart jar of "shine" in his handbag. He offered us a drink and we accepted. The Angel could tell that it was not the first drink the girl had enjoyed. She drank out of the fruit jar like a trooper. Of course, after a couple of drinks our inhibitions were considerably lowered. We worked our way into some heavy petting for the remainder of the trip to Memphis. The Angel hated to part company with that beautiful young lady. In Memphis, they had to go in separate directions. Her parents met her at the bus station and the Angel could tell they were not too happy with her appearance.

Oh well, it was on to St. Louis for the Angel. This part of the trip home sure was lonesome without that lollapalooza young lady. In pulling into St. Louis, the Angel caught a streetcar going south on Broadway to Lemay. He knocked on the door of Slim's apartment and was very happy when Slim answered the door. Slim was so happy to see the Angel that he went into an Irish jig, grabbed and hugged him. It was a great welcome for the Angel.

The Angel could not help digging Slim regarding his statement of about a year ago when he said the Angel went into the Navy because he was not man enough to serve his time in the Army behind a rifle. In other words, the infantry. Slim now noticed the cross rifles on his brass and the jump wings on his chest and said that he would have to eat his words. Their get-together was truly an occasion.

After a few hours with Slim, the Angel stated that he should go to see Flo. Flo was as surprised to see the Angel as Slim had been. The next stop was to hitchhike out to Stanton to see Mrs. John and the Old German. It was just great seeing all of them. After all, I had not told any of them that I was going to parachute school. They just could not visualize a person jumping from a perfectly good aircraft. Even thinking that the Angel was a little crazy, they were all proud of him. The Angel would stay with Mrs. John and the Old German during his leave time. After all, that was home to him.

To get back to the night life of the area. The Angel picked up the local newspaper and checked out the divorce column. When he saw the name of a young lady he knew, he would give them a call and ask for a date. They were thrilled about hearing from the Angel and was never turned down. His pitch was that he was going overseas and as a paratrooper, they may never have a chance to see each other again. Then, he would use a play acting gimmick. He would go into his spiel about the wings being his original wings. The spiel worked every time. By the time his leave was over, the Angel wished that he had purchased more wings at the PX before coming home on leave. It was fun and games all the way.

During the leave, the Angel did have to give thanks for his excellent physical fitness. He was in a bar with his date when a group of 4-F's (unfit for military service) came in. There were three in the group. They started making fun of the Angel's boots and wings. The Angel tried to ignore the situation but the 4-F's kept at him. It was embarrassing for the Angel's date also. Finally, the Angel had all the crap he could stand. He knew that surprise was the way to take care of the situation. Therefore, while pretending to be leaving the bar, he positioned himself for the best offense possible. The Angel knew that he had great hand speed and balance. He remembered Slim teaching him to bring the force of the blow through his body and to hit or aim your blow six inches behind your target. That way you would not pull your punch. When the Angel was all set, he exploded and three 4-F's were on the floor and out. To my date, I was a hero.

After being at home for ten days, it was time to head for Camp Stoneman, California. It was hard to leave, as the Angel was having a great time. He figured staying one more day would not hurt. He remained the extra day and then caught a passenger train for San Francisco. Even with a club car, the train was not as much fun as the bus trip from Fort Benning to St. Louis had been. In San Francisco, he spent a night on the town. He called the WAVE he had dated over a year ago and they partied. She was surprised to see him in a paratrooper uniform and headed back overseas. It was a pleasant evening and the Angel reported into Camp Stoneman on time the following day.

Camp Stoneman was the processing center for those of us being assigned to the Pacific Theater of Operation. They checked our medical records, brought our shots up-to-date and issued equipment. We still did not know where we would be assigned. However, being a jumper, the Angel figured it would be either the 11th Airborne Division or the 503 Airborne Regimental Combat Team. Finally, we were given line numbers and taken by ferryboat down the Sacramento River to Oakland Army Base. Our group spent the night there and boarded a Victory Ship the next day. Being back aboard a ship again made the Angel very happy that he was now a soldier.

Life aboard the ship very quietly fell into a transit routine. With the sound of reveille over the ship's public address system, the day would begin. First order of business was to get our toilets out of the way, then clean our compartments and stand by for inspection. Next, came a very long line as we waited for breakfast. Then, it was a matter of staying out of sight so you did not get picked for some detail. After detail selection we would settle down to poker or craps if you had money, and a game of hearts if you were broke. On this trip, the Angel became very good at hearts. We were only fed twice a day because it took so long to get through the line. When darkness came, we had to stay below deck until reveille sounded to start the next day's routine.

The ship's first stop was Pearl Harbor. This brought back memories for the Angel. Line number and name was called over the public address system for those lucky people who were going to be stationed in Hawaii. The next day we were off again—same routine. The next port of call was Wake Island and again we lost some troops, mostly fly boys. Then, it was on to New Guinea and we had more troops disembark. All this time the Angel kept looking for the DE263, USS Deede—the ship he had served on. He never saw it. Finally, the ship arrived at its final destination, Leyte in the Philippine Islands. Here, the troops had to disembark over the side and into Higgins Boats. We disembarked with only a musette bag for our personal belongings, as we were told our remaining gear would be transported to shore after all the troops had disembarked. The place we disembarked was called Tacloban. Once on shore we were taken to the 4th Replacement Depot for further assignment in good time. Our duffel bags came later and were dumped into our tent city street. If you did not grab your duffel bag in a hurry, it would just seem to disappear, as one of the old-timers who had been there awhile would make off with it.

The big gossip around the 4th Replacement Depot was about the Japanese parachute attack on the headquarters elements of the 11th Airborne Division. Some of the straight legs were worried about it happening at our location. Hell, the Angel didn't even have a rifle yet. What the hell was he supposed to do? Perhaps the powers that be, thought the Angel, could just stare them down. Other things about the 4th Replacement Depot were taking place that sure did not make the Angel a happy trooper.

One of those things that made the Angel unhappy was the fact that many of the qualified paratroopers were being assigned to straight leg units—some to the 77th Infantry Division, some to the 6th Infantry Division and other units. The Angel knew that he would have to find a way to be assigned to an airborne unit before he came out on a draft to a non-airborne unit. Yes, he would just have to take matters into his own hands. It is true that the commanding officer of the Replacement Depot did not care for paratroopers, as they had torn up his little tent city and assignments to non-airborne units were his way of punishing the paratroopers.

The Angel heard that the 11th Airborne Division was at a place called Bito Beach. This area was not too far from the Replacement Depot. The Angel, without orders, just packed his gear and caught some transportation to Bito Beach. As soon as possible, he reported to the 11th Airborne Division and informed them of what he had done. The Angel, never short on words, talked himself out of trouble. The Angel was placed on the perimeter of Division Headquarters until he would be assigned to one of the regiments. By talking with other soldiers in the area, he was sure he would be assigned to the 511th Parachute Infantry Regiment. While he was awaiting assignment, most of the talk around the area was about the raid by Japanese paratroopers that had taken place a few days before the Angel had arrived. The Angel was sure his assignment would be the 511th because it was the only jump regiment in the 11th Airborne Division. How disappointed he was when he received orders to the 187th Glider Infantry Regiment and told he would join them as soon as they returned from Balinsayoo. The Angel figured that this just could not happen to him—after all he was a qualified Fort Benning jumper. The more he talked, the more he received a deaf ear. Finally, he realized that it was the 187th Glider Infantry for him. About the middle of January, 1945, the 11th Airborne Division reassembled at Bito Beach. The Angel then reported into the 187th. During this time, there was a great deal of speculation about the next operation. The Bito Beach time, unknown to the Angel, was about to come to an end. The landing on Luzon was about to begin.

On 31 January, 1945, the 11th Airborne Division minus the 511th Regiment would land from the sea at a place called Nasugba and would head northeast toward Manila. The Glider troops would make an amphibious landing and secure a beachhead. As soon as the 187th and 188th Glider Regiments had secured the beachhead, they started their hike, perhaps attack is a better word, uphill and toward Tagaytay Ridge. The two regiments received considerable Japanese fire along the way. However, they would overcome these strong points and continue to march.

It was at one of these Japanese strong points that the Platoon Sergeant called on the Angel and three other fellows to overcome the situation. The platoon would lay down a base of fire and two of us would work our way to the right and left side oblique positions. When in place, the base of fire would be lifted and the two of us from the right and two from the left would assault the Japanese position. The strong point was a hut-like building raised from the ground by stilts. The Angel worked his way forward and lobbed a grenade into the hut. As soon as the grenade exploded, the Angel rushed forward and entered the hut. On entering, he fanned his fire and got off eight rounds from his rifle. He was sure the squad leader or the Platoon Sergeant would say, "Great job, Angel." He did not—instead he called the Angel all kinds of dummy.

The sergeants both told me that the hut would not stop the fragments of a grenade and the Angel had exposed himself by standing outside the hut when the grenade exploded. He said that I was lucky to still be here. The other item he came down on was for firing all eight rounds on entering the hut. He said that if the gooks were still alive I would have been standing there with an empty weapon. He said on entering without a specific target, to always hold back two to four rounds for anything still moving. It was good information and the Angel learned. Oh well, onward and upward toward Tagaytay Ridge. During the march to Tagaytay Ridge the Glider Regiment had to fight as they had never fought in the past. The objective was to reach Tagaytay Ridge and link up with the 511th Airborne Infantry Regiment. After reading military history, the Angel likes to compare the assault on Tagaytay Ridge and on to Manila as being like operation Market Garden in Europe with this exception. The 11th Airborne Division's move was successful. The Angel got to use some of the demolition training he received back at Fort Benning, Georgia. In some cases if we were receiving fire from a cave or rock enclosure, we would just blow it shut and continue to march.

Please bear in mind that it was 30-plus miles from Nasugba to Tagaytay Ridge and about the same distance from Tagaytay Ridge to Manila.

On February the third, the 511th jumped at Tagaytay Ridge and linked up with the Glider Regiments. As soon as the area was secure, the march started down Highway 17 toward Manila. From somewhere the 11th had gotten two and a half-ton trucks to assist in the movement. However, there was not enough trucks for the entire division so we had to shuttle, ride a way; walk a way; even at times run a way; until it was time to ride again. The recon platoon of the 511th led the way. The Angel would say in a light-hearted manner that the 11th had a front of 1,000 feet across and 30 miles long.

Our first view of Manila from Tagaytay Ridge looked as if the city would be an open city and not a city destroyed by the Japanese. In fact, the Angel had heard that the Japanese Commander had declared Manila an open city. This was not to be the case. Even before the battle for Manila had begun, the Japanese went on a rampage of complete destruction for the city. They engaged in atrocities, rape and pillage beyond anything that one could imagine. They absolutely ignored their senior commander's directive or orders that Manila be an open city. Thus, came the battle for Manila and hard fought it was!

On January the 31st the glider troops had hit the beaches at Nasugba; on the night of the fourth of February, the 11th Airborne Division had advanced to the Paranaque River and crossed a partly destroyed bridge over the river. The battle for that bridge and the crossing of that bridge brought the 11th Airborne Division up against the Genko Line.

This was not a bar room fight, no quarter asked for and no quarter given. The Division fought with no reserve. The 2nd Battalion of the 187 GIR as attached to the 511th PIR and the 1st Battalion to the 188th GIR. There was no reserve and no retreat.

During the battle for the Genko Line, the Angel was promoted to Corporal and made the BAR (Browning Automatic Rifle) man for his squad. He was now a noncommissioned officer at age 15. Now all he had to do was to stay clear of the bullets that were marked, "To whom it may concern." That would be no easy task.

By the 13th of February the 511th, with the 2nd Battalion attached, broke through the left end of the Genko Line by pure bull-headed devotion to duty. They had fought block by block, and once they had broken through the line they turned east to continue the attack toward Nichols Field and Fort McKinley. On 17th of February the 11th attacked Fort McKinley from the east and south. This was the area where Private Perez Jr. would win Medal of Honor. However, Private Perez would be KIA (killed in action) before he would receive this distinction.

It was during this time that the Platoon Sergeant told the Angel that he would be taking his fire team out on a recon patrol to try to find a place where there was a break in the Japanese field of interlocking fire. It was to be a night patrol. The Angel had always considered the night his friend. The Angel and the two riflemen in his fire team left on patrol after complete darkness had set in. The patrol would cross an area that had a stream on one side of a built-up berm and an area of water and silt on the other side. It was an area where one should not expose himself by crossing on the built up berm for they would surely draw fire. However, it was extremely dark that night and after discussing it with the other two riflemen it was decided to cross on the berm. The Angel and the riflemen figured the quietness and speed of crossing the berm would offset the noise that would be made by wading across in the water. The Angel and the two riflemen started across on the berm and were immediately fired on.

The damn Japs must have been able to see in the dark. They had the Angel and his patrol members pinned down and lying alongside of the berm away from the Japs. About this time, the Angel heard in the distance, THUMP!, THUMP!, THUMP!, THUMP!, THUMP!, THUMP! Six mortar rounds had been fired, but none had hit yet. The Angel figured if the mortar crew was using the ladder system, they would have waited until a round landed before adjusting their fire and walking it into the patrol. If they were using the bracket method, they would also observe the mortar round explosion and adjust. However, if they had this berm already zeroed in they could set their mortar and fire any number of rounds right on the berm we were on. Therefore, the berm would be their target and all the Angel and his patrol could do would be to pray. The Angel did not know if the others in the patrol prayed or not, but he knew that he had done some heavy bargaining with God. He must have heard our prayers for all six rounds landed in the water and silt just behind us a very short distance and they were either duds or the water and silt was of a consistency that they would not explode on contact. As soon as the

Angel counted six in the water, he and his patrol hauled ass out of there.

The next day the Angel had a very sore neck and was walking around like a sick chicken. He could not figure out why, until he remembered pressing his head into the berm while being mortared. That pressure had caused the sore neck.

By February 1945, all organized resistance by the Japs along the Genko Line had come to an end.

The 11th Airborne Division would pull off the most successful airborne operation in history in the next couple of days. This operation would be known and logged into history as the "Los Banos Raid." The raiding complement would be selected from units within the division. Unfortunately, the Angel's unit was not one of the units selected for the raid. His unit would remain on the Genko Line for a few more days before being moved to the Lipa area for mop-up operations in the mountain areas around Lipa.

In these mop-up operations, the Angel's unit would have to clear caves and strong point positions in the mountainous area.

The Angel's squad was in the process of clearing some of these caves. One day after clearing a couple of caves and finding nothing, they came to the third cave. One of the squad members would always charge ahead. He said it was to get the first crack at any souvenirs that may have been left behind. In the third cave he charged in and immediately came back-peddling out with a gook with a grenade in his hand trying to grasp the squad member in his arms. Members of the squad did away with the gook, the soldier hit the ground, the grenade detonated and the only one hurt was the Jap. He had met his maker. The soldier was not anxious to clear a cave after that. Not even to get first crack at souvenirs. The Angel did not know if any Japs remained in the cave or not. They threw in a couple of Willie Peter (white phosphorus) grenades and then used demolition charges to blow the cave shut. Were any Japs still in the cave? Who knows?

A soldier in combat does not know how keyed up he is until something happens that triggers a release from the stress that has built up over time. To prove this philosophy, an incident happened in Lipa that brought it home. A USO troop was in the area and they were putting on a show for the 11th Airborne Division. There may have been 1,000 or 2,000 in attendance for the show, for it was a real change in the routine. Well, some dummy down front threw a couple of coconuts into the crowd and shouted

"Grenade!" The entire audience took off as one and ran in great confusion for probably a mile. Oh well, it was a good tension relief!

Along about June, July and August some of the high point men could go home, not many, but a few qualified. This opened up some slots for promotions and the Angel was promoted to Sergeant and made a squad leader. Some just did not want the responsibility and therefore, turned it down. This was not the thought of the Angel; he was proud of a promotion!

During these months some other training was taking place in Lipa. A jump school was opened and started training glider men who volunteered for jump training. It was nothing like Fort Benning, but it would do. The school would also give glider training to some who were already jumpers. The idea was to have a unit that was qualified as both paratroopers and glidermen. The first part of August of 1945 the atomic bombs were dropped on two cities in Japan. Thank God for Harry Truman! The 11th was airlifted to Okinawa to get ready for the invasion of Japan. It turned out to be the occupation of Japan. Thanks again to Harry Truman! His action on dropping the atomic bomb saved many American lives.

One of the things we had to endure during our stay in Okinawa was the most serious typhoon that had occurred in many years.

Because of the typhoon our stay in Okinawa was not a pleasant one. Finally the airlift to Japan came about. The airlift was not without its problems. A plane, a B24 or B25, had crashed on takeoff from Lipa, and now on the last leg of the flight for the occupation of Japan a cargo plane crashed, killing the members of the 11th Airborne Division's Reconnaissance Platoon, an outstanding unit.

The flight from Okinawa was a stressful flight. We knew we were going as an occupation force. We just felt, hope against hope, that the Japanese also knew that this was an occupying force and that their ass had been whipped beyond a doubt. Yes, Pearl Harbor had been remembered. The Angel had not seen such a mixed reaction on the faces of the paratroopers and glidermen since his first jump back at Fort Benning.

The terminating point of the airlift was an air field at Atsugi, Japan, just a short distance from Tokyo. The 11th Airborne had the honor of being the first fighting unit into Japan. Upon landing, we found everything in fairly good order. We were into Atsugi on the 30th day of August, 1945 and the Angel had just turned 16 that month. The Japanese surrender papers had not been signed yet, but we knew in our hearts that WWII was over. Instead of the saying "Golden Gates in 48" it would be for some "The Golden Gate in 45." It did not rhyme as well, but what the hell! We all sure felt better.

At Atsugi, the planes that had been Japanese were lined up at the airport with their propellers taken off. On landing we immediately formed a perimeter defense for security of the air field. Some of the troopers started looking for souvenirs. The Angel can assure you that if the Japanese had set booby traps, they would have gotten some of us right after landing, but the fight was out of them. By the end of the first day in Japan some of the planes on the air field had been stripped of the rising sun emblem on the fabric of the plane.

The Angel doesn't know who, but someone had located a saki warehouse, and of course, the contents were the spoils of war. A large drum or barrel was found and cleaned out: one end was cut out, it was filled with saki and a low grade fire was built under it. It was placed in a hangar, and one could just walk by and fill his canteen cup when we wanted to. Let me tell you, it was a happy group of troopers. The 11th Airborne band met and welcomed the 1st Cavalry Division into Tokyo a couple of days later, playing "The Old Grey Mare, she ain't what she used to be." We had to rub it in a little as they were our "friendly enemies," so to speak. I do believe it was our frivolous attitude that caused General MacArthur, or some member of his staff, to exile the 11th Airborne Division to the northern part of Honshu and, later on when the 77th Division returned to the United States, to send the 187 GIR to Hokkaido with the 2nd Battalion being in and around Sapporo.

The rate of those returning to the United States for discharge accelerated with the point system becoming less and less. The replacements were not coming in as fast as those returning to the States. This had a tendency to cause the units of the 11th Airborne Division to become under-strength. Of course, this made assigned duties come around more often than usual. Regulations tightened up on a constant basis. This tightening of the regulations made it difficult for the troopers to have fun and enjoy their stay in Japan. Of course, most of these regs were not adhered to by the enlisted men of the 11th Airborne Division.

One regulation the Angel remembers that was not adhered to

by the enlisted men was the regulation on nonfraternization. This meant that a soldier was not supposed to date or be with a Japanese person of the opposite sex. The fine was considerable if caught. Of course, this was a reg that was impossible to enforce. When in a Japanese town it was a common sight to see a trooper walking down the street with his moose (a shortened GI term for girl) walking a pace behind and a pace to the left of the trooper. The trooper always had a very large contented smile on his face. Life was good. Even though life was good for the individual soldier, the thought process was to get out of Japan and back to the states.

About this time, to help maintain the unit to strength, new regulations on extension of service or re-enlistment became known to the troopers. Ever since graduation from jump school, the Angel had a desire in his heart to go to Europe. He expressed a desire to look into enlisting for the 508 Parachute Infantry Regiment now in Berlin, Germany. His buddies considered him a little touched in the head for even thinking this way. However, the Angel thought, what the hell, why not? He checked into battalion personnel about re-enlisting and was sent to regimental personnel. Here he ran into a clerk that he knew by sight, but not by name.

He asked the Angel if he was right in the head or had he gone Asiatic (a little crazy). When the Angel asked about a one year enlistment and assignment to Europe, the clerk stated that for one year you could only enlist for your own vacancy. He stated that it would take a three year-enlistment to get to Europe. That was longer than the Angel wanted to commit for at this time. Therefore, the Angel asked if they couldn't bend the regs some. They both went over the regs with a fine tooth comb. Finally, the clerk said he was going home the next week and he would type up the enlistment for one year and assignment to Europe after re-enlistment leave in the states. If it was not caught by the officer administering the oath, perhaps we could pull it off. It went through like a charm, and the next week the Angel was on a ship back to the states. Incidentally, the clerk was on the same ship. The Angel was headed for a 90 day leave and assignment to Berlin, Germany with the 508 PIR. However, things would not turn out exactly as the Angel thought they would.

On the ship back to the states it was extremely difficult to maintain discipline. The soldiers were mostly high point men and were going home for discharge. In short they just did not care anymore about military discipline, devotion to duty and all that old crap. The war was over for them. In fact, the Angel was chided about re-enlisting into the regular army.

The Angel had been sending money home to be placed in a bank and he had a goodly sum on his person. The money on his person he had to watch very closely because some stealing was taking place aboard the ship. To pass the time, the Angel got into a crap game and everything fell his way. It seemed the Angel could do no wrong. Yes, before he dropped out he had made 22 straight passes. He had broken the game. Now comes the sad tale. The Angel was a soft touch and he loaned out a substantial amount of money on IOU'S. Now, like a fool he was playing against his own money. This was something a gambler never does and the Angel was about to learn his lesson, the hard way. Of course, right at this time the Angel was flying high. He paid soldiers to stand in line for chow so he would not have to leave the game. He bribed members of the crew to prepare steak dinners for him. The world looked rosy. This went on for the entire 14 days that it took to get from Yokohama to San Francisco. When the Angel processed through Oakland Army Base and prepared to go on leave, he was left with a pocket of IOU'S that were worthless. The men who had given the IOU'S scattered to the four winds and the Angel was left holding the bag. The Angel now had, and felt, about gambling ad nauseam. He had learned his lesson, never again. He took the loss in a good natured way, after all c'est la guerre.

Before catching a bus for St. Louis, the Angel remained in San Francisco a couple of days and dated the WAVE whom he used to work with at the 12th Naval District Headquarters. The Angel was her hero and a good time was had by all. All good things and times must come to an end, and after a couple of days the Angel said a tearful goodbye to the pretty young WAVE and caught the express bus for St. Louis. He was anxious to again see Slim, Flo, the Old German and Mrs. John, and he knew they would be happy to see him. The Angel's mind was turning again. Before the bus was out of the city limits of San Francisco he was figuring a way to use the jump wings he left in the states for his recent overseas tour. A good trooper always takes advantage of the situation at hand.

The situation that was presently at hand was how to meet a good-looking young lady who happened to be a passenger on the same bus. During the first rest stop the Angel started a conversation with the girl and before the rest stop ended the girl agreed to sit with the Angel when they returned to the bus. Before they arrived in Cheyenne, Wyoming, they knew each other extremely well. In fact, the girl agreed to lay over with the Angel in Denver, Colorado, and do the town for a couple of days. May I say here that a good time was had by all. When they decided to continue the trip it was because the young lady had a deadline to keep and she was already a little late. So it was on to St. Louis for the Angel and New York for the girl. Of course, between Denver and St. Louis some very heavy petting took place.

Upon arriving in St. Louis the first thing the Angel did was to have his uniform pressed and boots shined to a high gloss. He did not want to meet Slim with a rumpled uniform from traveling. The Angel considered himself a very sharp trooper. He was proud of his uniform and the fact that he was a paratroop sergeant. He knew that Slim was a fastidious dresser and the Angel wanted to look his best when he saw Slim.

When he did see Slim, military courtesy was forgotten as Slim grabbed the Angel and hugged him with tears running down his face. You could tell that Slim was overcome with the meeting. Perhaps it was because the Angel had not maintained contact with Slim while he was overseas.

The next move was to see Flo and here the same situation happened as did when he met Slim. She was very happy that he was back in one piece. The Angel told Flo that she need not worry, as he was invincible. Of course, this was just paratroop braggadocio talking. A false front—the Angel could remember a tight spot or two where he had bargained with God to get him through a situation. There are no nonbelievers in a foxhole. The Angel knew that an airborne soldier would be a fatalist and a believer at the same time.

Slim decided to go to Stanton with the Angel so he could spend a weekend with him before returning to work. Slim, being the fun-loving man that he was, bet the Angel that he could pick up a girl at the bus station before the Angel could. The Angel accepted the bet and they were off. The Angel figured this young paratroop sergeant would have no trouble beating this 45-year-old man. Well, the Angel was wrong. Slim had a girl and was out the door before the Angel even struck up a conversation with the one he had selected. Slim would not let him live this down. Along in the wee hours of the morning Slim and the Angel finally caught a bus to Stanton.

The meeting with the Old German and Mrs. John was great!

They were extremely happy that the Angel had made it through the war intact. However, Mrs. John was not happy that the Angel was remaining in the Army as a regular. Mrs. John had been an adult back in the late 1800's and she had a tendency to look on regular soldiers as bums and never-do-wells. She remembered her brother who had been in the Spanish American War and had come home an alcoholic and to die at an early age from drinking. The Angel assured Mrs. John that this would not happen to him. Neither the Old German or Mrs. John could understand why the Angel would continue to jump from aircraft. After all, they figured the war was over and the need for paratroopers should end with the war.

It was a great time to be home on leave. Almost every day one of the men who had been drafted for the duration and six months would show up in Stanton, and this was cause for celebration. The honky-tonks in the area always gave free drinks to the men who had served honorably. All of those from Stanton had an honorable discharge on their release from service. At this time, discharges were color coded. The honorable discharge was white. The bad conduct discharge was blue. The dishonorable discharge was yellow.

The Angel only knew of one person who had been dishonorably discharged and he was from Union or Washington, Missouri. He had gone "Absent Without Leave" (AWOL) from a POE (Port of Embarkation). For this he served time in the stockade and was kicked out of the service. Around the area in the honky-tonks he had a reputation of being extremely boisterous. He had in the past been a "ham and bean" boxer and had caused a lot of trouble for some of the men who had served honorably. They did not deserve this. He also knew that the Angel was 16 and figured him for an easy mark. He took the opportunity to belittle the Angel. The Angel stood fast but did not reply. When he said that the only thing that fell from the sky was bird shit, the Angel smiled as if he was going along with the belittling words. He worked the antagonistic individual around to the edge of the porch they were standing on, and there the Angel let him have it. He sailed off the porch and into the front of a parked car. The Angel was right after him and in short beat the hell out of the no good son-of-a-gun. He never harassed another returnee from the war. Slim was especially proud of the Angel because he recognized that the Angel had used a tactic that he had taught him years ago. That was to give yourself any advantage you could and to use the element of surprise.

With the weekend over, Slim had to return to work in the ship yard. The Angel decided to remain with the Old German and Mrs. John. He made their home his base of operations for the remainder of his leave. Of course, they encouraged him to stay with them.

Early on in the leave, the Angel had a pocket full of money, and it was all going on having a good time. Mrs. John had a heart to heart talk with him telling him to take it easy, to get his rest.

On one occasion, the Angel was out with a couple of girls until the wee hours of the morning before he made it home. The next day at around 10:00 in the morning, the girls came to the door and asked Mrs. John to tell the Angel they were there. Mrs. John did not appreciate these girls coming so early for the Angel. The Angel awoke to Mrs. John running the girls back to their car with a broom stick and shouting, "You hussies get out of here, let that boy alone, he needs his rest." It was a spectacle to behold. Mrs. John had them on the run, the Angel never let Mrs. John know that he was aware of what she had done and she never mentioned that the girls had been there.

One good-looking girl around town had a 1941 Mercury convertible. The Angel came on to her in a big way. First, she was extremely beautiful. Secondly, she had transportation. Thirdly, she had money. In fact, she had all the prerequisites of a good time.

The Angel and this lady were a hot item for about a month. Then one day she said that they would have to cool it because her husband was on the way home from Okinawa where he had been a civilian employee for the Department of Defense. The Angel had not known that she was married. Therefore, he immediately called a halt to the dating frenzy that had transpired between them. It was probably a good thing too, because when the Angel saw her husband he was the biggest and best built man the Angel had ever seen. The Angel was not ready for aut vincere aut mori (either to conquer or to die).

By this time, the Angel's leave was rapidly coming to an end and his money was rapidly running out. Also, some of the girls were getting wise when they would meet each other and both would be wearing jump wings. After all, there was only one paratrooper that was home at this time, and that was the Angel. It had been a glorious leave, one that would always bring good memories to the Angel. The Angel's orders told him when and where to report. The last weekend of his leave he spent in St. Louis with Slim and Flo. When Slim found out the Angel was broke, he gave him money to continue his good time for the weekend and to return to the destination of his orders. It was now January of 1946 and servicemen were returning from overseas in large numbers. The Angel was happy that he was one of the first to return as the newness of the returnees was rapidly wearing off.

The orders that the Angel had ordered him to report to Fort Leavenworth, Kansas, for further shipment to the 508 Parachute Regiment in Berlin, Germany.

The Angel had a friend that knew a conductor on the Rock Island Railroad and he fixed it up with the conductor for the Angel to ride in the caboose to Kansas City. From there he could catch a bus to the Fort. Everything went well on leaving St. Louis, so the Angel thought he would catch some much needed sleep. While coming into Union, Missouri, he was shaken awake by the conductor and told he was sorry, but the Angel would have to leave the train as an inspector was coming aboard and if he caught the Angel on the train it would cost the conductor his job. The Angel understood the situation and exited the train on the side away from the oncoming inspector. Because the conductor's heart was right, the Angel thanked him and got off the train. Now, what to do. The Angel asked the first person he came across, the direction to Highway 50. He walked the mile or do to the highway. He stuck up his thumb and caught a ride on the first car that came along. As luck would have it he was going to Kansas City. The Angel sat back and enjoyed the trip.

Upon arrival at Fort Leavenworth, the Angel reported in and was given the duty of barracks NCO for those people who were being released from the Disciplinary Barracks and were attempting to soldier themselves back into the good graces of the US Army. Some had been in for murder, some for being AWOL, etc. The Angel was given the assignment because they needed a paratroop sergeant to keep them in line. It was not easy duty and the Angel had to break some heads to get their attention.

After about two weeks, the Angel received further orders to report to Camp Pickett, Virginia, where they were putting the 508 PIR packet together for shipment to Europe. The month-long stay at Camp Pickett was fun and a learning experience. In order to avoid being put in charge of details like ash-and-trash or keeping the coal bins filled, the Angel would always fall out for formation with a pair of trousers under his arm. When told of a detail he would be in charge of, the Angel would say that he had an appointment with the post tailor shop to shorten his trousers. It worked every time. On other occasions, he would say that he had an appointment at the hospital or dentist. It worked like a charm. However, on one occasion the Angel outsmarted himself. He was talking to a friend and did not pay attention to the ambulance he got into to ride over to the hospital. The one he entered was for the venereal disease patients. When the ambulance arrived at the hospital, it drove into a barbed wire enclosure. We were run through a line and each person on that ambulance got a penicillin shot. The Angel tried to tell them there was a mistake, but the medics turned a deaf ear to him and gave him the shot in the rump anyway. The Angel vowed to be more careful after this. After all, the shot was not given con a more (with love or tenderly).

Being paratroopers, we were just naturally a feisty, rough-and-tumble group of soldiers. This led the Angel into an altercation at a honky tonk in Crewe, Virginia, between the Angel and another trooper. The Angel and some other paratroopers asked some of the natives of the area where the excitement was. The natives all agreed that the liveliest place around was a joint in Crewe. The troopers pooled their money and hired one of the natives to take us to that place. When we got there it sure did not seem too lively; it was just a run-down old building with a rough dance floor. He said that we should just wait until dark. As soon as darkness came, he asked us outside. He directed our attention to hills. At first it looked like a group of fireflies in the distance. He told us that the lights were lanterns and flashlights of people coming out of the hills and heading to this honky-tonk for a Saturday night good time. He spoke the truth, for within one-half-hour the place was jumping.

During the night the Angel struck up a conversation with a couple of sailors who were home on leave. Since the Angel had been in the navy, they were discussing the ships they had served on. During this conversation a perfectly arrogant paratrooper in the group started to belittle the sailors. The Angel told him that these sailors were his friends and that he should back off. He then started to belittle the Angel for having friends like the sailors. The Angel could see where the conversation was heading and arguing would not help the situation, so he hit the trooper. He went down but not out. It turned into a real dog fight. The fight was tit for tat for awhile. Then, they went to the ground. He was strong—for the Angel came out on the bottom. However, the Angel was in position to apply about 20 short rabbit punches to the back of the head and neck area. The other trooper rolled off of the Angel out as cold as a cucumber. During the fight I heard someone say, "They are paratroopers—they were born to fight—let them have at it." Later on that trooper and the Angel became very good friends. I guess it came from respect for each other.

Just a short way from Camp Pickett was a town called Blackstone, Virginia. It was a very nice town of about 3,500 people. The big draw to the town was a girls' college. One Saturday afternoon the Angel and a friend were in town when some girls started shouting at them from the dorm windows. Of course, the bantering went on between the troopers and the girls. They invited us up to their room, but of course, the lady in charge would not let us through the lobby. On the dorm was some trellis work and vines. My friend and I decided to go up the trellis and with the encouragement of the girls, we climbed to their room. Of course, the lady in charge had called the law. He asked us down. We asked him up and had a standoff for awhile. Finally, he went to his car and got a shot gun. We decided it was time to come down. By now the girls' heads were protruding from every window. The law was an alright guy. He laughed and said that was the most excitement he had seen since he came home from the war. He drove us back to Camp Pickett and told us to stay out of trouble and left. There are good people in this world.

By now we had a sizeable group of paratroopers waiting for shipment to the 508 PIR in Germany. The group was called into the post theater one day and it was explained to us that the 508 was coming home from Europe and that those of us who had reenlisted for the 508 PIR had a choice—we could either be discharged or we could sign a waiver of assignment promise and be shipped to the 11th Airborne Division in Japan. Since the Angel had been in the 11th, he decided to return for the remainder of the year. Within two days, three passenger cars full of paratroopers headed west as a troop train. Our destination—Camp Stoneman, California.

The Angel was unhappy that he did not get to go to Europe but in a way, he was looking forward to returning to the 11th Airborne Division and duty in Japan.

The train ride across the United States was something else.

The priority of getting troops overseas had deteriorated and our troop train was on a very low status of priority. Therefore, it took us about eight days to cross the country. The Angel remembers spending about ten hours on a side track in Chicago. This gave the paratroopers plenty of time to purchase beer, whiskey and get acquainted with some young ladies. When the train finally did get going we had about ten troopers who did not make it back to the train. Some returned to the train at stops west of Chicago and some just went on to Camp Stoneman and reported in early. To this day, the Angel does not know how it happened but we all made it across the states and reported in as directed. I guess we all made it without anyone going AWOL because of Deo volente (God willing).

For the Angel, Camp Stoneman was a replay. He had gone this route before. It was processing, shots, checks, dental checks and finally a line number for boarding the ship. There was the ferry-boat ride to Oakland Army Base and boarding the Liberty Ship. Then, under the Golden Gate Bridge again. With the one night in Oakland Army Base, the Angel tried to get in touch with the WAVE he knew in the 12th Naval District. However, when he called he found out she had been discharged and had gone home. The Angel figured this as love lost in aeternum (forever).

Back aboard the ship the Angel volunteered to work in the butcher shop. He did this because now he ate with the crew and they ate the best. He would have none of the troop swill on this trip. Also, he would not gamble on this trip. He had learned his lesson.

Within our group of troopers we had one who was extremely talkative. He constantly wore his jumpsuit even when most of us just wore fatigues. He wore the patch of the 17th Airborne Division on his right side and the patch of the Parachute Command on his left side. He claimed he had a Silver Star medal awarded for the jump across the Rhine River into Germany. He also claimed a Bronze Star medal for the same operation. The lad was a very boastful-type person. Well, someone managed to get into his records and found out the individual had only recently completed jump school. With this information, the lad was taken into the head of the ship, worked over, stripped naked and his jumpsuit thrown overboard. Then, the word got out and he was silenced by all the other paratroopers on the ship. When we got to Japan the false hero requested that he be assigned to a non-jump unit in Japan. We, of the airborne, did not need this type of man.

Once docked in Japan we debarked the ship and were trucked to the Angel's old nemesis, the Fourth Replacement Depot—the same one the Angel had problems with in Leyte. He was in luck. The Colonel in command was not the same one and the replacement depot now operated much better than before. This time jump-qualified men were being sent to the 11th Airborne Division and not to some leg unit.

When the Angel and the other paratroopers from this shipment received their orders, it was to the 11th Airborne Division in Sendai, Honshu, Japan. On this trip one young soldier received a lesson in trust. As the train was pulling out of the station in Yokohama, a Japanese man running along the side of the train offered 50 yen for one pack of cigarettes. The young trooper jumped at a chance to make some money. He grabbed the money and threw the pack of cigarettes out the window. After the train had left the station the young trooper was on a high regarding how easy it would be to become rich on his tour of duty in Japan. At this point, the Angel asked to see the money he had received. The Japanese slicky boy had done him in. He had given the trooper 50 sen and not 50 yen. The 50 sen was worth about a penny. We had a good laugh at the expense of this young trooper. Arrival in Sendai was like coming home, as the Angel had left there only about four months ago.

It was now March of 1946 and most of the men who had been there when the Angel had left were now in the states and discharged. The 11th was in the process of rebuilding and almost every company was under-strength. When the Angel received his orders it was for the 188th Glider Infantry Regiment. It was a very good unit but since the Angel had been in the 187th Glider Infantry Regiment before, he wanted to go back to the 187th. A little talk with an understanding personnel officer got the Angel a change of orders. He was now going to the 187th Para/Glider Regimental Combat Team now located in Sapporo, Hokkaido, Japan. The Angel remembered that he had given the First Sergeant a hard time when he had left back in November. He was hoping that the "Top Kick" would be gone by now. His luck had run out. The First Sergeant was still there, and with a big smile, said that he had been waiting for the Angel because he knew he would return like a bad penny. He assigned the Angel to the position of squad leader, second squad, second platoon of "G" Company. When the Angel went to his billets he had another shocker. A trooper who had been a Private First Class in the Angel's squad when he left was now his Platoon Sergeant. The Angel considered his situation as viva la bagatelle (success to trifling).

The Angel settled down to making his squad the best in the regiment or at least trying to. It would be a hard job with the strength of the squad. A squad at that time was 12 men. The squad he took over was at half strength or six men. About half of these would be on guard duty daily, but you do the best with what you have.

The second battalion was stationed in the old Japanese Marine Barracks just at the edge of Sapporo. We had a two-and-one-half-ton truck as a bus to carry us into town on our free time. One of the things that caught the eye of the troops was the way the Japanese relieved themselves when they had to go the latrine. In Sapporo it was extremely cold and damp and the Japanese had an overlapping slit in back of their winter garments so if they had to go to the latrine they just went to the side of the road, squatted, pulled the slit open and took their crap. I suppose they considered it a natural function and nothing to be ashamed of. The latrines for the soldiers had been built by Japanese carpenters. They must have thought we were all giants for when you took a crap your feet would not touch the floor. The Japanese were very good at using anything they came across. One of the things that was noticed by the round-eyed soldiers from America was the way they built the latrines. They built it with flaps on the outside so that they could lift the flap and take out and replace the half barrel of human waste. This they used as fertilizer on their gardens. The odd part was that you could be sitting on a hole and hear someone underneath making noise. When you looked down and between your legs, there would be this Japanese gentlemen smiling up at you and waiting to take the barrel when you had finished. The Angel always said that this created a pucker factor with him.

The Angel was totally embarrassed on one trip into Sapporo for an evening and night of fun. One very obviously pregnant Japanese girl jumped in front of the truck to stop it. The driver stopped the truck in time to avoid running over her. She ran around to the rear of the truck and looked the passengers over until she found one she knew. The one she knew was the Angel. She shouted at the Angel, "Angel sahn! Come Quick! Drunk American soldier, have sex, hitee, hitee my friends! Come Quick! Come Quick!" Even though very embarrassed the Angel got out of the truck and followed the girl. She was right, the soldier was beating up on the girl. The Angel took him upside the head a couple of times, turned him around and kicked his ass and sent him on his way with these words, that if he ever heard of him doing anything like that again, he would kill him. Because of the pregnant girl, the Angel took a lot of ribbing, but it was good-natured ribbing, and everyone could see that she had zonam solvere (had lost the virgin girdle).

One evening a soldier from the Angel's squad asked the Angel if he would like to go into Sapporo for a night on the town. The Angel always ready for fun said, "Sure." During the course of the night, the Angel and the other soldier gravitated toward and into the "Off Limits" area of Sapporo. As bad luck would have it, this was the night the Military Police scheduled a raid on the area. The soldier from West Virginia and the Angel hauled ass from the geisha house they were in and ran like hell down the street with the MP's after them. The Angel shouted to the soldier to run down an alley. The MP's were not likely to follow where it was dark and they could not get their jeep into the alley. After shouting this the Angel took off down an alley, and the MP's did not follow. The Angel was sure the soldier from West Virginia had done the same. The Angel returned to his barracks and hit the sack for the rest of the night.

The next morning at reveille formation, the First Sergeant ordered the Angel to come to the orderly room. In the orderly room, he told the Angel that one of our men had been picked up in an "Off Limits" area last night and that the Angel was to be the prison chaser that would take the man from the stockade to Regimental Headquarters to have charges brought against him. When the Angel reported to the stockade for his prisoner it turned out to be the soldier from West Virginia. The two of them had quite a talk on the way to Regimental Headquarters with the soldier under the gun. If he had followed the Angel, he would not be where he was now, but would have gotten away clean.

One of the places the soldiers used to hang out was a bar and dance place that was across the street from the theater. You entered and bought tickets; a ticket usually would get you a tin cup of beer (about a quart) or a dance with one of the mooses. However, you could not leave with one of the girls. There was always an MP there to prevent trouble. The beer came from a barrel that was pumped up with a tire pump and served like a draft beer. It was fun going there just to listen to the troopers talk to the Japanese girls. The trooper would approach the girl and say, "You old horse faced son of a gun, how would you like to cut a rug with a real man?"

The girl would usually respond by saying "Oh, 'Merican soldier speak good for me, we dance Joe," and off they would go dancing up a storm. It was good clean fun and no one hurt.

One night in the middle of the week, the Angel was in the enlisted men's club in Sapporo talking to friends and drinking beer. The enlisted men's club in town was only allocated so much beer per week, and when that ration of beer ran dry, the club would be closed until the next week. The troopers were very protective of their beer. On this night a group of British sailors came into the club. Their ship was docked in Otaru not far from Sapporo. The sailors were drinking up the troopers' ration of beer as if it was going out of style. It had to happen; the troopers cut off the beer supply to the sailors and a fight erupted. It turned into a glorious free-for-all between the troopers and the sailors. Heads on both sides were broken. Finally, the MPs got the fight under control, the troopers back to their barracks and the sailors back to their shop. The crux of the situation did not take place until reveille the next morning. That was when the First Sergeant told the Angel that his squad had been selected to take a goodwill tour of the British ship in Otaru. It was a sight to behold: the night before breaking each others heads and the next day putting on a good-will show. Not an unfriendly word was spoken on either side that day.

Time moved on and we did things that would never be thought of in today's army. One of the things we did was to take horse cavalry training and to run horse-mounted patrols into the mountains. In fact, we found a lost tribe of people that even the Japanese did not know existed on Hokkaido. They drank bear blood for strength. They also tattooed their upper lip. They were weird but friendly people.

One day after returning from patrol and submitting the Angel's after action report for the S-2 section, the Company Commander called the Angel to the orderly room. He told the Angel that he had reviewed his records and had noticed that the Angel was not a high school graduate. He said that it would please him if the Angel would report to the post education office and take the high school level GED (General Education

Development) tests. The Angel thanked him and went directly to the education center and started taking the GED tests. He passed them with very high scores and was now considered a high school grad at 16. Back in Missouri the class he would have been in was still in high school.

One morning at the reveille formation, the Angel was told to report to the S-2 and S-3 sections at Regimental Headquarters at 08:00 hours.

This he did and was briefed on the situation to the North where refugees were crossing from the Soviet Union territory into Hokkaido. There were seven in the Angel's squad including himself. They also assigned a cook to the Angel's squad. After briefing the troops and drawing our basic load of ammunition and a jeep with a trailer and plenty of "C" rations, we were off to the North. Our job was to apprehend the incoming refugees, tag them and get them back to the CIC (Counter Intelligence Corp) for debriefing. Everything went well for a time, then someone shot up the town that was close by with a BAR. This brought on the CID (Criminal Investigators). It almost had to be someone on the Angel's outpost. The investigators brought people in from the town that had been shot to hell and had a line-up of the Angel's patrol. The Angel was sure that he had trained his squad better than to pull a trick like the one that had happened. The shooter turned out to be the cook that had been assigned to the Angel's patrol at the last minute. The last the Angel heard of him after his court martial was that he was in transit to the Military Prison at Fort Leavenworth, Kansas.

Upon the patrol's return to Sapporo, the Angel was selected to conduct a recon patrol primarily for road conditions on the east side of Hokkaido. This patrol turned into the best assignment during his tour of duty with the occupation army. The patrol consisted of a driver, a Japanese American and a Japanese National. We were out for two weeks on this patrol and in most cases we were the first Americans the Japanese people had seen. When we rolled into a town, the town would turn out in force just to see us. The next item of business would be a large banquet with all the local officials present. When we moved from town to town, the people would be alongside the road cheering us on and filling our trailer with produce. It was a great time for a 16- year-old Sergeant! Upon return to Sapporo and after completing the after action report the Regimental Commander requested that I give him a verbal report of the patrol. He wanted to know if the patrol had encountered any animosity from any area while on this patrol. The Angel informed him that the opposite was true, that we were well received. He congratulated each member of the patrol with a job well done.

A day or two after returning from the patrol, the Company Commander called the Angel to the orderly room. He had an assignment for the Angel. The 187th Para/Glider Regimental Combat Team had a man go AWOL (Absent without leave) in combat. He had been AWOL for over a year when he was apprehended in the Philippines. The Angel was given the duty of picking the prisoner up in Sendai and escorting him from Sendai to Sapporo. The Angel did not know the prisoner as he had not been in the Angel's company. On the trip from Sendai to Sapporo one had to make a number of changes in mode of travel. It would be train travel from Sendai to Aomari, then by ferry to Hokadate and train again to Sapporo. The prisoner said he had heard of the Angel and what would the Angel do if he decided to run. The Angel told the prisoner that there was one way to find out and that was to go ahead and run. Perhaps if he did, the Angel could save the price of a court-martial. No more was said about running from the prisoner. General Swing, our Division Commander, sentenced the man to death. However, the Angel believes the sentence was commuted when the man was shipped to the Disciplinary Barracks at Fort Leavenworth, Kansas.

By this time, the Angel and a couple of others were the only men in the company that had been in combat with the 11th Airborne Division. The First Sergeant was still there and one of the platoon sergeants was still there; and that was all the combat veterans remaining who had been with the 11th in the Philippines.

This started to cause a problem, for in the Second Platoon, the men started to come to the Angel with their problems and the Angel could see the Platoon Sergeant losing control of his men. This was the soldier who had been a PFC in the Angel's squad when the Angel had returned to the states on reenlistment leave. He was a good man but he did have a control problem. The Angel could see only one way of correcting the situation and that was to remove himself from the scene. This he did by volunteering for the 187 P/G RCT boxing team. This would move him to Sendai and division special troops. The Angel was carried on the morning report as belonging to the same company he had always belonged to, but he would be carried as TDY (temporary duty) to the boxing team. The Platoon Sergeant would have to take control of his platoon now; it would be a forced issue.

Being a member of the 187 P/G RCT boxing team allowed the Angel some special perks. For example, when the troops were eating stew, the boxing team was eating steak. The team was on a high protein diet. The training schedule was great, no formations. We would report to the gym each morning about 9:00 a.m. for a work-out on the light and heavy bags, then we would spar a few rounds with other members of the team. We would knock off about 11:00 a.m. and rest until the noon meal. In the afternoon it was road work from about 1:00 p.m. until 5:00 p.m.. then back to your room to rest. At about 7:00-8:00 p.m. we'd go into town for fun and games. It was not regimented at all. On each Wednesday evening we would be on the fight card for a match with one of the other units in Japan. We did a lot of train and plane travel to the location of the boxing matches. The Angel trained down to about 160 pounds, middle weight, but being a youngster of 16 he could not hold this weight and gradually lapsed over into light heavy weight.

The Angel was extremely proud that he finished each bout on his feet. Oh, he dropped a decision now and then, but he answered each bell. One of the Angel's extremely difficult fights was at Kobe Base on Honshu Island. The Angel was matched with a black man. The Angel figured it would be a walk over when he saw his opponent for the first time. The opponent was extremely tall, and extremely skinny. He had very long thin arms. The Angel boasted that the guy would not make it half way through the first round with him. When the bell rang for the first round, the Angel came out of his corner ready to feel the man out. Those long thin arms of his almost tore the Angel's head off. The Angel just could not get in to him. At the end of the first round, the Angel's corner man told the Angel he had probably lost the first round. He said that this would not be a pretty fight. He told the Angel to follow by a counter his blows and to clinch with him and do as much damage as the Angel could inside, then throw him away on the break from the clinch and repeat this over and over. It was not a pretty fight. It was one to be remembered but not be proud of. The Angel got the decision from the judges and the referee for taking rounds two and three. The Angel said that he sure wanted to look behind that fellow to see what in the hell kept him on his feet throughout the fight. If it had been a professional fight, the Angel is not so sure he would have won, as the man may have outlasted him. Well, we will never know.

On Wednesday night the fight card was at the Theater in Sapporo. It was the 187 P/G RCT versus the 24th Division. The 24th Division lost every fight on the card. The Officer in Charge of the 24th Division boxing team came back into our dressing room crying foul and claiming poor officiating for their poor showing. About this time General Swing came into the dressing room to congratulate his boxers. He listened to the OIC from the 24th Division cry foul for a little while. He then ordered the 24th OIC outside of the dressing room and in a very level voice said to the 24OIC that the 187th boxing team had well trained boxers and that if he shut his mouth and spent the time gained on training his boxing team, perhaps they would make a better show the next time they opposed the 187 Rakkasans. This sure made our boxing team happy to have the Old Man on our side all the way. He was the kind of leader that could lead you through hell and make you happy you made the trip.

It was about this time that the Angel was approached by a representative of a fight promoter that wanted to put the Angel under contract to fight out of San Diego, California, after his term of service was completed, which was only a few more months. The Angel gave it some thought and then decided not to turn pro. To this day, the Angel believes that was the best decision he ever made. At times, it is a small thing that causes a person to make a decision. For the Angel, he did not believe he had the killer instinct that a pro boxer needs. He had been known to let an opponent come back after having him down. Also, after each fight, the Angel's hands would swell and be very painful for a couple of days. The Angel figured that amateur boxing was great, but professional boxing just did not get the job done in his mind.

The best incentive the Angel had for staying on the boxing team was the fact that each team member had his own room complete with a house boy to cater to the boxer. The room was always spotless, your uniform pressed and your boots shined. Yes, life on the team was great. It was great because each of the boxers on the team had vis vitae (the vigor of life).

About a month or six weeks prior to the time the Angel was scheduled to return to the continental United States, he was returned to his company in the 187th P/G RCT. Shortly after returning to the company he received his orders to return stateside. Yes, back to the land of the big PX (Post Exchange). While he had been gone from the 2nd Battalion a couple of things had happened that were of interest.

One of the troopers from another company had assisted in the break out of a friend from the post stockade. They had then gone into Sapporo and cut the throats of four gooks and threw their bodies into the river. Then they tried breaking the one in the stockade back into the stockade. If they would have been successful, they would have gotten away clean. However, they were caught. It crossed the Angel's mind that if they would have done this one year earlier, they would have received medals. Instead now they would receive a General Courts Martial. Life has its weird twists.

Another thing that happened while the Angel was on TDY to the boxing team was rather funny but did get the troopers in big trouble. The trooper took a jeep from Service Company motor pool without a trip ticket. He came across the Company Commander walking to Regimental Headquarters and offered him a ride. The CO accepted the ride. The trooper asked him if he had ever been to a Japanese cat house. Of course, the CO said "No," although this was probably a lie. Well, the trooper said that he would soon be in one. He drove at a high rate of speed into Sapporo's off limit area and ran the jeep through the sliding doors of the geisha house. The trooper from Alabama now said to the CO that he could now say that he had been in a geisha house. The trooper made his point, but it cost him six months in the stockade and two-thirds of his pay for six months. In other words maximum for a Special Court Martial.

The date of departure finally came for the Angel. This would be his third round trip to the Pacific Theater of Operations since 1943. The Angel again volunteered to work in the butcher shop on the ship and his voyage was uneventful. He ate well and stayed out of the crap games. After all, he was a veteran of troop ships.

Upon arrival at Oakland Army Base he and a couple of buddies from the 11th Airborne made the town and made it back to the base well after daylight the next day. When they arrived, they were calling off names and destinations for the Angel's group. The Angel was going to the Separation Center at Camp Beale, California. Upon arrival at Camp Beale the processing was hurried and extremely chaotic. If someone would have asked me to reenlist regular army I would have. No one asked. I was asked if I would like to enlist in the US Army-Enlisted Reserve Corps for three years. The Angel did just that, after he was informed he would not have to make weekly or monthly drills at some armory. That he would just be considered ready reserve. They swore me in, gave me my WD AGO Form 166 dated April 1946 and sent me on my way.

Two things happened at Camp Beale that did make me angry. The first one was they took the Angel's General Joe Swing Cap. This was the cap accepted in the 11th Airborne, and they took the Angel's Samaarai sword, which made him angry as hell. I am sure those rear stateside son-of-a-bitches kept them.

THE YEARS BETWEEN
WORLD WAR II AND KOREA

After out processing was completed at Camp Beale, California, the Angel purchased his bus ticket to St. Louis. He was expecting the trip to be one long party as the two trips he had made previously. This was not to be the case. The mood of the country had changed completely. During the war the mood had been live for today and to hell with tomorrow. During this trip the mood was somber. It was, "Get me back to my wife, my children or my parents and let me start life anew." By the time the bus was 50 miles out of Sacramento, the Angel missed the comradeship of other paratroopers. He was very sad and almost in a state of melancholia. After all, the military had been his home from age 13 to age 17.

The Angel did not know what was ahead, but he knew that since 1943 he had been an outstanding sailor and soldier. He had lead 40 men in combat. What now? He settled back for a long and uneventful trip. Yes, he was one of them now. A civilian. A person who did not know what the uniform of the day was. They were a chaotic mob and not a regimented formation. It would take some getting used to, for sure.

During out processing at Camp Beale they had lectured the returnees regarding the 52/20 Club: $20 per week for 52 weeks and the lecture had included the GI Bill for education. Perhaps one of these programs would ease the hurt and make the transition from noncommissioned officer to raggedy-ass civilian easier.

The Angel's spirits were lifted somewhat by the reception he received from Slim and Flo and a couple of days later from the Old German and Mrs. John. He knew they loved him and would always be there for him. It was a good feeling.

The first thing the Angel did after the welcome home party was to visit the local unemployment office and sign up for the 52/20 Club. During this visit the Angel became acquainted with a fellow paratrooper who said that he had been accepted at Washington University right there in St. Louis. He said that he had used the shot gun approach to getting into the university of his choice and that he had applications from other schools that the Angel could have if he wanted to apply for entry for the second semester of the 1946-47 school year. The Angel decided on the University of Kansas at Lawrence, Kansas. The Angel said he selected that school because he liked the Jay Hawk emblem of the school. He was playing it lightly because he did not believe he would be accepted. After all, he was only a GED high school grad. How surprised he was when he received a letter to come for an interview. The letter gave a time and date for him to be there. With the help of a friend who knew someone working in a clothing store, the Angel purchased his civilian wardrobe. He made it very conservative, you know, dark blue suit, red tie, white shirt, etc. He wanted to give the appropriate good impression at the coming interview.

The interview went extremely well and after awhile he indicated that I would be receiving my letter of acceptance and given a date for registering for the second semester. The interviewer told the Angel that it might be a good idea to stick with survey courses for the next couple of semesters. After some small talk, the interviewer asked if the Angel enjoyed football. Naturally, the answer was in the affirmative. He then gave me a couple of tickets for the upcoming game between Kansas and Missouri: the Jay Hawks and the Tigers. They are friendly enemies. Now the Angel had to find him a girl to go to the game with.

The Angel had a room in a hotel in Lawrence for the weekend so it was no trouble to stay for the Saturday game. He left the interview with a thank you and a hand shake, and with two tickets to the game. He walked out on the campus and sat down on a bench. Within 15 minutes a tall, slim young lady sat down on the same bench and started reading a book. The Angel struck up a conversation with the young lady and in a short period of time they were talking as if they had known each other for years. One topic of conversation lead to another until finally it got around to the upcoming football game. The Angel then asked if she would like to go to the game on Saturday. The answer was definitely yes. She said that she lived in Topeka and she lived at home, but she would meet the Angel right here on this bench before the game. She was as good as her word.

The day of the game, she was at the bench before the Angel arrived. When he saw her she was beautiful. She was dressed in the mode of the day for female college students. You know, sloppy-joe sweater, bobby socks, short pleated skirt and saddle shoes. She was a vision to behold. After a little small talk it was off to the game. The game was a close one and a lot of cheering was taking place. On a Kansas touchdown the Kansas side of the field went wild. My date jumped up to cheer by throwing her hands violently over her head and screaming. This action caused a falsie to come out of her brassiere and go bouncing down over the seats in front of us. What should the Angel do now? Being a gentleman, he went to the bottom of the stands, retrieved the falsie and brought it back to her. She was so embarrassed that she was crying. She sobbed out that she wanted to leave the game. Therefore, the Angel escorted her out of the game and to the bench where they had met. We talked awhile, but she could not get herself composed and finally she said with regrets that she had to go home. I saw her after that, but it was just with a nod and a hello as we passed.

With my letter of acceptance in my pocket I returned to Stanton to stay with the Old German and Mrs. John until the second semester started.

The Angel must admit that getting adjusted to civilian life did not come easy. The Angel was a little on the wild side. The Saturday after the Kansas football game, the Angel was living it up at the local honky-tonk when he decided to go alone to a dance at the intersection of Highway 30 and County Road B. The Angel had a fun time at the dance and about 2:00 a.m. Sunday morning he started back to Stanton. A carload of six followed him on the highway. They would zoom around the Angel's car, then slow up making the Angel go around them. The Angel was never one to go wild in this manner. It could get someone killed. Therefore, with the element of surprise as his ace in the hole, he pulled off on the shoulder of the road and took one-half of a spring leaf from under his car seat. When the other car stopped, he went back to meet them. The six got out and came to meet him. The Angel did not go into small talk with them for that would give them the advantage. Without saying anything, he hit the first three with the spring leaf; they were down and out. The other three ran like ruptured ducks. Slim had always said, "If you can't avoid a fight, at least get in the first licks." It was good advice.

The second semester at Kansas University would begin in January of 1947, a couple of months away. The Angel would stay in the 52/20 Club until the start of school and then he would be on the GI bill. Some of the Angel's peers could not understand how he could be in college before his classmates had finished high school. To say that some were envious would be putting it mildly.

The Angel noticed that by new year of 1947 most of the guys who had returned home from the military were starting to blend into the civilian society. Even the Angel was not quite so wild. He was not drinking so much, fighting as much or chasing women as much. The rough edges of his personality were being honed down. The Angel started dating a young lady who was a teacher in the Stanton School. She was definitely a looker and just an all around great girl. The Angel had about a half dozen dates with the young lady during December of 1946 and January of 1947. However, the long range situation did not work out.

The reason it did not work out was that the Angel, while carousing in a bar in St. Clair, Missouri, met her cousin. From that time on the Angel and the cousin were constant companions. The cousin was a girl who knew the ways of the world and did not mind teaching them to the Angel. She was a petite blond, with an olive complexion and brown eyes. She had a hold on the Angel and would not let go. She had also been divorced. The Angel now knows that he should have pursued the teacher and not fallen into the charm of her cousin. Everyone figured that when the Angel left home to go to the University of Kansas he and the girl would be split up, and that would be all she wrote regarding their relationship. It did not work out that way.

In January of 1947 it was off to school in Kansas. The academic challenge at KU was not that great, and the Angel was continuing to march academically in good order. When asked by the other students what he expected to major in he would answer, "I'm here to major in girls and to minor in the GI Bill." When it came time for spring break, the Angel was back home in Stanton with the Old German and Mrs. John. However, all of his time was spent with the little brown-eyed blond divorcee. Even on some weekends, the Angel would drive the four or five hours that it took him to drive from Lawrence, Kansas, to Stanton, Missouri, just for a few hours with his lady. Looking back it was crazy, but at the time it seemed perfectly normal. Yes, it was a very heavy infatuation.

By the end of the semester, the Angel was chopping at the bit to get back to Stanton and to his main squeeze. The Angel's grade point average was fine. It was 3.2 for the semester. Now it was home, find a job and spend time with the girl over the summer break. His goals were met the first week he was home. The Angel went to work for Koss Construction Company out of Des Moines, Iowa, as a concrete form setter. This meant swinging a sledge hammer 8 to 12 hours daily, and he still found time for the girl.

Setting those concrete form pins with that sledge hammer kept the Angel in outstanding physical condition. He looked almost top heavy with a 32-inch waist and a 54-inch chest. The money on this job was extremely good for that time. The Angel put his time in working and being with his woman. However, there still lingered a desire for the military in his heart.

Along about August of 1947 the Angel's girl, his main squeeze, started putting the pressure on to get married. The Angel indicated that he was not ready, but the pressure continued. In September it was back to Kansas University for the first semester. What a shock it was going from big money on construction back to the income from the GI Bill. It was difficult to adjust. Of course, the girl continued to pressure to be joined in matrimony. The big pressure came from the crying fits she would have. The Angel finally gave in and said they would get married, but not to put on a big show. In other words, keep it very small. In the first part of October the act was accomplished. The Angel was now 18. The Angel should have known cito-maturium cito-putridum (soon ripe, soon rotten).

After the wedding, the Angel moved the girl, his wife, to student housing in Sunflower, Kansas. This was government housing for GI Bill students. It was about 10 miles from Lawrence, Kansas. He settled down to being a husband and a student in that order.

The semester moved along in good order. However, the girl started to badger the Angel to move back to Missouri. She was very good at using oriental philosophy to get her way. She practiced the art of using a small but constant pressure over a long period of time and any object will eventually move in the direction of the pressure. She used the Angel's mind set of philology against him just to get her way. It worked.

The Angel said that he would register into the Rolla School of Mines for the second semester of 1947-48. That put them about 40 miles from their home. The girl was happy about this, the Angel was not. However, he tried to make the best of what he considered a bad situation.

After the first semester at KU was completed, and over the Christmas break, the Angel moved her back to Missouri. He started school in Rolla in January. The Angel found the curriculum more difficult than it had been at KU. This school demanded more attention to detail. It was a small school and one could not get lost in the crowd. However, the Angel applied himself and did relatively well with his GPA (grade point average). The Angel also found that he had to take on extra work because the GI Bill would not cover all the school and living expense.

Along about March of 1948, the Angel was reminded that he was still a member of the US Army Ready Reserve. He was invited to return to active duty to be an escort for soldiers who died or were killed during World War II. The criterion used for selection as an escort for those killed during World War II was outlined in the letter received by the Angel. You had to be a noncommissioned officer who had gone through at least two major campaigns during WWII. You also had to have "RECOMMENDED FOR FURTHER SERVICE" on your DD 214 (Discharge Information Form). If you were interested, you had to fill out the attached document and return it to the reserve center in St. Louis. Without a second thought the Angel filled out the form and returned it to the reserve center. Within a week he was contacted and told where and when to report for his physical for return to active duty. With the receipt of the letter the Angel started to feel that old military pride again. On the date of his physical he was there and standing tall. After the physical, it was back to Rolla to await the call to active duty.

It did not take long for the call, about a week. The Angel reported to the reserve center in St. Louis to pick up his orders. He also had to withdraw from school and terminate the income from the GI Bill. His orders directed him to report to Fort Sheridan, Illinois, for assignment to the 5017 ASU (Army Service Unit) Escort Detachment. After a short course on how to conduct oneself in escorting WWII remains, the Angel was given his choice of working out of the Chicago quartermaster distribution center or the Kansas City, Missouri, distribution center. The Angel selected the Kansas City Quartermaster Depot at the intersection of Independence and Hardesty Avenues.

Now came the shocker for the girl the Angel married. He would move her back to Sunflower, Kansas. She was livid with rage when the Angel broke the news to her. However, there was no arguing now; orders are orders. The move was made and the Angel was extremely happy to be back in uniform. He just felt that he belonged, it seemed so natural. The area that the Kansas City Quartermaster would cover in escorting the remains of WWII dead was from the Appalachian Mountains in the east to the Rocky Mountains in the west. There was always some overlap between distribution centers. The escort would make one or two trips each week depending on the length of the trip. The escorts were kept extremely busy for in the year we had for active duty, there would be approximately 275,000 remains returned to the United States for burial. These remains had been KIA (killed in action) during WWII. They initially had been buried overseas then, at the request of their next of kin, they were being returned to the United States for burial. We escorts treated these remains with the utmost dignity and respect, for they were all heroes who had given their all for their country.

Escorting war dead was a unique learning experience for the Angel. One week he would be in a home with dirt floors, and the next be in a home with caddies parked in the driveway.

While the Angel never had a bad trip, this was not true for some of the escorts. A friend of the Angel's had a trip to New Mexico as an escort for a Native American. After the ceremony, he was given a pony and told to ride it to town and to let it go and it would return to the reservation. Needless to say, the escort had never been on a horse in his life, much less riding bareback while carrying a suitcase. Another friend of the Angel's had a trip to Tennessee where the next of kin to the remains he was escorting belonged to a religious sect that had no respect for the symbol of our country, the flag. The next of kin would remove the flag from the casket, the escort would put it back on the casket. It turned into a Mexican standoff. Finally it was settled when the escort called the Quartermaster Depot for instructions. He was told to return to the Depot as soon as possible. This allowed the issue to die. The Angel had a trip to Crowe Agency, Montana during the ceremony, the Angel was made an Honorary Chief; to the Angel this was indeed a great honor.

Within the escort detachment there was a lot of competition for trips into Kansas. The reason was money. At that time Kansas was a dry state. If the escort wanted to make a buck or two, he would purchase whiskey in Missouri, place the whiskey in the void space between the casket and the shipping case, and sell it when he reached his destination. In fact, the Angel never heard of a case where the funeral director would not buy it.

A military escort had to be an extremely adaptable individual. On a trip to Minnesota that the Angel made, Murphy's Law was definitely the rule. The father got down drunk and could not make the funeral. Therefore, the escort had to be at the mother's side. Then on the way to the cemetery, the minister's car slid into a ditch and he was a no-show. The funeral director asked the Angel if he could handle the graveside ceremony. The Angel responded, "Sure"; at 35 degrees below zero, he could handle anything to get out of the cold. The Angel conducted the service and had them back into town in short order. On a trip to Nebraska, the Angel became snowbound. He wired the Quartermaster Depot in Kansas City, snowbound, send per diem, and they did. The Angel was in town about a week and a half before the roads and the railroad were clear. On a trip to Kansas, the next of kin wired the Department that the Angel reminded them of their son and could the escort, the Angel, stay with them for a couple of weeks. The request was granted.

For some reason all of the escorts could not adapt to the duty. Post traumatic stress was not heard of at this time. The Angel now believes that this was a problem with some of the escorts. We had more people go off of their nut with escort duty than the Angel had ever seen or heard of in a line unit.

Just a few of the things that happened during the Angel's tour of duty as a military escort that probably happened because of post traumatic stress. The supply sergeant at the QM Depot went off of his nut and started giving things away from the supply room. The Angel himself got a couple of new poplin shirts out of the deal. The supply sergeant was shipped off to the psychiatric ward and from there, who knows? Another individual featured himself as a criminal investigator and he would hide in a wall locker, and when you came into your room at wee hours of the morning, he would jump out at you. He was another for the physic ward. Another escort, while on a trip, threw a banquet at a hotel in the town where he had escorted the remains. He invited everyone in town to the banquet. He then told the hotel manager to send the bill to his boss, Uncle Sam. He was another candidate for the nut ward. One of the officers at the QM Depot used to ask different individual soldiers to purchase, on a daily basis, six half pints of whiskey for him from the drug store across the street from the QM Depot. Then he would have the soldier hide them in different places around the depot. Therefore, he was never more than a few feet from a drink of booze. These were all men who had seen heavy combat during WWII. Wherever they are today, the Angel wishes them well.

Along about the 19th birthday of the Angel, the woman he was married to informed him that he was going to be a father. The Angel was thrilled at the prospect of having a family. The woman he was married to would receive all her prenatal and childbirth care at the Station Hospital at Fort Leavenworth, Kansas. Yes, the Angel had his head in the clouds he was so happy.

The first of the new year, the year of 1949, escort duty had slowed down to the extent that the QM Depot in Kansas City was phased out as a distribution center for war dead and the escorts were shipped to Fort Sheridan, Illinois, for escort duty out of the Chicago QM Depot Distribution Center. The Angel and his wife decided that she would stay in Sunflower, Kansas, so she would be near Fort Leavenworth for her prenatal care. This turned out to be the right decision. On the last day of February 1949 the Angel was informed that his wife was in the hospital at Fort Leavenworth for childbirth and that he should be granted leave to be with her. The Angel arrived at the hospital on the first of March expecting to see his child and his wife. This was not to be, as the wife was having an extremely difficult labor. She had been in labor about 48 hours when the Angel arrived. The Angel had to make the decision on whether to allow normal childbirth to proceed or to take the baby by an unnatural procedure. The Doctor suggested that we wait a few more hours and then get our heads together again regarding what avenue of approach to take. A nurse gave the Angel a room so he could rest. About the time he dropped off to sleep, he was awakened by the nurse and told it was time. On March 2, 1949 Michael Eugene entered the world. His head was misshapen and bruised and he had a terrible black eye, but he was here. The Doctor had used forceps to bring Mike into the world kicking and screaming. He told the Angel that the head would clear up in a day or two, and it did. No one could have been more proud of his youngster than the Angel. He was walking on clouds. After about three days, the Angel took his wife and son home to Sunflower. Then he had to go back to Fort Sheridan. His one year of active duty would be coming to an end in about six weeks, and the Angel would revert back to the ready reserve again. For the time remaining, the clerks in the orderly room scheduled the Angel on trips as near to Sunflower, Kansas, as possible. They did this so he could spend as much time with his wife and son as possible. That is what the Angel enjoyed about the military; they operated as a team, a team that knew and practiced empathy. The Angel would miss the active duty.

During the year of active duty as an escort for WWII dead, one thing happened that hurt the ego of the Angel. The Doolittle Commission was meeting in Washington, D.C. to study the unification of the military services. The idea was that all services would have the same uniform and no appendages to the uniform would designate an elite organization within the service. That would not allow airborne troops patches, or airborne tabs, no ranger tabs, no division patches. It also did away with the backbone of the Army, the buck sergeant rank. The rating patches were extremely small and blue on gold for Combat Troops, gold on blue for non-combat troops. Over all, it was a joke!

When the regulation was published those on regular army status and ranked as buck sergeant were promoted to staff sergeant. However, those on active duty as members of the Enlisted Reserve Corps would become corporals again. It was not fair but it was the regulation. It hurt the ego of the Angel to remove the three stripes of a sergeant and replace them with the two stripes of a corporal. The pay did not change, but the prestige of the individual soldier did.

About six weeks after the birth of Mike, the Angel's year of active duty expired and he was released back to the Ready Reserve. He returned to Sunflower to look for work. He was accepted for training as a Kansas State High Patrolman. His discharge had him old enough, but his true birth certificate did not. He was told to reapply when he was 21. He then applied and was accepted for employment at the Buick, Oldsmobile, Pontiac plant in Kansas City, Kansas. He took the job as a final shipping inspector. The hourly wage was $1.85 per hour. Excellent wages for that time and place.

Again, the Angel missed the US Army. The feeling of wanting to be with and around his comrades in arms was constantly present. Oh well, totidem verbis (in so many words) he would stick it out at the BOP Plant and perhaps the feeling of the desire to soldier would go away in time. In August of 1950 the Angel would finally be able to vote; he would be 21. However, something happened before he reached this goal. On June 25, 1950 the North Korean horde crossed the Yalu River and went south across the 38th parallel and caught South Korea and the United States by surprise. Most of our troops had been living the soft life in Japan. They were not hardened in and ready for combat. Most of the units both in the US and in Japan were understrength and not combat ready.

The Angel heard about this invasion while working his shift at the BOP plant. At the end of his shift he immediately went to the Reserve Center and volunteered to come back on active duty. He requested that his assignment be with a paratroop unit. Therefore, the Angel was surprised when he received his orders to see that he was not assigned to a paratroop unit, but assigned to the 439th Engineer Battalion, a reserve unit that had been called to active duty. It was a Kansas unit and the Angel's orders read for him to join "A" Company in the city auditorium in Emporia, Kansas.

The 439th Engineer Battalion was a reserve unit called to active duty. It was really Sand Ore Construction Company put into uniform. They were not the greatest soldiers in the world, but they were outstanding at any type of construction. It was reserve units and personnel like these that really pulled Korea out of the fire. At first, the Angel was extremely sad that he was ordered to this unit because he considered the men of the airborne (para-troopers) uniquely elite. He considered them as the bedrock of the United States Army and the true guardians of our democratic way of life. He could not understand how he wound up in a straight leg outfit. However, the longer he stayed with the 439th Engineers the better it became. The companies from Hays, McPherson, Salina and Emporia, Kansas, were ordered to pro-ceed to Camp Carson, Colorado, to stage for overseas movement to Korea. There we would process all of our equipment for ship loading and ship the equipment to California for ship loading. As soon as this was accomplished, the personnel of the battalion would be shipped to Camp Stoneman, California, for shipment to Korea via Japan.

At Camp Carson, the Angel again volunteered for the boxing team. The team trainer at the time was Lon Jenkins, the former World's Lightweight Champion. The Angel had now matured to the point where he could fight as a middle or light heavyweight. After a couple of fights, he was called to Post Headquarters and was asked to transfer to the post military police unit to fight for Camp Carson and perhaps for Fifth Army. They stressed that this would keep the Angel from shipping to Korea. The Angel just could not do this. It would have been chicken shit of him to dodge Korea just to be a jock strap for a non-combat unit. He turned the request down abruptly.

The Angel was granted a short leave to return to Sunflower,

130

Kansas, to move his wife and son back to Sullivan, Missouri. It was on this leave that he was informed that he was going to be a father again. The feeling was great and again, the Angel had his head in the clouds. It was hectic, but he got his wife moved and settled in the short time he was allowed. He returned to Camp Carson just in time to make the shipment to Camp Stoneman. This would be the Angel's third time for processing through Camp Stoneman for shipment to the Far East.

At the time of shipment to Korea, things did not look good. The North Koreans had pushed our troops and the South Koreans back to the Pusan Perimeter.

The Angel, who had now been promoted to Staff Sergeant was dispatched to accompany the shipment of the battalion engineer equipment to the west coast and to oversee the loading of the equipment on a victory ship. After the equipment was shipped, the Angel joined the personnel of the battalion at Camp Stoneman. It was now in October of 1950. The equipment would go directly to Pusan, Korea and the personnel would go to Funsbashi, Japan until notified that the equipment had arrived in Pusan. Everything went together like clock work, and the 439th Engineer Battalion joined their equipment in Pusan and moved to Station Nathan Hole on the Pusan Perimeter. From this place the unit started to push north against the North Koreans. They were whipped badly and knew it. Yes, we expected to be back in the states by Christmas. This was not to be. The battalion received a request for two engineer NCO's who had been trained in demolition to accompany Task Force Walker on a patrol that would range for 40-50 miles beyond the MLR (main line of resistance). When they reported to the CO of the task force they were given their duty. The North Koreans were moving north so fast that they could not place mines in the road as well as they should. It was the other NCO and the Angel's duty to ride the lead tank and be on the lookout for the anti-tank or anti-personnel mines. If and when they located a possible mine they would go ahead and place a quarter pound block of TNT along-side or over the mine and explode it.

Even in combat there are light moments. While entering Wonju a North Korean officer with very thick glasses came out and down the road we were on, as if coming to meet us. When he saw the mistake he had made he turned and ran, one of us on the tank was armed with a carbine and the other with an M1 rifle.

The NCO with the carbine was first to open fire. You could see that he was hitting his target because little puffs of dust would come out of his back. However, he never went down more than to his knees and then back up and running. When the M1 grand opened up on him that was all she wrote. The papers in his brief case were sent back to the intelligence unit.

Just south of Wonju there was a bridge leading from one tunnel to another tunnel. The bridge was about 130 feet high and maybe 1,500 feet long. By blowing the bridge we could slow the movement north by the North Koreans. This task was given to the Angel and the other NCO. The other NCO did not have formal training in demo and it had been since the Alabama area at Fort Benning in 1944 that the Angel had demo school. Some of the formulas for cutting steel were a little hazy in his mind. However, he remembered P=3/8A and this was the formula he used. The Angel figured the amount, but it seemed small, so he doubled it. It still seemed small and not enough for such a large bridge so he doubled it again. He placed the charges so they would blow in and he offset them so they would act like a cut with scissors. We had the task force move to what we considered a safe distance down the road, and he blew the bridge. The charge was definitely more than needed for it put a piece of rail from the railroad track through the hood of the jeep. The blast had the entire task force looking for cover. Little did he know that in a short while, in fact, as soon as the North Korean line was north of Wonju, his unit would be given the mission of rebuilding the Kil-rah-Chon bridge. However, before they were to go to work on the bridge the Chinese entered the war. The Angel and his engineer section received orders to join the 1st Marine Division north of the 38th parallel. The Angel reported to his assigned post at the Changjin Reservoir. All of a sudden there were Chinese all over the damn place.

If the scuttlebutt of the time was correct, then some General Officer should have been discharged from the service with other than an honorable release. Scuttlebutt said that there was a lack of communication between X Corps and the 8th Army, thereby allowing the Chinese to infiltrate south between X Corps and the 8th Army this maneuver effectively cut off the 1st Marine Division and the 7th Army Division. Good movement on the part of the Chinese. The Angel knew now that he would not be home for Christmas and he would not be there when his second youngster was born.

With the entry into the war of the Chinese, it was, to say the least, a chaotic situation. In the Angel's engineer section he received some weird orders. He was to follow the main body of troops and create land slides, blow bridges and in general do anything to slow the Chinese down on the forced march to Hungnam. The Angel was told that if ships ordered to Hungnam were not there when he arrived, he was to blow up his equipment and lash some empty drums together making a raft, ride this out on the tide and he would be picked up by our forces somewhere in the sea of Japan. Thank goodness the ships were there! It was now back to Pusan and rejoining the 439th Engineer Battalion at Andong, and with Operation Killer in effect, the movement was north again to Mai-po-u and on to Wonju. Now we could work on rebuilding the Kil-rah-Chon bridge.

The rebuilding of the bridge was a feather in the hat for the men from Kansas and Sand Ore Construction Company. The bridge was rebuilt in about three weeks or a month and train traffic could now move material north and south. The building of the bridge was fun to work on and to watch it go together. The Angel noted that the first 25-foot section had engineers swarming all over it, but by the last section, about 130-feet high, only eight men would still climb and hang steel. The Angel was one of the eight. On completion of the bridge, the CO brought in some ROK soldiers to man the perimeter while the engineers had a big party. It was a true morale booster. The Colonel must have pulled rank, either military or political, to bring in as much good booze as we had. It was a grand party.

Upon the completion of the Kil-rah-Chon bridge, the battalion moved to a position north and east of Seoul. Before we really got started with the bridge, we noticed elements of the 24th Division moving toward the south. When we questioned them as their destination, they said they were moving to a secondary line of resistance. If that secondary line was south of we engineers, then what the hell were we doing in front of it? Then the word came that the 6th ROK Division had not held the line and had cut-a-chog's allowing the Chinese to flank the 2nd Division who caught all the hell. The 6th ROK Division was not known as a good fighting unit, in fact, some thought that the 6th ROK was the best division the North Koreans had. A little humor there! The Capital ROK Division fought well, but the 6th ROK Division was number 10.

The 439th Engineer Battalion finally was ordered back to the site they had in Wonju and given the mission of building an air strip just south of the MLR. The line was on the high ground and the engineers were immediately behind them building the strip so ammo and other supplies could be flown almost right to the line.

The Angel was working his section when a runner from Battalion headquarters found him and told him to report to battalion as soon as possible. In fact, he was to return with him as the Angel had an emergency at home. The Angel immediately thought of Slim who was in the VA hospital in Springfield, Missouri. At battalion headquarters the Angel was out processed in short order. He was informed that he had been recommended for the Bronze Star Medal and that it would catch up with him when it was approved. For the Angel it was back to the air strip to catch a plane to Japan.

Something happened on the way from Korea to Japan and to this day, the Angel does not know if the thing that happened was real or if the air crew of the plane was just having fun. One of the engines on the C-119 started running very rough. The flight engineer got a red light on his console. He pushed a button and the light went off, but in a minute or so it came back on. The Engineer tapped the co-pilot, pointed to the red light and made motions for the co-pilot to put on his chute. The co-pilot did and then took control while the pilot put on his parachute; he sat back down and motioned for the flight engineer to put on his chute. The Angel looked around and could not find a parachute. The Angel decided that if it was a game, he would play along with it. So he continued to sit by the hatch that goes down into the cargo bay of the plane. In the Angel's mind he knew if they started to come by him that two of them would be riding one chute to the water below. Finally, the red light on the console went off and things returned to normal. Even the engine was not running rough now. It was on to Kyushu, Japan.

The Angel was a sorry sight and some of the airmen seemed almost afraid of him. He still had about a month of combat grime on him and was still carrying his weapon.

From Kyushu he was given transportation to Camp Drake for out processing. This consisted of turning in my rifle, fatigues, etc. Then going through the delousing line, then the clothing issue line for a clean uniform, and finally my orders for 30 days of emergency leave with travel time. The uniform the Angel was issued was clean, but it did not fit. The trousers must have come from some short-legged individual because on the Angel they came to about an inch above his boots. The shirt must have been about a 14 or 15 in size and the Angel was an 18, the only thing that fit was the tie and socks. Even the underwear did not fit. Once through the line it was off to catch a plane back to the land of the big PX.

The plane was a TWA charter flight and our first stop over was on Wake Island for refueling and a chance to stretch our legs. Then off to Hawaii. In Hawaii, the Angel's flight had an extended stop over of several hours. The Angel took advantage of the time to buy a tailor-made uniform so he would not look as if he was a complete bum. While waiting for the uniform to be altered, the Angel almost missed his flight to Travis Air Force Base in California. When he arrived back at the passenger terminal in Hawaii they were calling his name over the public address system to report to Agriculture to make sure he was not carrying agricultural products back into the United States, especially fruit of any kind. After holding the plane's departure time for the Angel and a friend he had become acquainted with on the flight, they were off on the last leg of the trip. The Angel still did not know what his emergency at home was; could it be that Slim had taken a turn for the worse?

After arrival at Travis Air Force Base the Angel's orders were stamp dated and he was on his own for the remainder of the trip to Sullivan, Missouri. The Angel and the fellow he had met on the flight decided to chance a space available flight to any base in the mid-section of the United States. The trooper that the Angel had met on the flight informed the Angel that he was going into town to do some serious drinking, and he did. The Angel remained at the base to be sure that if he was manifested on a flight, he would not miss the flight and be placed at the bottom of the list again. A manifest for a flight to San Antonio, Texas, was called over the public address system. The Angel was not on the list, but his friend was on the list. His friend was in town and was going to miss the flight so when the aircraft was loading and the last name of the Angel's buddy was called, the Angel sounded off with his first name and middle initial and boarded the aircraft. He was now on his way to Texas. The Angel never saw his buddy again. In San Antonio the Angel ran into a fighter pilot that told him he had one empty seat and if the Angel wanted to go to the Naval Air Station at Olathe, Kansas, he was welcome to go along. What a ride! In Olathe, the Angel was lucky enough to catch a space available flight to Scott Field, Illinois. He then hitched a ride into St. Louis and from there a bus to Sullivan, Missouri.

When the Angel arrived in Sullivan it was very early in the morning and traces of dawn was just starting to break for the day. Here one must remember that less than 72 hours had elapsed since the Angel was in the line in Korea trying to stop a break through by the forces from the north. About this time an old logging truck without a muffler started his engine and the sound was identical to tank engine start-up. Without thinking, just using one's inborn sense of survival, the Angel hit the ditch along the side of the road. When he realized where he was and what he had done, the Angel very sheepishly crawled out of the ditch and continued his walk hoping that no one had seen him.

Evidently the Angel's cousin who lived next door to his family knew that he was coming home before he knew it. She had been watching for the Angel to come walking down the road for some time. She wanted to contact the Angel before his wife had the opportunity. The Angel was still unaware of the type of emergency that had brought him out of Korea. His cousin was about to enlighten him on the reason for his emergency and it was a shock, like getting hit in the face.

His cousin informed him that he was brought home because his wife was running around on him. The Angel did not want to believe this, but he knew his cousin would not concoct a story that was not true. The Angel also found out that a couple of his cousin's had worked his wife's lover over very badly, then stripped off the clothes of the Romeo and ran him down Main Street as naked as a jaybird. When the Angel heard this he simply went next door, picked up his children and brought them next door to his cousins. The Angel's cousin then told him that he should go to Union, Missouri, and see the judge, that he knew about the situation. This he did that very day.

The judge was a very congenial type of person who had a number of questions regarding Korea. It seems that the Angel was one of the first returnees from Korea, and the first for this particular area. He also gave the Angel some very good advise. He said that I could stay with the woman, which he did not recommend. He also suggested divorce. When the Angel asked about custody of his children, he said that the Angel should not worry as he would be the judge who heard the case. He gave the Angel a list of lawyers that would take my case. The Angel selected one and the case started moving. The Angel now knows that he should have gone to the bank first, because while he was talking to the judge, the Angel's wife depleted the bank account and only left two dollars and some change in the account. Within a week the Angel was divorced and with permanent custody of his children. She had the money, but he had the children and that was the most important thing. The judge now told the Angel to have some fun, that he deserved it, just returning from Korea and all my problems.

For the next couple of weeks, the Angel stayed with the Old German and his wife Mrs. John. He spent as much time as possible with his children and the time did fly by. One weekend he drove to Springfield, Missouri, and checked Slim out of the hospital for the weekend. The Angel could tell that Slim was not in good shape. However, he still had the Irish spark and sparkle for life. On the way home he had the Angel stop at a haberdashery store in Rolla, Missouri, and he bought a complete new outfit. Suit, shirt, underwear, socks, belt, hat, a whole wardrobe for a gentleman of that time. Then as we were driving into Stanton, Missouri, Slim had the Angel put the top down on the car. As he said, "I want these son-of-a-bitches to know that I'm still alive." During the weekend a couple of locals who thought they could make a name for themselves by challenging Slim to fight. Slim stated that he would like to change clothing before the fight so he went to his sister's to put on some old clothes and to get a pistol. He then returned to town and asked the two who wanted to make a name for themselves to come out in the gravel. Slim called them out, but they had crap in their necks; they would not answer the call. When the Angel asked him later what he would have done if they would have answered the call, Slim said that he would have fought them fair and square until he felt his strength going, then he simply would have shot them. Slim had a logical mind. Yes, that is exactly what would have happened.

At the end of that week the Angel returned and signed in Slim at the Veterans Administration Hospital in Springfield. The Angel could tell that Slim was in bad shape. The Angel figured that Slim would be lucky if he made it another month. The Angel noticed that Slim had been put into the ward referred to as the

137

"Dead Man's Ward." Once assigned to that ward, it was a ward of no return. Slim said that he could beat the odds, but deep down he knew he could not. It was a hard thing to do, to shake hands and say goodbye to Slim. Slim knew that it was back to Korea for the Angel. Slim's advice to the Angel was to keep moving and to keep your head down.

As soon as the Angel returned to St. Louis, he purchased his ticket back to Camp Stoneman, California. By Saturday of the week the Angel reported in, he had completed in processing and had a line number for boarding his return to Korea ship. The next day, a Sunday, was to become the nadir of the Angel's life. He received word from the Red Cross at the VA hospital that Slim probably would only last about 72 hours and that the Angel should be granted a 30-day emergency leave.

All of the money the Angel had was $1.25. The Red Cross at Camp Stoneman would not open on a Sunday to grant a loan for the emergency. What to do? What to do? The Staff Duty Officer granted the leave and the Angel took off hitchhiking. The events of the next 72 hours made the Angel believe that a guardian angel can be assigned to look over an individual.

The Angel no more than hit the road when he caught a ride to Reno, Nevada. That Sunday evening the Angel figured he may as well be broke as having only $1.25, so he tried the blackjack table. The $1.25 ran up to $200—pure luck! The Angel knew when to get out of the game, so with $200 he hit the road again. Now, he was just trying to stay ahead of the bus schedule. Coming out of Reno, he was given a ride with an old man in an old and beat up pick-up truck. Somewhere between Winnemucca and Battle Mountain, he drove off into the desert and left the Angel stranded in the middle of a desert and at night. With cars going by at 80 or 90 miles per hour, it would be difficult to get one to stop. Finally, at about three or four o'clock in the morning one stopped. It took him about one-half mile to get shut down. However, he backed up to meet me. This ride took me into Salt Lake City, Utah. After break-fast, a good shower and shave and a press of my uniform, it was back on the road again. While hitchhiking, a car stopped and the man said that he was a car dealer. He also said that some older man who had been on vacation had become ill and had returned to Liberty, Missouri, by charter aircraft. He was looking for some-one to drive their car through for them. The Angel said that he was the man for the job. It was a new 1951 Ford sedan. He gave me money for gas, food and for taking on the job. The Angel put the car across Colorado and Kansas in short order. By the time he arrived in Liberty, Missouri, the car was well broken in. The Angel, who had left California with $1.25, arrived in Missouri with over $500 in his pocket. This was very good money for that time. My guardian angel had seen me through. In Liberty, Missouri, the Angel caught a bus to Springfield, Missouri, arriving in time to see Slim who was still alive.

The Angel was given a guest room in the hospital. He was with Slim until about 10:00 p.m. Then, at Slim's request, he went to his room for some much needed rest. At 10:00 a.m. the next day he was back with Slim. The Angel and Slim visited all day until 5:00 p.m. Slim then said that the Angel needed a shave and to take some time now to freshen up. While the Angel was shaving, he was notified by a nurse that Slim was no longer of this world.

The Angel felt that he was in the bottom of a very deep hole and that there was no way out. Over the past two months he had really taken a beating. He had divorced his wife, had his money taken from him and now had lost his father whom he respected very much. Thank goodness his father had been able to see his grandsons once before he gave up the ghost in this life. However, even at this nadir in the Angel's life, he felt as if he was standing at the South Pole and that any movement he made would be up.

The Angel made the funeral arrangements for Slim. He had him buried in the family cemetery at Cherry Valley, Missouri, at the right side of his father, the Angel's grandfather.

The funeral put the Angel even further in debt. However, thanks to an esteemed aunt who went his note, he was able to borrow enough to get him through this tough time. It seemed that almost as soon as Slim was put away positive things started to happen.

The two never-do-wells who had been running with his ex-wife were both killed in separate automobile accidents. The world was better off without them.

The Angel also had a chance meeting with the judge who had presided at his divorce. When the judge found out that the US Army was going to send the Angel back to Korea, he was beside himself. He asked for a copy of my orders and observed that I was to return to Camp Stoneman, California, for shipment back to Korea. He became even more angry, asked for a copy of my orders and again took the Angel out to dinner. The Angel does not know what happened, but in a few days he received a change of orders. He now was to report to Fort Leonard Wood, Missouri, at the end of his leave. He also noted that the type of assignment he had was called a compassionate reassignment so that I could spend time with my two sons and continue to pull my duty. The Angel was assigned as acting First Sergeant of the 5017 ASU at Fort Leonard Wood.

Wedding Day 1955
"Oh happy day."

The Angel, his beautiful
bride, Flo, and his little
brother

Left to right–
The Angel's father-in-law,
mother-in-law, beautiful bride
and the Angel, 1955

The Angel in Stanton, MO
1955

The Angel's son Pat
whom he loves very much
1957

The Angel's son Mike
whom he loves very much
1957

The Angel, his wife and
two sons at the Alamo
1959

The Angel, file photo, 1963

The Angel and others being decorated by Secretary of the Army Vance. Left to right– General Freeman, Secretary Vance, Colonel Clement, and receiving the decorations is the Angel.

Downs Barracks, Fulda, Germany 1963

*14th Armored Cavalry Regiment,
The Angel was 1st Sgt. of the 58th Engineers.*

The Angel being congratulated on receiving an award by Col. Bohrdley, commanding officer of the 14th Armored Cavalry Regiment. 1965

The Angel receiving an award from Col. Schulton, United States Army "V" Corp. through Col. McCoy, 14th Armored Cavalry. 1964

The commander of the Savanna Army Depot giving the
oath of enlistment to his son as the Angel observes.
1966

Michael Eugene Richardson,
son of the Angel, Cadet,
U.S.M.A. West Point, NY,
Class of 1971

Patrick Oliver Richardson,
son of the Angel, Cadet,
U.S.M.A. West Point, NY,
Class of 1973

The Angel loves his wife,
his children, and his
grandchildren
1969

Flo and the Angel's bride,
Mary Lou (Amundson)
Richardson
1965

Flo as she appears today
83 years of age

The Angel.
Masters of Science Degree
(1970 Bachelor)
1974 Masters Degree from the
University of Wisconsin-Stevens Point

1973

THE POST KOREA YEARS

The assignment to Fort Leonard Wood was a plum of an assignment. However, with good things starting to happen, there had to be some stumbling blocks along the way. I was informed that the cousin I had placed my sons with was now having family problems of her own. Her problem, with the fact that the Angel's term of service was nearing an end, prompted the Angel to make a decision to take a discharge to see if he could get things ironed out. If he could do it within 90 days, he could return to the US Army with no loss of rank.

The Angel took the discharge and immediately went to work for Koss Construction Company out of Des Moines, Iowa. The money was good, but the hours were long and hard. It was 12 to 14 hours a day, then home to the Old German and Mrs. John's home to wash diapers. The Angel started to feel trapped. However, positive things were now happening. Another cousin came through when he and his wife approached the Angel and said that a man could not be expected to do what the Angel had been doing. An amount of money for child care was agreed upon and they took over the care of the Angel's boys. The cousin had a boy and a girl about the same age as the Angel's boys. They got along fine.

With his sons in outstanding hands, the Angel could now start thinking army again. However, when the Angel got in touch with a recruiter, he was informed that he had been out slightly over 90 days and would have to suffer the loss of a grade, that would be from Staff Sergeant back to Sergeant. The Angel said that he would try the other services. These regulations were all the same so the Angel tried the US Army Reserve just as he had done before. He enlisted in the reserve for two years with immediate call to active duty and in the grade of Staff Sergeant. Therefore, no reduction in grade—things were looking up.

The Angel reported to Fort Sheridan, Illinois, for in-processing and then was assigned to the 484th Engineer Battalion at Camp Atterbury, Indiana, as a Platoon Sergeant. This was a great assignment and the Angel settled in for what he hoped was a "Homesteader Tour." The people in the area were very friendly and it was only about 250 miles from his children so he could see them often. The area was also short-track racing country. The Angel became very interested in the sport and with those who participated in it. On one occasion, the owner of one of the cars had a driver who could not make it to race night for some reason or other so he asked the Angel if he would drive under the name in an upcoming race. It was to be on a quarter-mile dirt track. The Angel said he would be honored to drive for him. The race came and went; the Angel did not win, but he also was not the last car in the race. It was fun and when the Angel was asked to race again, he said sure. He was also asked if he had a friend who would like to race. The Angel stated that he could find a friend who would drive.

On the night of the race it had been raining and the track was very muddy. The Angel and his friend were asked if they wanted to watch the race. They both said no, that they would drive. The race was off and going well with the Angel even though it was slippery as hell. After a few laps the Angel noticed a car going end-for-end on the track; it was his friend. After the race the Angel found out that his friend was in a local hospital and that perhaps he would not make it. He did pull through after several days in the hospital and then came the crunch. Because he had not gotten permission of the Commanding Officer to race while off duty, his injuries were not considered in the "Line of Duty." Therefore, he was determined to be "Line of Duty No." He would have to pay for his medical treatment and have all the days he had lost from duty for his injuries added to his enlistment. It was a bad situation to say the least. That was the end of his racing and the Angel's also. However, the Angel has always been glad that he tried it for now it was out of his system.

While at Camp Atterbury, the Angel received a speeding ticket from the Post Military Police. Normally, this would not have been a big thing but the Angel received his ticket for speeding with a motor grader. The Angel had been cutting ditch with the grader and improving a tank trail. At the end of the work day he left the work sites to return to the Battalion Motor Pool. On the way in there was a long and rather steep hill. The Angel took the hill without cutting back on the throttle. The hill had a 25-mile per hour speed limit. The Angel was clocked out at 45 miles per hour by the MPs. It was the joke around the battalion for the next week or so. The Commanding Officer just told the Angel to try to cut back on the speed some for if it happened again he would have to take action. The Angel was not dumb—from then on he paid attention to speed limit signs.

Camp Atterbury was the homepost for the 31st Infantry Division (The Dixie Darlings). This division had been federalized due to the Korean War and now that the war was slowing down, the 31st was deactivated and returned to Alabama, for the division was the Alabama National Guard unit. When this happened there was not a need for the 484th Engineer Battalion to remain at Camp Atterbury. Therefore, the 484th was ordered to Fort Knox, Kentucky. The Angel did not mind this change of station as he was still close enough to visit his sons often and the area was great.

It was at Fort Knox that the single NCOs got together and came up with a plan that they called the "Pig Pool." Each week three of the married NCO's would be selected as judges for the pool. During the week the single NCO's would try to get a date with the ugliest woman they could find. They would also give the judges ten dollars each for the pot. The single NCOs had to bring their date to the NCO Club on Saturday night and treat her like a queen all evening long. The judges would decide on the winner and the winner would collect the pot on Monday. You could not bring the same woman back for judging more than one time. It worked extremely well. In fact, an NCO from one of the tank units once asked the Angel, "Where in the hell do you engineers get those women you bring to the club on Saturday night?" He was not told about the "Pig Pool."

One occasion that the Angel remembers extremely well started to take place in Louisville, Kentucky, on a Wednesday night. The Angel and a friend were visiting some potential spots looking for a winner for the "Pig Pool" on the coming Saturday night at the NCO Club. The Angel figured it was his lucky night, for into the honky-tonk came the ugliest girl he had ever seen. He immediately told his friend he was sure she was a winner and for him to stay away from that one for she belonged to him. Using as much charm as he could muster, he came on to the girl. They spent the evening dancing, talking, and in general, laying the gab on heavy. Finally, he asked her for a date on the following Saturday night to go to the NCO Club dance. She accepted and the Angel knew he had easy money coming. Yes, it would be impossible for anyone to have an uglier date for the pool.

The following Saturday afternoon the Angel borrowed a friend's car to pick up his date. She lived in the country between Louisville and Fort Knox. The car was a 1949 Studebaker, you know, with one of those wraparound windows in the back of the car. It was the soldier's pride and joy and he admonished the Angel to be careful with it.

The Angel, following the directions the girl had given him, located the farm and drove up the driveway to pick her up. All of a sudden the girl ran from the house slamming the screen door open. She ran across the yard, jumped the fence and hurriedly got into the car. All in one breath she shouted, "Get out of here quickly, Daddy's got a gun!" Don't you know that car would not go into reverse. So, the Angel drove forward down through an orchard and then back by the house. The father was now out with his shot gun. As we went by him, he blasted in on us with the gun. The shot knocked out the rear glass and chipped the paint and metal around the car where the rear window had been. The Angel must admit it shook him up some. In a couple of miles he had to stop for a stop sign so the Angel figured he would try the reverse gear to see why it would not work before. This time it slipped right into gear as easy as could be.

Needless to say, the Angel won the "Pig Pool" that night. However, it took all the "Pig Pool" money and then some to fix the car that the soldier had loaned the Angel. At the end of the NCO Club dance the Angel took the jeune fille (young girl) as close to her home as he dared, kissed the girl good night and never saw her again. The Angel hopes she remembers the occasion fondly. For even though she was ugly, she was a queen for the night.

The NCOs of the Engineer Battalion had another gimmick that they would pull on a young lady who was too haughty to dance with them. Often, there would be a table of young women present at the NCO Club on Saturday night. The NCOs of the Engineer Battalion would ask them for a dance. If the girl said no then another NCO from the Engineer's would ask. If the answer was still no, then they were fair game. For in the crowd and during the night, at least three engineers would stumble and accidently spill their drink down the cleavage between the young ladies' breasts. They were fast learners and after a couple of Saturday nights, the engineers were seldom turned down. It was crude, but it worked.

Fort Knox was a great assignment, but all good things sooner or later come to an end. Even though the 484th Engineer Battalion was under strength, it was still being levied for personnel to go to Europe. The Angel came down on one of these levies.

Was he happy? Yes! He had always, in the back of his head, wanted a tour in Europe.

Something else was very peculiar at that time and that was the missile field. The Angel and one other NCO were the only two in the Battalion that met the criteria for missile training. He and the Angel were ordered to Post Headquarters to be interviewed by an officer from Fort Bliss, Texas. The end result of the interview was that the Angel had a choice. He could either take the levy to Europe or missile training at Fort Bliss. Here, the Angel made a bad choice, he selected to go to Europe. Why was it a bad choice? Because, if he had selected missiles, he would surely have been appointed as a warrant officer on completion of the missile course. However, the Angel shed no tears, for who really knows what road to take when a road forks. The Angel chose to follow the road of travel and adventure.

With the choice the Angel made, he was off to Europe, more specifically, Germany. The trip was uneventful and the Angel's orders read to report to Camp Kilmar, New Jersey, for shipment to Germany on the USNS Darby, a military transport. Crossing the Atlantic Ocean took several days and with that we had a one-night layover in Plymouth, England. The officers and the NCOs were allowed to go ashore until midnight of that day, then it was back to the ship and off for Bremerhaven, Germany. Upon debarking from the ship we were quartered in Bremerhaven until our assignments came through. Within 24 hours the Angel's orders came through for him to report to Panzer Cacern in Kaiserslautern, Germany. The Angel was shipped to Kaiserslautern to await further orders. Three or four days after arrival at Kaiserslautern the orders came through for the Angel to report to the 293rd Engineer Battalion located in Baumholder, Germany. Upon his assignment the Angel found out why it had taken so long for the assignment to come through. In Europe there was a day that was referred to as integration day. On this day the 293rd Engineer Battalion had been a Negro unit. On this day 85 percent of the Negro personnel of the 293rd were assigned to other units and the shortage in the battalion was made up by shipping white soldiers into the 293rd and other units. The 293rd after this day would be 85 percent white and 15 percent Negro. The mix came about in one day and with very few problems. The US Army in Europe was now integrated. The planners of this move knew what they were doing.

The Angel had one rather funny thing take place shortly after his assignment to the 293rd. He had his platoon working on a tank trail when he felt the urge to go to the toilet. Not having one in the area, he had to go to the woods and dig a cat hole. The Angel was relieving himself when he was charged by a wild hog. Without taking time to tidy up or to get his pants up, he ran for the trail where his platoon was working. Well, the hog stopped the charge but not before the Angel's troops saw what was going on. The troops did tease him for awhile, noticing his bravery before the charging hog. The teasing was good-natured and it made good comic relief time for the troops. They now knew that their Platoon Sergeant was only human.

Germany, of course, was a land of very good looking girls and the Angel really appreciated the fact.

The Angel, now being a divorced man, could play the field and this he did. The Angel had three young ladies that he was proud of. One was from the Wiesbaden, Mainz area, one from Brussels, Belgium and one from Braunschweig, Germany. They were all outstanding young ladies and the Angel sincerely hopes they are well and happy today.

The little town of Baumholder that was just outside the gates of the military post was a typical town that you can find outside the gate of any military post. It was over-patrolled by the military police. Fights could break out at any time and usually did. The curfew for the soldiers was midnight and any breach of the curfew would bring about a delinquency report; this was usually followed by company punishment. On one occasion the MPs picked up the Angel and a friend before curfew and held them until after curfew to write them up. This definitely was not right, but it did happen. When the DR came down, the Angel and his friend were called before the Company Commander who stated that he was going to give them a company punishment. The Angel explained the situation to the CO but he would not come around. The Angel then stated that he would take a court martial instead of company punishment. This was the right of the Angel to do so. When he made this request the CO backed off for he knew he could not make his case with the court martial. The case was dropped with a letter of apology placed in the Angel's 201 Personnel file. For the Angel, there was still multune in parvo (much in little).

The Angel was in the barracks one Saturday afternoon when a couple of his buddies came by and asked him to go with them to the Golden Angel, a bar in Baumholder for a few beers. The buddies who came by were the S2 NCO (Intelligence NCO) and the S3 NCO (Operations and Training NCO). After a few beers they indicated that they were going to submit their applications for Officer Candidate School and that they would like to have the Angel submit with them. Right at the time, the Angel was not overly excited about becoming an officer. Among the career NCOs there was a saying that "being an officer would not be bad if you did not have to be a Second Lieutenant before you could be an officer." Of course, this was a joke among the senior NCOs. When the S2 NCO said that he would type the application if we would give him a copy of our 398 Form (Personal History Statement), the Angel and the S2 NCO said, "Okay, go for it." The S2 Sergeant did a good job and within a week our application for OCS was in the mill.

The first hurdle to cross was going before the selection board. For some reason still unknown, the S3 Sergeant did not pass the board. Well, that was one down, two to go. The next step was to take the physical examination required. Here, the Angel ran into trouble because somewhere along the line he had picked up a hernia. This did not disqualify the Angel, but he would have to have the hernia repaired before he could attend OCS. He checked into the hospital at Baumholder ASAP (as soon as possible) for the operation. It was two weeks in the hospital and four weeks of convalescence leave. The S2 Sergeant pulled his application temporarily so he and the Angel would go together at the end of the Angel's convalescence.

During the first week of the convalescence leave the Angel was approached by some German business men that he knew who asked him if he would like to make some good money while he was on leave. The Angel's reply was that they were talking his language; as long as he did not have to kill anyone, he was ready to listen. The first thing that they asked was did he have a friend who could get leave right away and he did. The next thing mentioned was he willing to take some risk. He and his buddy were. Then, they laid out the plan.

The Angel and his friend would be sent to Tangiers (a free port), from there we would be put in charge of two converted PT boats with an Arab crew. The PT boats would be painted a flat black to make them harder to see of a night. We would make two runs during our leave time, from Tangiers to Corsica (Corse) and from Tangiers to Sardinia (Sardegna). We would deliver our load, be sure of the money and return to Tangiers. Then, back to Germany to finish any leave we still had not used. Sounded easy. Our load would consist of nylons, cigarettes and tomato catsup. We would follow the coastline of North Africa until we came to Philippeville. Here, we would refuel and make the run true-north to our destination where we would receive our challenge and would give the counter sign.

The first trip was a piece of cake. The smaller boats took on our cargo, we received the money, the pot was right and we were out of there in short order. The second trip we ran into a little trouble, but a few rounds in the general direction of the Italian Police caused them to rethink the situation and they backed off. Now, it was back to Tangiers, pick up our money and return to Germany. All was well that ended well and our little escapade ended extremely well. In fact, so well that when the Angel reported in from leave to duty, he found that he had been promoted to Sergeant First Class.

From the nadir of divorce and Slim's death, the Angel was now riding a high. Not only had the Angel been promoted, but he had been selected for temporary duty with the Resident Engineer for the Baumholder area.

The Resident Engineer had requested and had personally scrutinized the records of all the noncommissioned officers in the 293rd Engineer Construction Battalion. From this he had selected two noncommissioned officers to work as engineer inspectors for all new construction within Western Area Command. The inspectors would work with the German contractors to make sure that they built within the plans and specifications of the contract. The Resident Engineer had selected a Master Sergeant, who was also a Reserve Officer, and the Angel.

The Angel was responsible for contracts that exceeded 50 million dollars. With this, duty, honesty and integrity were the key words to live by. The inspector that the Angel replaced was now in the Disciplinary Barracks in Fort Leavenworth for accepting kickbacks from the German contractors. The Angel would not fall into this trap. Once the German contractors found out that the Angel could be a hard-ass and could not be bought, they would not argue but would build to the specifications. They also came to respect the Angel and his method of operation.

The duty was absolutely great and the prestige of the duty

was beyond comparison. The inspectors had outstanding quarters and each morning a staff car with a driver was assigned to each of the inspectors. Our driver would take us to the Resident Engineer's office for the morning briefing, then out to the construction sites for the day. At the end of the day, we would turn in a written report. The staff car and driver were always available to us. The duty was great and the Angel began to wish he had not applied for Officer Candidate School but he had, so when the orders came through for OCS, the Angel packed his duffel bag and got ready for the move back to the states.

However, before he departed, the officers, enlisted men and the German contractors threw the Angel a very big farewell party. At these parties one is usually engulfed with an abundance of praise. This party was no different. When the Resident Engineer said that the Angel was possessed of bel-esprit, the Angel did not know what in the hell that was. Later on upon looking it up and by asking, the Angel was informed that it meant he had a brilliant mind. Before leaving, the Angel was presented with a letter of commendation for the work he had accomplished for the Resident Engineer.

The Angel and the S2 Sergeant from the 293rd Engineer Construction Battalion were now off to Fort Benning, Georgia, and OCS.

When the Angel had applied for OCS he had given three branch choices to be commissioned in. His first choice had been Corps of Engineers; second choice, military police; and third choice, infantry. When his selection came down he had been selected for infantry. This, being the Angel's third choice, did not make him overly happy.

When the Angel saw that he had been selected for infantry OCS, his first reaction was to turn the appointment down. After all, he was now a senior NCO with probably the best duty assignment in Europe. Besides, he really did not care that much about being an officer. However, the S2 Sergeant talked the Angel into hanging in there and accepting the appointment. Also, the Angel was anxious to see his sons and the appointment to OCS would give him time to do just that via the delay-in-route that he would get on his way to Fort Benning, Georgia. So, it was back to Bremerhaven for surface transportation back to the states, again aboard the USNS Darby. Once in the states, he used his delay-in-route time to be with his sons as much as possible. Then to Fort

Benning and reporting into the OCS area at Harmony Church, which is a part of Fort Benning.

The pettiness of OCS was noticed immediately as two young officers who were being held over from the preceding OCS class met us at the orderly room door. These gentlemen had been in the army about eight or nine months as compared to the Angel's nine years. They put us at a brace which was accepted. The next situation was uncalled for. They physically ripped the insignia of our rank from our arms. Then, they physically ripped the medals and campaign ribbons we had been awarded from our chest. This included the Combat Infantry Badge, Bronze Star with V device, Army Commendation Medal, etc. This was hard to take from someone who had been in the army less time than the Angel had stood in the chow line. Yes, it was hard to take, but the Angel decided to play their little game.

In the OCS company we had four tack officers, the two from above who had just finished the cycle before us. We also had two tack officers who had seen combat in Korea. These two knew what they were doing. The other two did not have a clue as to what the army is about. The one thing that really pissed the Angel off was the way they treated a highly decorated Master Sergeant who was taking the course just as the Angel and the S2 Sergeant were. The Master Sergeant had been rather badly wounded in Korea and one arm, that had been part of the wounds he had received, was not completely healed and did not have the strength of the other arm. These young tack officers would cause the Master Sergeant to do push-ups until the MSG could do no more, then they would verbally berate the MSG and probe the wound scar, which was not entirely healed, with their swagger sticks. This was completely uncalled for.

Along about the 12th week, the S2 Sergeant came to the Angel and said, "Piss on this crap, Angel, I'm quitting this moxnix outfit." I must say the Angel did not blame the S2 Sergeant from the 293rd Engineer Battalion. It was too bad for he would have made an outstanding officer.

About the 18th week, the Angel was ordered to report to the personnel section, where he was informed that they noticed that his term of service would expire before his graduation date, and that in order to graduate he would have to reenlist. The Angel startled the Personnel Sergeant when he said, "No, he would take the discharge." By the end of that day, the Angel was transferred to the 1st Officer Candidate Regiment for discharge processing. The Angel figured that because he was in the upper 10 percent of his class, they did not want the other officer candidates to know that he had accepted a discharge over being a Second Lieutenant. However, deep down the Angel knew he was a much better NCO than he would have been an officer. After all, usually officers request what is to be done, and the NCO gets the job done. Everyone knows that the NCO is the backbone of the Army.

The Angel knew that he was not out of the military forever. His plan was to return to Stanton, Missouri, and spend some time with his sons before reenlisting as a senior NCO in the Corps of Engineers. This was his plan of action and this was exactly what the Angel did. The Angel knew that by reenlisting he would be able to pick his Post, Camp or Station providing a vacancy existed in his MOS (Military Occupation Specialty).

After a couple of weeks with his sons, the Angel decided it was time to return to the US Army. Therefore, he went to St. Louis for processing back into the military service. His first request was for duty assignment to the Granite City Engineer Depot just across the river from St. Louis. The first request was denied due to no vacancy in the Angel's MOS. His second request was for Fort Leonard Wood, Missouri. Here they had all kinds of vacancies. Yes, they had vacancies in almost every engineer MOS. The vacancy that the Angel accepted was as First Sergeant of a line Engineer Company in the 361st Engineer Construction Battalion. With the vacancy accepted, the Angel's processing back into the army was completed.

Once the Angel arrived at Fort Leonard Wood he found out that the last AGI (Adjutant General Inspection) his company had received was an unsatisfactory rating from the inspection. Therefore, he knew that he would look good if he could bring the unit rating from unsatisfactory to an outstanding on the reinspection. It would be a tough job, but the Angel had confidence in himself. The Angel threw himself into the job at hand. At first his tactics were resented by many in the unit, but after awhile, the attitude of the troops did an about face and you could see pride in the eyes of the troops. This was both individual and unit pride. In fact, the troops started to refer to the Angel as Mister RA (Mr. Regular Army) and you could tell they were saying it with pride. Needless to say, when the AGI reinspection took place the unit was rated as outstanding. The Angel had truly found his niche as First Sergeant.

Shortly after the unit had received its outstanding rating for the AGI, the Angel was summoned to report to the 20th Engineer Brigade Commander. The Brigade Commander put the Angel at ease and started a give and take conversation. After warm up verbiage the Brigade Commander said, "Angel, I have had my eye on you for awhile; you are doing a bang-up job in bringing your company around. I know that you only have newly commissioned Second Lieutenants in your company. I know it was you that brought the company around to the envy of every First Sergeant and Company Commander on the post. Therefore, I would like to recommend you for Officer Candidate School." The Angel had to laugh. The Brigade Commander asked in a rather gruff, command voice, what the hell the Angel was laughing about. When the Angel told him that just a few months before he had been in OCS and what had happened, they both had a good laugh. When he dismissed the Angel he just stated that he should keep up the outstanding work.

After being in the 361st Engineer Battalion for about a year, the battalion was redesignated the 62nd Engineer Construction Battalion. It was just a paper change, same unit just a different number.

No matter how hard one pursues unit excellence there is always Murphy's Law to contend with. One of the things that would jump up to bite the Angel was his selection of an I&E person for the company. I&E (information and education) was an area we got into each Saturday morning immediately after inspection and just before giving the troops off until Monday at reveille. It was usually a lecture and discussion regarding current events. It would keep the troops aware of what was going on.

As the First Sergeant for the company the Angel screened the records of his troopers to see who might be the best person to appoint to the job. He located a young soldier who had a Bachelor of Arts Degree with a concentration in Political Science and History. The soldier also had a Master of Arts Degree in Literature. The Angel figured he had the perfect man for the position. He called the soldier into the orderly room and asked him if he would be interested in being the I&E soldier for the unit. The soldier said "Sure." The first Saturday he had the theater ready for his representation, training aid and all. The Angel was sure he had selected the right man. However, it was not to be. The soldier became so wrapped up in his presentation that he walked off the stage and took a bad fall. When he climbed back on the stage he had lost his audience.

During the question and answer session, the troops really came down hard on him. One soldier asked the question, "If Russia attacked Turkey in the rear would Greece help?" Again, the audience broke up. To save the young trooper more embarrassment the Angel took over the chair.

The Angel still wanted to use the soldier in a way that would use his intelligence to some degree. Therefore, he made the trooper the company mail clerk. In taking the mail to the post office he fell down the steps from the mail room to the first floor. Again, he was black and blue all over. Again, what to do with the young man? In talking it over with the Company Commander, the CO said to put him on the mine warfare committee to teach mine warfare. The Angel advised against it, but the CO said to give him a try. The Angel did and the young trooper in placing a booby trap stepped on his own booby trap. The booby trap was using an M-8 simulator (like a firecracker). The M-8 had enough explosive power to cause his foot to swell from the concussion. What to do with the fellow now? The Angel made him the CO's driver, and you have probably guessed it. He turned the damned jeep over. The job the Angel finally had to go to keep the trooper from hurting himself was to make him the latrine and barracks orderly. He did this job very well.

On another occasion, and a different situation, the Company Clerk thought that by playing up to the CO he could bypass the Angel. The Clerk finally figured that the company could not operate without him. When the Angel laid out some work for him to do he ran to the CO stating that he did not have time to do the work. The CO being a Second John and about the same age as the clerk, was emphatic toward the clerk. When the Angel explained the situation to the CO he finally said for the Angel to take care of the situation. At the start of the discussion, the Angel had hooked the screen door on the orderly room so the discussion would not be interrupted. When the CO said for the Angel to take care of the situation he did. He walked back into the 1st Sergeant's room in the orderly room, took the clerk by the nape of the neck and the seat of his pants and headed for the door with him; forgetting that the screen door was hooked, he threw the clerk through it and told him to report to the First Platoon Sergeant for duty. He was no longer the Company Clerk. It was not difficult to find a man to replace him.

In the military unit, training is essential and goes on constantly. Since the military does not operate on an eight-hour day nor on a daylight only schedule, it is essential to have night training problems on a regular basis. The troops were not too happy when night problems were ordered. The Angel put his mind to work to try to figure out a way to boost the morale of the troops regarding night problems. What he finally came up with was as follows:

First, he would take a collection from the troops to buy a barrel of beer and some picnic items, ie: hot dogs, etc. The mess sergeant would make the purchase while the night problem was conducted.

Second, he would have lights strung in the company street.

Third, when the troops returned to the company area with the night problem complete, it would now be time to start the company party.

Fourth, he would allow the troops to sleep in until noon on the following day.

This created a situation that was so well received that the troops actually looked forward to night problems.

The Angel and his tactics became so well known on both the training and the TO&E units on the post that he was selected to be First Sergeant of the Exhibition Detachment to the Missouri State Fair in 1953. It was an honor to be selected for this detail.

Yes, the Angel was content with his tour of duty at Fort Leonard Wood for it allowed him to soldier and to be with his sons on the weekends. It could not have been better.

In April of 1954, the Angel found out that his company had been alerted to proceed to Camp McCoy, Wisconsin, to form teaching committees to teach engineer subjects to the Reserve and National Guard units that would receive their training at Camp McCoy. With his sons in mind, the Angel tried to remain at Fort Leonard Wood. However, this was not to be, as he was ordered to Camp McCoy as essential personnel for the mission. A good soldier follows orders and the Angel was an outstanding soldier. What the Angel had tried to avoid, "Assignment to Camp McCoy, Wisconsin," turned out to be the best move the Angel had ever made. As it happened this was where the Angel met the lady he would spend the rest of his life with.

In May of 1954 the convoy of engineer units going to Camp

McCoy departed Fort Leonard Wood for a two-day convoy to Wisconsin. This included a night layover in Quincy, Illinois, at the Armory. The trip was uneventful except to say that the girls from Quincy treated the engineer soldiers very well. In some cases perhaps too well. The units closed on McCoy within their ETA (estimated time of arrival) and the advance party had our billets ready on our arrival.

The first few days were spent in beautifying our area and in last-minute training of the teaching committees, becoming familiar with the Post, etc. By the time the units arrived to be trained we were set up and ready for them.

With things moving so smoothly the Angel found time to visit the teaching areas. At the floating bridge site the Angel had a situation happen that was rather amusing to him. The Division Commander was on the site. He happened to be a man very small in stature. A group of officers and NCOs were standing in a group observing the work. The Angel was right behind the General. For some reason the General kept moving back. He bumped into the Angel. Of course, the Angel gave ground. Again the General moved back and bumped into the Angel. The third time it happened the Angel thought, why should I move, so he stood fast. The General bumped into him again and again, but the Angel would not move. Finally, the General turned around and his eye contact was about where the Angel's belly button was located. He very slowly looked up until he made eye contact with the Angel. At this point he was looking up and Angel was looking down. He seemed to be a bit confused. Then he excused himself and departed the training site.

The first weekend after our arrival one of the Platoon Sergeants and the Angel were out looking the area over and getting acquainted with some of the locals. They stopped at a place called "The Chicken Hut," in Necedah, Wisconsin. When they asked the locals where there was to go that would be jumping that night, one of the locals invited the Angel and the Sergeant to a wedding dance at the "Skyway" in Wisconsin Rapids. The Angel thanked him for the invitation and said that they would be there. This invitation would change the life of the Angel for at this dance he met the girl that he would marry. Of course, he did not know this would happen, but life takes mysterious turns. The Angel dated the young lady throughout the summer. However, toward the end of the season and before his unit returned to Fort Leonard

Wood the Angel and this girl would have a falling out, a parting of the ways. This split came about because the Angel was just a little too aggressive and the farmer's daughter did not want to move that fast. After the split the Angel found her constantly on his mind. However, he figured that feeling was like a bad cold and would go away in time.

The Angel now spent a good portion of his off duty time at a hang out for the engineers called the "Ace of Clubs" at Wyeville, Wisconsin. It was just a honky-tonk where everyone felt at ease. On the first of the month, the NCOs would get together and purchase two, three or four barrels of beer and they would throw a beer bust for the entire area. Free beer really brought out the natives in the area. The NCOs were really surprised at the result because they found by throwing the beer bust on the first of the month their money was no good for the remainder of the month, for everyone in the area would buy them drinks when they entered the club. The Angel was now happy that his request to stay at Fort Leonard Wood for the summer had been rejected. He felt at home in the area. The Angel figured memento mori (remember that you must die) so have fun now.

Along in the fall of the year, orders came through for the Battalion to take its ATT (Army Training Test) at Camp McCoy and then return to Fort Leonard Wood for regular engineer duty. Most of the troops were rather sad to leave Wisconsin. However, orders are orders and so they were carried out. The return to Fort Leonard Wood was uneventful.

Shortly after returning to Fort Leonard Wood, the Angel was asked by the S3 Sergeant if he would like to attend the Engineer Supervisor School at Fort Belvoir, Virginia. The Angel said "Sure," as long as promotions were slow he may as well go. Several of the NCOs had turned the school down because of its high academic standards. The Angel looked on it as a challenge.

The school in Fort Belvoir turned out to be a well run, academically tough course. The school covered about 20 engineer subjects. Fort Belvoir was also a spot where the off duty time was outstanding.

To fill in the off duty time, the Angel became acquainted with a couple of girls from the WAC (Women's Army Corp) detachment. One of the girls was from Watkins Glen, New York, and the other was from Normal, Illinois. They were outstanding young ladies and very accommodating to be with. However, with all good intentions caused the Angel to be called before the WAC Detachment Commander. You see, the girls had agreed to do the Angel's laundry and ironing, and on an inspection of the WAC quarters, the WAC CO had found my fatigues in the girls' lockers. When she asked the young ladies about my fatigues being in their lockers, they told her that they were doing them for the Angel. This made the WAC CO extremely unhappy. Therefore, she called the Angel on the carpet for using her girls as the Angel's laundry maids. Needless to say, the Angel had to find other ways to keep his fatigues washed, starched and ironed. It was a small thing, but the Angel took quite a razzing around the NCO Club about the WAC CO calling him on the carpet. It was really a big joke among his fellow classmates.

The girl from New York reminded the Angel of the young lady he had dated in Wisconsin. In fact, they looked so much alike they could have been taken for sisters. The young lady from Wisconsin was on the mind of the Angel on a daily basis, but he had not had contact with her for four or five months; therefore, he was trying to push her out of his mind. Then on Christmas of 1954 he received a Christmas card from her. All of her good points came to mind and from then on a letter writing contact came to the fore.

Finally the Engineer Supervisor School came to an end. The Angel graduated second in a class of 40, and received his orders back to Fort Leonard Wood, Missouri. It was back to being First Sergeant of "C" Company, 62nd Engineer Battalion. Yes, it was back to seeing his sons every weekend. He had missed them very much while he was at Fort Belvoir, Virginia. They were fine, intelligent boys who made the Angel very proud to be their father.

On one weekend Flo and the Angel's stepfather came out to Stanton to spend a weekend with the Old German and Mrs. John. The Angel liked and enjoyed being with his stepdad. During the day, the Angel asked his stepdad if he would like to go to the local honky-tonk for a beer. The stepdad said, "Sure," so they were off. The place was known to be a rather tough place but that was no worry on the part of either of them. After a few beers the Angel had to go to the latrine. When he exited the latrine he saw a commotion taking place by the bar. He noticed that five supposedly tough individuals were pushing his stepdad around for no apparent reason. The Angel took three down with three blows and the other two ran for the door like rabbits. The Angel's stepdad enjoyed telling about the situation until his dying day. He was a good man, not strong, just good.

The Angel was now 25 years of age. His mind was turning more and more to the joys of married life. Sure he had been running around and he had no shortage of girlfriends. He got along extremely well with the fairer sex. However, he had been burned once in marriage and he did not want that to happen again. This time he would be extremely careful of what he could be getting into. Therefore, he made himself a matrix listing all of the good qualities one would expect of a wife. Then he listed the 10 girls he had dated that he liked and enjoyed being with. The young lady from Wisconsin was by far in the lead. The Angel now took a 10-day leave to return to Wisconsin and to win the hand of the young lady. The Angel was well received and the more he was with her the more he loved her. One day the Angel and the young lady were walking by the lake, the Angel had his rifle with him just in case a target of opportunity should crop up. Well it did, and sitting there by the lake the Angel proposed marriage to the young, good-looking lady. She said she would have to think it over for awhile; she did, for about 10 minutes, then she said "Yes." This made the Angel very happy indeed. They set the date for December; therefore, the Angel had many things to accomplish and did not have much time to accomplish them. He wanted to get off to a good start.

The Angel knew that if he remained around Fort Leonard Wood, where many girls knew him, it could create a trouble situation, so he had a to find a way to get out of the area. This was not too difficult as he was a qualified paratrooper. He was also the holder of the Combat Infantry Badge, and he had participated in more than two combat campaigns, and he was 25. Therefore, he was more than qualified to volunteer for the 77th Special Forces Group (airborne). They were the Green Beret soldiers. This would get him and his wife to be to Fort Bragg, North Carolina. It was a change of area and had better dependent housing than Fort Leonard Wood. The Angel passed through the screening process with flying colors. However, the unit was so secret at the time that the career counselor at Fort Leonard Wood could not find the location of the green beret unit, so he had orders cut sending the Angel to Fort Benning, Georgia. At Fort Benning, it took about a month to find out that the Special Forces

Unit was at Fort Bragg. It was a real snafu (situation normal all fouled up). In the meantime, the Angel had contacted the young lady from Wisconsin and they had moved their wedding date up to the month of October.

The United States Army is very good about granting leave to marry, so the Angel had no problems there. When the time came, he was off to Wisconsin by way of St. Louis to pick up Flo and head north. They arrived at the home of the parents of the girl from Wisconsin a couple of days prior to the wedding ceremony. It was a beautiful ceremony. The Angel now knew that he would be devoted to one woman for the remainder of his life. He was now 26 and ready to settle down with his wife and sons.

Yes, the Angel had married a wonderful and beautiful young lady and she would be coming into a ready-made family. She would be taking over the raising of two boys ages four and six. The boys took to her immediately with absolutely no problems. She was their mother and that was that.

The Angel had to report in at Fort Benning, Georgia, for some specialized training, and his new wife could not follow him there because of the nature of the training. However, with training completed, he was granted a delay-in-route to go to Stanton, Missouri, to get his wife and sons and to proceed to Fort Bragg to the 77th Special Forces Group (airborne) immediately after Christmas and New Year of 1955.

Here the Angel found out that good housing was as hard to come by as it would have been at Fort Leonard Wood. The house he had to move his family into was really a shack. You could lie in bed and count the stars through the cracks in the ceiling. The place was heated by soft coal and most of the heat went up the stove pipe. The Angel felt badly about moving his family into such a place, but it was all that was available at the time. The girl the Angel had married moved into the shack with tears in her eyes but with the fortitude to make it do until something better was available. She was a real trooper. The Angel came home one day after duty and found his wife and sons standing outside in the cold and crying. The chimney had plugged up and the coal smoke was all through the house. It was really a downer. Fortunately, they only had to live in the place for one month. The next place they moved to was more livable, but still not the greatest.

The Angel's duty consisted of training in Special Forces operations type of training. He was also the instructor in homemade demolitions, and he was good at it. In demolitions one must consistently stress safety. Yes, there are bold demo men, and there are old demo men; but there are no bold, old demo men!

The Angel remembers one incident that happened that he was not too proud of. With the stand full of students and VIPs (very important persons) the Angel put together his bomb. He thought he was taking the time to do it right, using just the right blend of theatrics to spice up the presentation. He melted the waxes and packing compound and put it neatly around the center portion of the bomb, inserted the cap and fuse. He had those in the stand shout "FIRE IN THE HOLE" three times and he lit the fuse. The fuse burned down and the cap exploded, but the bomb did not explode. How humiliating for the Angel! Thank goodness the next one put together worked like a charm.

Along about March of 1956, the Angel was on his teaching site when the S3 Sergeant came out to the site. He said that he had two allocations for slots at the Army Language School in Monterey, California. The Angel had a choice; he could take Polish or Chinese-Cantonese. He selected Chinese-Cantonese. After all, he had been to the Far East four times. He and his wife and sons departed for California on Easter Day 1956.

The trip would be an education for his wife and sons. The trip was uneventful, but fun and it was extremely interesting for the boys. However, when we were going through the Painted Desert and the Petrified Forest we left Route 66 and took an old and unused road into an area of greater interest. This turned out fine and was a great learning experience for the boys. On the way back to Route 66, the Angel decided to take a short-cut across the desert. Then, all of sudden, he hit a prairie dog hole and the front wheel of the car dropped into the hole bringing us to an abrupt stop. When this happened everything in the car flew forward including the boys. The older boy hit his chin on the dashboard of the car right where the name of the car was located. His chin hit the letter "R" and cut it into his chin. For years after the incident he had the letter "R" practically branded on his chin. Since his last name started with the letter "R" this was a novel thing for him. The Angel finally managed to free the car and get back to Route 66.

On arrival in the Monterey, Pacific Grove, Carmel area the Angel was astounded at the rent they were asking. His solution to the problem was to buy a mobile home. The one he bought was located on 17 Mile Drive. He was now settled in and ready to report for duty.

Chinese-Cantonese, as taught by the Army Language School, was an extremely difficult language to learn, but the Angel, never one to avoid a challenge, hit the books head on and burned the midnight oil studying. The course was one-year in duration without let up in the work needed to keep up. About six months into the course the class took a field trip to China Town in San Francisco. The trip was supposed to build confidence in our ability to use the language. What did happen was that when a Caucasian walked into a place of business and started speaking in Chinese-Cantonese, the place would become extremely quiet and the locals would not talk. The Angel learned later that they would not talk because they were afraid that the Caucasian may be an agent from the Department of Immigration and many of the Chinese were in the United State illegally. They looked on the Caucasian as a latet anguis in herba (a snake that lies hidden in the grass).

The time flew by and before long the year had passed. It was a beautiful place to live and even though the course was tough the Angel did well. He graduated as the top Caucasian in his class. It was now time to return to Fort Bragg, North Carolina, and to his Green Beret unit. This trip would be an adventure because this time he would be pulling a mobile home. In April of 1957 they departed Pacific Grove and headed east with a wife, two sons, a car and a mobile home. Just another adventure and learning experience.

On the first day out they made it to Tehachapi, California. Here they rented a space in a mobile home park. The space was narrow and would be very hard to get into. The Angel, ever confident, backed the mobile home in, but he went too far and backed the mobile home through a fence. This was just a start to the problems. It was cold and windy and the electric plug-in for the site had shorted out so we were without heat. Thank goodness, it was only for one night. The next morning we were off bright and early. The odyssey on the return to Fort Bragg was now on again. The second day we found a place to hook up the mobile home behind a service station. The third night had a little more suspense attached to it for we located on the Arizona-New Mexico state line in an Indian reservation. Of course, we had a number of Native Americans who gathered around to observe the Angel and his family. The Angel was at ease and enjoyed the banter, but his wife was more apprehensive and insisted that she would sleep with a butcher knife under her pillow. She was going to protect the boys at all risks to her. Of course, nothing happened and it was just another night on the road.

The next day with everything going so well we were pulled over by the law just after crossing over the Oklahoma State Line. To this day, the Angel does not know why, for he just looked us over and waved us to proceed. While crossing Oklahoma we sighted two tornadoes at the same time, one on each side of the road. The Angel pulled over to the side of the road and got his family into a place that would give them some protection. After they passed it was on the road again, until we were a short distance from Springfield, Missouri; now we hit a snow storm. It was an April storm, wet and slick. However, we did get to Springfield and spent the night there with frozen water pipes. The Angel's bride was now getting a taste of what it is like to be a career soldier's wife.

The next day, with the snow melted, it was on to Stanton, Missouri and a reunion with Mrs. John and a visit to the grave of Slim and the Old German.

We left the mobile home in Stanton and the Angel and his family drove to Wisconsin so his wife could visit her folks. Then back to Stanton and on to Fort Bragg.

Everything went well until we were going up a mountain to Ashville, North Carolina. Here it was a two-lane curvy road and a road gang was working on the road. Wouldn't you know, they stopped the Angel right in the middle of the road. The Angel had to back the car and the mobile home into a "V" configuration to get started up the mountain again. It was a touch and go situation, but they made it into Ashville.

The trip from Ashville into Fayetteville and Fort Bragg was uneventful and the Angel and his family reported back to the 77th Special Forces Group (airborne).

The Angel was not too happy with the change that had taken place during his one year assignment to the Army Language School. One of the things that made the Angel unhappy was the way that details were allocated to the units. They were allocated on a number basis and not a rank basis. Therefore, the 77th Special Forces being heavy in NCOs had to furnish so many soldiers regardless of rank, to details such as ash and trash, etc.

Therefore, instead of training, a good portion of usable time was spent on trivial details. This went against the grain of the outstanding NCOs of Special Forces. After a few months of this, the Angel went looking for a new home. He found it as NCOIC of the 182nd Military Intelligence Detachment to the 82nd Airborne Division. When this change took place the Angel became the Order of Battle NCO for the 82nd Airborne Division. Now if he could look forward to a promotion he would be in tall cotton. This did not work out as the Order of Battle slot on the TO&E for the 82nd MID was the rank that the Angel now had. So it was enjoy the assignment, but continue to look for a promotable slot. Here the Angel was again going to outsmart himself.

Missiles were the big push in the Army in 1959. So on his ETS the Angel reenlisted for the Nike Ajax and Hercules course at the Air Defense School at Fort Bliss, Texas. After graduation from the course in the top ten percent of the students, the Angel was assigned as an instructor in the Air Defense School. This was enjoyable duty until the school started to increase the duty of instructors to include driving the students to the firing range in a bus, teaching all day, then driving them back to Fort Bliss in the p.m. Another senior NCO and the Angel decided that they would teach or they would drive the bus, but not both. When we were ordered to the Motor Pool to be qualified and licensed to operate a bus we made an agreement to back the bus through a chain link fence that surrounded the motor pool. The Angel was called first to drive and he did just that, backed the bus through the fence. The Angel's friend was up next and he did the same thing. The Motor Officer knew that he had been had, so they decided that we two instructors would be given drivers for the transport of our students. The young motor pool officer had not learned or had forgotten that if you mess with a career senior NCO that you will come out on the wrong end of a dirty stick. It was a learning experience for him.

After working and having an assigned duty as missile instructor, some things happen that can bring stress to the instructors. One day the Angel was assigned to have a VIP (very important person) shoot from his pad. In the countdown everything was green light on the section cabinet until the countdown got to missile ready to go light. The light was red. The Angel took all the necessary steps to see that the light would change, it did not. Now the OIC is at him through the two-way radio from the IFC to the missile launch area. The Angel checked all the electrical hookups, they were correct. He tapped all the relays; they seemed to be OK. The OIC is still shouting at him. Finally, in anger the Angel stepped back and slammed the sections cabinet door as hard as he could saying "To hell with the son-of-a-gun." When he did this the missile ready to go green light came on and the Angel shouted "Fire, Fire;" they did and the missile got a kill on the target. The Angel received a letter of commendation for the successful VIP shoot.

One difficult situation for the Angel was teaching conversion packets. That is teaching the Chinese or the Turks the proper way to fire the Ajax and the Hercules Missile properly. You learn very early that the first thing you do when you get them on the range is to collect all of their screw drivers, for if you do not, they will take the missile apart while your back is turned. By taking all the screw drivers away and only giving one to one student at a time, you could control the instruction. One reason the Angel was given the Chinese packet to teach was due to the fact that the Angel was a graduate of the Army Language School. However, the person who assigned the Angel to the Chinese packet did not take into consideration the fact that the Angel was trained and could speak Chinese-Cantonese and the Chinese soldiers he was teaching spoke Chinese-Mandarin. They are like two different languages. Just the usual SNAFU for personnel and assignments.

The Angel continued to desperately try to get an assignment to the St. Louis Defense packet, but to no avail. Then one day he found out why he could not get assigned to the St. Louis Packet. He was being held for another assignment.

A friend of the Angel's came out to the missile firing range one day, all in a huff and he was looking for the Angel. This friend was holding a position in the assignment section of Fort Bliss, Texas. He was in a huff because he had advance knowledge that the Angel was being held for assignment to Thule, Greenland. The Angel sure did not want this assignment. The friend told the Angel that he could hold on to the levy for two days, and if the Angel had any outstanding IOUs that he could use to get off the assignment, now was the time to use them. The Angel knew a Sergeant Major (E-9) and a Colonel stationed at Fort Sam Houston, Texas, that were assigned to the Fourth Army Recruiting District. The Angel was granted a pass to see them personally. He loaded his wife and children in the car and headed for Fort Sam Houston, Texas, before the day ended.

When he arrived, he went immediately to the Colonel's office and asked to see the Colonel. His request was granted and he went right in. After the door was closed it was like old time week in the office. After about a half an hour of reminiscing about past assignments, the Colonel asked the Angel what could he do for him. The Angel stated that he was coming down on orders for Thule, Greenland and he sure did not relish this assignment. The Colonel asked the Angel if he thought he could be a successful recruiter, and if he could swing the assignment for him could the Angel be as loyal to him as he had been on past assignments. The Angel thought for just a fraction of a minute before he answered the Colonel. When he answered the Colonel's question he answered in the following manner. He said, "Colonel, if I can work for you again, I would be as loyal to you as I have been in the past. In fact, Colonel, so loyal that if you tell me a piss ant can pull a freight train, I will put him in harness and give it a try." The Colonel smiled and the Angel knew that he would not be going to Greenland. The Colonel smiled and said for the Angel to return to Fort Bliss and his orders would be awaiting him for assignment to the Recruiting Station in Tulsa, Oklahoma. The Colonel also let the Angel know that he expected him to be a 100 percent-plus recruiter, and that if he did not maintain a 100 percent of quota over a three-month period, he would personally call the Angel and tell him to report to Fort Sill, Oklahoma, for further assignment. The Angel was happy; the location was great and the duty would be tough, but the Angel, who was always in the top 10 percent of any endeavor he undertook, was not worried about a tough assignment. After all, he would be with his family. The trade-off for this assignment was long, hard hours for the privilege of being with his family. The Angel took to recruiting like a hog to slop.

When the Angel reported to the Recruiting Main Station (RMS) in Oklahoma City he was issued the tools of this trade, a staff car, a briefcase, credit cards and a pat on the back and was told by the RMS Commander to report to Tulsa, Oklahoma. When the Angel reported to the NCOIC (NonCommissioned Officer in Charge) he was somewhat shunned. The station had about six recruiters present for duty and a heavy quota to fulfill. The fact that the Angel had served in the Military Intelligence Detachment of the 82nd Airborne Division caused the recruiters to believe that the Angel might be a ringer assigned to look for recruiting discrepancies. Of course, this was not the case.

After a few days, the other recruiters became used to the Angel and accepted him as a regular. One thing that helped was one of the recruiters had gone through missile school with the Angel. The two of them became very close friends. The Angel remembers one of the older recruiters telling him not to unpack his duffel bag because the Angel would not be there long enough to unpack. Well! The Angel had the opportunity in the near future to say goodbye to the individual.

Recruiting turned out to be a wonderful job for the Angel. There was never a dull moment. One situation that is memorable to the Angel was as follows:

The Angel took a part-time job through Burns Detective Agency for the weekends. He would work as Charge of Quarters for the DX Sunray building from midnight Friday night until noon on Saturday and from noon Sunday until midnight on Sunday, 24 hours each weekend. This particular Sunday night the Angel placed his pistol in the glove compartment of his staff car. The next morning the Angel had an early appointment to take an applicant to the RMS in Oklahoma City for processing into the US Army. From the particular section of Sapulpa, Oklahoma, the Angel had been coming up with a number of rejected applicants; however, he was sure he had one that would pass the AFQT (Armed Forces Qualifying Test) this time. The applicant was a post grad student in math from Langston University. Surely, he would make it mentally. On the Turner Turnpike from Tulsa to Oklahoma City, the Angel was trying to motivate the applicant on testing procedures. You know, on the test eliminate the obvious and select one of the two answers remaining. If he had no idea on the two remaining to go for the center one. The Angel could see that the applicant was paying no attention to him, he was just sitting there gazing out over the prairie. This caused the Angel to become angry. The Angel pulled over to the side of the road, reached over and took his pistol from the glove compartment, placed it to the temple of the applicant and said, "If you don't pass the AFQT test today, I am going to blow your damn head off on the way back to Tulsa." The applicant would now pay attention to the Angel. Yes, the Angel had his undivided attention. The Angel waited on the applicant to be tested. When the applicant came out of the testing room he had a very large smile; he had passed the

AFQT by one point. Yes, he was going to be a soldier and, perhaps best of all, he would not be riding with the Angel on the trip back to Tulsa.

Another time, a potential applicant from Locust Grove, Oklahoma, gave the Angel a call and indicated that he was ready to go to Okie City for testing and enlistment. The Angel immediately got into his staff car and headed for Locust Grove to pre-test the applicant. He pre-tested well so the Angel filled out the papers for him to go to the RMS. It is best to operate while the applicant is hot to enlist. Therefore, the Angel was going to take him back to Tulsa and put him on a bus to Okie City that very day. On the way back to Tulsa the Angel went through Pryor, Oklahoma, to check out the Sheriff's office to ascertain that the applicant did not have a police record. He was clean. Therefore, the Angel started for Tulsa. On the way out of Pryor the Angel had to stop for a stop sign. When he stopped the applicant leaped out of the car and ran. The Angel was disgusted and returned to Tulsa empty handed. About two days later, the same boy from Locust Grove called to apologize for his demeanor and stated that he was now ready to go. The Angel said, "Good reasoning," and he would see him in about an hour. Before the Angel left the recruiting station he took all of the clips from the door handles of the staff car. He then drove to Locust Grove to pick up the applicant. The applicant was waiting and got right into the car. On the way back to Tulsa, through Pryor, the Angel stopped for the same stop sign. The applicant again tried to open the door but the handle came off in his hand. The light turned green and the Angel was on the way back to Tulsa with the applicant. He passed all of his tests, physical and mental, and turned out to be a very good soldier. Yes, the recruiter had to always be one step ahead.

One extremely hot and sultry day, one of those days when the temperature is well into the three digit numbers and the heat index is off of the scale, the Angel was driving from Nowata, Oklahoma, back to Tulsa. He noticed a young man on a tractor plowing a field. The dust was boiling up and the sun was beating down. The young man was wearing a pair of pants, cut off above the knee and cowboy boots, nothing else. When he noticed the car with the US Army printed on it he began to wave frantically for the Angel to stop. The Angel did stop and the boy, without shutting the tractor off, came running across the plowed field to where the Angel had parked the car. The first thing he asked when he reached the car was if I was a recruiter from Tulsa. The Angel said yes and what could he do for the young man. "Take me to the army," he said. The Angel asked when did he want to be tested and go. He said, "Right now." The Angel asked him if he wanted to turn off the tractor motor before he started for Tulsa. He said, "Hell no!" His dad would find it running or it would run out of gas. The Angel asked if he wanted to go home for a change of clothes. He said, "Hell no. It was now or Never!"

The Angel took him at his word and it was go now. The Angel took the boy back to Tulsa, processed him and shipped him that very day. He shipped him just the way he was, wearing shorts and cowboy boots and nothing else, except a film of dust that covered his body from head to toe. When the boy came back to see the Angel after basic training he said that the army was a snap compared to the way his father worked him. The Angel kept track of the boy and found he had made an outstanding career soldier.

On another occasion, the Angel had an appointment to see a young man from the vicinity of Locust Grove. When he arrived at the young man's house, the boy's mother said that his dad had made him go to another farm they had to fill a silo. Again, it was a nasty, hot day in Oklahoma. The Angel asked for directions to the other farm and was told that it was in the vicinity of Jay, Oklahoma. The Angel drove on to Jay and located the farm. The boy and four other young men were filling silo. When the Angel drove up to the silo all five boys ceased what they were doing, loaded into the staff car and stated that they, each and every one, were ready to enlist and again, it was now or never. That was the last of the silo filling for those boys, for it was back to Tulsa to process them for shipment to the RMS in Okie City. There was never a dull moment in recruiting. If you played it like a game, you would have fun and always make quota.

One day the Angel dropped by the draft board office in Pryor, Oklahoma, Mayes County, just to bat the breeze with the draft board clerk. She stated that a young man was looking for me and that he was waiting for the Angel in the local pool hall. The Angel walked over to the pool hall and asked about the man that wanted to see him. One of the young men at the first pool table said he was the one. After his game and his collection from the other players, he was ready to talk to the Angel. After he and the Angel had come to an agreement, he said that he would take the EST

(Enlisted Screening Test). While he was taking the test, one of the other individuals in the pool hall was constantly bad-mouthing the military. The boy finished the test and had a very high score. However, the bad-mouthing continued from one of the others in the pool hall. The Angel finally became a little angry at the man and told him to shut up or put up. The Angel indicated that the only reason the man was bad-mouthing the military was because he was too damn dumb to pass the test himself. Yes, the challenge was there. The ego of the bad-mouther would not let him back down and taunts of the others in the pool hall really got to him. He agreed to take the test. The Angel tested him with the EST#3 and graded the test with the answer sheet from EST#4. Of course, with this slight of hand, he failed the test miserably. The Angel then told him in front of the others that he was indeed too dumb for the US Army and should shut his mouth since he could not enlist even if he begged to. Yes, he lost face, the Angel gained face and the young man who took the test first was processed into the US Army.

The Angel found out that a recruiter could not pass up a potential enlistee into the army if he wanted to be a successful recruiter. Case in point. Bright and early one morning the Angel arrived to open up the recruiting station for the day. There he found a dirty looking individual sleeping in the doorway. The Angel shook him awake and asked him what the hell he was doing there. The fellow, who looked like an uneducated bum, said he was there to join the army. The Angel thought, join the army, sure! The guy was probably a mental group five; you know, one of those whose comprehension would be about ten seconds long. However, the Angel, being a person who would give anyone a chance to pass or fail, asked the boy into the station and told him to go to the latrine and clean up some. After he had failed the Angel's inspection of cleanliness about three times, he finally became somewhat acceptable. At least he did not smell too badly. The Angel then gave him some money for breakfast and told him to come back if he still felt the same about going into the army after he had eaten. The Angel figured that was the last he would see of him. This was not to be the case. After he had breakfast, he was right back at the recruiting station. The Angel figured he would give him a chance and that he would probably fail and EST anyway. So, he administered the EST to the boy. He passed with a very high score. The Angel figured that anyone who looked as bad as he had would surely have a police record, but when he checked he found out that this was not the case. Now the Angel was interested, as he processed the boy and sent him to Oklahoma City, thinking that he just might not show there. This was not the case. He reported into the RMS just as he had been told to do. He passed the physical and on the AFQT test he was in mental group one. He enlisted for six years. One year after our chance meeting in the doorway of the recruiting station, he dropped in to see the Angel. He had gone to OCS and was now a Second Lieutenant assigned to the 82nd Airborne Division. He stated that since he owed me a breakfast, he would now pay it back with interest by taking the Angel to dinner in one of the better restaurants in Tulsa. It was a good feeling for the Angel just to know that he played a small part in this fine officer's success.

All SNAFUs (situation normal—all fouled up) were not humorous. The Angel remembers one situation that was really pathetic. The Angel had processed and shipped a young, intelligent and pretty Creek (native American) young lady for enlistment into the WAC (Women's Army Corps). She was shipped to Fort McClellan, Alabama. In going through Birmingham, Alabama, she had to change buses. During the layover between buses she had to go to the bathroom. This is where the foul-up happened. The bathroom at that time was segregated. She had used the "white only" bathroom and had been detained by the police for doing that. She had tried to explain that she was a Creek Indian. This being her first trip out of Oklahoma or even Creek County, she was scared out of her wits. However, she did remember the Angel and placed a collect call to him to explain the situation. The Angel talked to the policeman that had apprehended the girl, but he was a hard head and would not listen to the situation. The Angel then placed a call to the Federal Attorney for the Birmingham area. He got it all straightened out and called the Angel to let him know that the situation had been taken care of. It is a shame, but for some the playing field is not level.

You never know where training you have had in the past will come to the fore. While in the 77th Special Forces (Airborne), the Angel had received cross training as an "A" team medic. He had graduated first in his class, but never had the opportunity to use the training until he came on recruiting duty.

He had an appointment to interview a young man for enlistment in Bristow, Oklahoma. When the Angel arrived at the place of the interview the subject was not there. The Angel asked some who were at the designated place where the young man was. They did not know, but told the Angel where his mother lived. When the Angel drove up to the mother's house he found a catastrophe. The mother (a very large woman) had fallen through the porch and had torn her thumb very badly. The Angel asked if he could take her to the hospital or to a doctor. She said that she did not have the money for that. After the Angel got her out of the hole in the porch (which was not a small job), he said he would suture the thumb back to the hand if she would allow him. She said, "Thank God for you Angel," and the Angel found a needle and bent it some. He then found some regular sewing thread and proceeded to sew it back to the hand. After suturing it to the rest of the hand, he told the lady that he would return in five to seven days to remove the stitches. The Angel followed through and returned to take out the sutures. It was a very good job. She had her son there waiting for the Angel so he could be processed for the army. For the remainder of the time the Angel was in Oklahoma, every time one of her boys or girls would come of age for the military, she would call the Angel and have him process them for the army.

One of the problems encountered by recruiters was what we called the itinerant prospects. The young men who used this dodge were usually headed for California and had no or at least very little money. They would enter the first town in a state. Then, they would call the recruiter for the area and indicate they were ready to enlist. The recruiter would process them and put them on a bus to the RMS with meals and hotel tickets. They would use the meal and hotel tickets, but never show up for processing into the US Army. Instead they would hitchhike to the next state and repeat the procedure. Yes, they were very good at what they did. They had all the right answers.

The Angel found the law enforcement officers in Oklahoma to be very accommodating and easy to work with. For instance, on the occasion of the Angel's promotion, he threw a party for recruiters in Tulsa. The Angel was now the Station Commander at Miami, Oklahoma, but he maintained close contact with the staff in Tulsa, as he had worked with them for two years. Here, the Angel will have to admit that he drank a little more than he should have. On the return to Miami he used the Will Rogers

Turnpike. As soon as he cleared the pay gate on the turnpike, the red, flashing light appeared in the rearview mirror. The Angel was sure this would be a DWI charge. He pulled over to the side of the road. The officer approached the car and stated that he thought it was the Angel and that he had been waiting for him for some time. He knew that the Angel had been promoted and he was waiting to see that the Angel made it safely back to Miami. Therefore, I was to follow him to the Miami turn off. He made sure I made it safely home. In the Angel's estimation he was and, perhaps, is yet an outstanding officer.

On another occasion and by a different officer, another thing happened to raise my esteem for Oklahoma law officers. The Angel was running his usual itinerary. It seems that when one is on an itinerary he is never on time. This time I was speeding more than I should have been when the Angel noticed the flashing lights. He pulled over, waiting and cursing himself all the while. When the law officer approached the car he said that he could tell by the car that the Angel was an army recruiter and he had some questions to ask for his son who was military service age. What had initially looked like a bad situation turned into an enlistment. Yes, Oklahoma law officers, take a bow! You are the greatest!

In all situation there has to be a beginning and end. The Angel's beginning on recruiting duty had been with the interview by the Colonel at Fort Sam Houston, Texas, and ended when the Cold War with the Soviet Union heated up in 1961-1962. In 1962, all personnel records were checked to see how long it had been since the soldier's last completed foreign tour. The Angel had been overseas to Korea in 1950-1951, but it had not been a completed tour. He had been in Germany 1952-1953, but this also had not been a completed tour. Therefore, they took the Angel's return date from WWII and added the two incomplete tours which brought my return date to 1947. Therefore, the Angel was ripe and ready to be picked and picked he was. He received orders to 7th Army Headquarters in Viahegen, Germany. The Angel was ready to go as it was a good post and promotable slot. However, all good things do not stay that way. During processing and en route someone out-politicized the Angel and his assignment was changed to the 14th Armored Cavalry at Fulda, Germany. This was listed as the longest wait in Germany for dependent housing and the Angel already had all the rank this career counselor slot called for in their Table of

Organization and equipment. The Angel was a little downhearted. It was the length of separation from his family that bothered him the most.

The waiting period for housing turned out to be not as long as originally predicted and the duty was the best in Europe. The 14th had a border mission and, therefore, did not fall into the old training cycle that most of the other units in Europe had to endure. Also, the 14th was an extremely proud unit and this blended with the Angel's personality all the way. At first, the Angel was a little put out as this was the first non-airborne combat assignment that he had been relocated for. This too became a very small part of any dissatisfaction that the Angel may have felt. In fact, the Angel was happy to have been assigned to a proud and up-front unit and the 14th Armored Cavalry Regiment was that. Yes, they were proud and it showed in the military bearing of the individual soldier assigned to the 14th. The Angel was the Career Counselor for this proud unit and, because of this pride in the unit, the 14th consistently lead the way in reenlistments in the V (Fifth) Corps. The 14th was a ticket-punching assignment for its commander. Just about every commander's next assignment, after being commander of the 14th, was an assignment that called for a promotion into the flag grade position of a Brigadier General.

The 14th Armored Cavalry Regiment worked hard, trained hard and played hard.

The Angel, as Career Counselor (by regulation), could not be placed in a position that caused him to take disciplinary action toward one that he may later counsel for reenlistment. The same regulation outlined the manner in which his office was furnished. It was to be furnished with the best office furniture available in the unit. This regulation would, on occasion, cause problems with some of the field grade officers who had problems with an NCO having better office space and furniture than they had.

On one occasion, the S4 (Supply) officer of the regiment ordered the Angel to change offices with him. The Angel politely brought the regulation to the Major's attention. He ordered the change to take place immediately. The Angel alerted the V Corps reenlistment officer (a Colonel) of the situation. This Colonel called the Commander of the 14th and this Commander called in the S4 officer. It was a gentle rear end chewing for the Major and a reclaiming of his office by the Angel. The Angel made it a point to wish the Major a good morning every day. However, the Major did not speak to the Angel for the remainder of his assignment with the 14th Cavalry. When the word got out to the other NCO's in the unit, they claimed that the Angel was an NCO with bel-esprit (a brilliant mind). However, the Angel would say that he was just following regulations.

One outstanding soldier in the 58th Armored Engineer Company was about to be processed and returned to the United States for discharge. He was a fine soldier who was devoted to duty and had a good sense of humor. It would have been a shame for the US Army to lose such a man. Therefore, the Angel worked on him very much and very hard, but it seemed that he was not making inroads into the soldier's mind. Then, something hap-pened and the soldier came to the Angel's office and stated that the 58th was having a company party in about a week, and if the Angel would wrestle and defeat a full grown hog at the company party, he would re-up for another hitch. What the devil, why not? So, the Angel answered the soldier in the affirmative and the bout was on. One thing the Angel should have asked was how big the ring was going to be. He figured it would be a 16x16-foot ring or even a 20x20-foot ring. When the Angel showed up at the party to wrestle the hog, he found a ring of 50x50-feet. This meant that he would have to catch the greased hog in this large area and then pin him for 30 seconds before he could be declared the winner. When he saw the hog, it was about 250 pounds and literally cov-ered with lard. When this, the main event of the party, was on, the Angel climbed into the ring with the hog and tried to catch the son-of-a-gun. When he would catch the hog it would slip out of his grip. This went on for about one-half hour. The hog and the Angel were both panting profusely. Finally, the Angel got hold of two of the hog's legs on the same side and up-ended the hog. Then, it was down on the up-ended hog and hold the hog in place. Both the hog and the Angel were worn out, but the Angel had his reenlistment of a fine soldier.

The next day the hog died and a collection was made to pay the German who had rented us the hog. The Angel felt badly about the hog for he knew the hog was a fighter with a will to win. Yes, the Angel had something in common with the hog. Neither would give up, both had a will to win.

A couple of months later, the entire 14th Cavalry celebrated its activation date with a regimental day of fun and games. In general, it turned out to be a drunken brawl. The Angel, along with the others, was feeling no pain and in general, was having a good time. Along in the evening hours after partying all day, the Angel was talking to the S2 (Intelligence) NCO. He and his wife were about to return to their quarters and the Angel was trying to convince them to stay until the end of the party. About this time, one of the clerks from Headquarters and Headquarters Company kept butting into the conversation. The Angel informed him at least three times that he was not welcome in the conversation at this time, that it was between the S2 Sergeant and the Angel. The next time he broke into the conversation the Angel up-ended him with a right upper cut to the jaw area. The clerk was down and out and the S2 Sergeant's wife ran helter-skelter through the party area shouting that the Angel had just killed the S2 clerk. The Angel and the S2 Sergeant finished their conversation and continued to party. The clerk finally came to and was no worse for the wear. It was just another party to release built-up tension and it worked.

After two years as the Career Counselor for the 14th Armored Cavalry Regiment, the Angel was in his office one day when in walked the Sergeant Major for the unit. He said that the Regimental Commander was having a command problem with the 58th Engineer Company and was going to relieve the Commanding Officer of the 58th, along with the First Sergeant. The unit was presently in the field at Hanau, Germany for its annual bridge training in conjunction with the annual CMMI (Command Maintenance Inspection) and the AGI (Adjutant General Inspection). The unit had received an unsatisfactory in all three areas.

The Colonel said he needed a tough First Sergeant to whip the 58th into shape. He said he had gone over my 201 (personnel) file and noted that on at least three prior occasions the Angel had been a First Sergeant. He said if the Angel could whip the outfit into shape, he would give the Angel a free hand. The assignment would have to be voluntary on the Angel's part, as his MOS (Military Occupation Number) was 075 Recruiter, Career Counselor. The Colonel also used the argument that the Angel was one of the very few NCO's in the 14th that had been a First Sergeant in an engineer unit.

The Angel did not have to think twice before he said yes. This was his lucky day for he considered the position of First Sergeant the most difficult and yet the greatest challenge in the US Army. Now, the Angel would have a chance to see if he could bring a unit that had been given an unsatisfactory to a unit that would attain an outstanding on CMMI and AGI on a reinspection that would happen within the next 90 days. It would be an inspection with no warning.

The Colonel had also said that the 58th would be without a commanding officer until the slot could be filled and that the Angel, while being the First Sergeant, would also be the acting commander. Because the Angel was an enlisted man, he could not sign the morning report, but the Regimental Adjutant could do that.

When the Angel said that it would indeed be an honor to work with the 58th, the Colonel said that his helicopter was waiting for the Angel on the parade field to take the Angel to Hanau and to bring the Captain and the outgoing First Sergeant back. The Colonel said that all the Angel had to do right now was grab his ready bag and get aboard. So, in minutes it was off to Hanau and a definite challenge. The Angel was apprehensive, but charged up, the adrenaline was running.

Within minutes the Angel was at Hanau, where he reported to the outgoing commander and informed him and his First Sergeant to report to the commanding officer of the 14th Cavalry ASAP. In fact, they were to be on the helicopter and were to report directly to the CO. The Angel never saw them again. However, he did hear about them. The 58th CO was given another chance by being transferred to another unit in Germany. After all, being a young and inexperienced officer, he had allowed his First Sergeant to lead him down the primrose path to failure. He deserved a second chance. The First Sergeant went before a board for inefficiency, but beat the board and was also transferred to another unit in Germany.

The Angel, on taking over, immediately called a meeting for his platoon sergeants, the supply sergeant and the mess sergeant. It was an open meeting with no holds barred. The Angel found out that the senior NCOs of the unit had received no backing from their former CO or First Sergeant. The outgoing First Sergeant was constantly out with the privates, pfcs and spec. fours. It was so noticeable that some in the unit felt that he may have been a little funny. He exercised no control. The Angel also found out that he had good NCOs, they just had to have backing. The young soldiers soon found out that when their sergeant told them to do something they could not run to the First Sergeant to have it overridden or countered.

On the Angel's first night with the company, one soldier, fortified with snaps, tried to cut the lines on the Angel's tent. In doing so he cut his wrist. One of the platoon sergeants brought him to the First Sergeant; the Angel had him hospitalized at the 97th General Hospital in Frankfurt, Germany. When he returned to duty the Angel gave him the maximum in company punishment over the signature of the Adjutant. The troops now realized that "Sergeant Good Guy," the career counselor, could do a 180-degree turn as the First Sergeant and commander of the 58th.

One of the spec. fours that had been buddy-buddy with the former First Sergeant refused a lawful order from his Platoon Sergeant and the Sergeant brought the culprit to the Angel. When the Angel listened to both sides, he knew the senior Sergeant had a problem with this wise guy. As the spec four stood there and started to berate the Sergeant with profanity, the Angel simply took him by the neck and squeezed the air off until his legs started to buckle; he then let him have some air. When the Angel dismissed the spec four he ran down the row of tents shouting that the Angel tried to kill him. However, he never refused or challenged a request from his Platoon Sergeant again. He now knew his Platoon Sergeant would receive backing and he turned out to be a very fine soldier.

The Angel's soldiers in general were now walking with a bounce in their step and pride in their eyes. Yes, they were coming around rapidly and in good order.

One day at the NCO Club one of the tank commanders from the First Squadron approached the Angel regarding a transfer into his unit. Of course, the Angel asked what the problem was that he was having in the First Squadron. The Angel found out that his tank and another tank commander's tank had run together on a night problem. He had been read Article 31 of the UCMJ (Uniformed Code of Military Justice) regarding the situation. As an outstanding soldier and tank commander, he was bitter about this for he did not know what the investigation might include.

Well, the Angel needed an outstanding tank commander to train and motivate the other tank commanders in the 58th Engineer Company. The Angel spoke with the tank commander's

Sergeant Major and his First Sergeant. They agreed that he was an outstanding soldier and that a transfer at this time would benefit both the 14th Armored Cavalry and the 58th Engineers. The Article 31 investigation would be dropped by the First Squadron and the 58th would gain an experienced tank commander. This was great, for the 58th was the only unit in the 14th Cavalry that maxed the TCQC (Tank Commander Qualifying Course) at Grafenwehr, Germany by qualifying 100 percent of its tanks, the M60AI with dozer blade up front, as distinguished tanks. How proud the unit was of this distinct honor!

Shortly after the 58th returned to Fulda, Germany from its yearly training in timber trestle, bailey and pneumatic float bridges at Hanau, Germany, and at the reveille formation of the 58th Engineers, the buses with the CMMI and the AGI inspection team pulled into the 58th's area. The Angel knew it was time for the reinspection. The Angel figured he had the unit in shape, but he still kept his fingers crossed. The inspection was going extremely well when one of the Platoon Leaders, a recently assigned Second Lieutenant, came running into the orderly room without knocking. He, in a shouting tone of voice, said that a trooper had gone berserk in the arms room and was threatening anyone who tried to enter. The Angel excused himself and walked very quickly to the arms room, and without thinking knocked the trooper cold as a cucumber. He put the 45 automatic pistol back in the rack and dragged the young trooper out into the hall. The inspection party was coming into the far end of the hall so the Angel dragged the trooper into a squad room and put him into a wall locker.

The next day the 58th was scheduled for an inspection in ranks. It was going very well when the inspection party stopped in front of the trooper who had gone berserk the preceding day. The inspector asked the trooper what had happened that his jaw was swelled up to about three times its actual size. The trooper stated that he had fallen down the steps in the building last night. The inspector told him to report on sick call as soon as the inspection was complete and moved on to the next trooper in ranks. The Angel gave a sigh of relief. After the inspection had terminated, the Angel sent for the trooper via the company runner to have him report to the First Sergeant in the orderly room. The First Sergeant thanked the trooper and then informed him that it would probably be better to start board proceedings to get him out of the army, he was just too unstable to be a career soldier. This was a hard thing to tell the trooper as the Angel had been the one to bring him into the army in the first place. However, the trooper agreed that the board procedure would probably be the best for everyone involved. The Angel also talked to the Second Lieutenant, man to man, and told him that he was the troop's leader and he should have been the one to take action. He would not always have a senior NCO to get his rear end out of the fire.

When the report of the outcome of the CMMI and the AGI inspection came back through channels the 58th was given an "outstanding" in all categories. The Angel had accomplished what he wanted in less than 90 days. The 58th Engineer Company had gone from unsatisfactory to outstanding in all areas of the inspection.

The Regimental Commander called the Angel to his office and thanked him profusely for shaping up the unit. He also informed the Angel that a Captain was en route from the United States and he would be assigned as the commander of the 58th. He also stated that he had been assigned to a post that should assure him a promotion to a one star rank. Yes, the "Old Man" was going to be a flag officer and that was great news for the Angel. However, the Angel was not happy about losing his patron, for to get things done in short order the Angel had stepped on a few toes and he knew that once the Colonel was gone, the dogs would start circling. This included the Sergeant Major, the personnel NCO. Oh well, thought the Angel, omnia vinci labor (duty overcomes all things).

Yes, one of the dogs that would be circling when the Colonel left would be the Sergeant Major for he had come to the Angel once to furnish men to build a garbage rack behind Post Headquarters. The Angel said that this was a Post Engineer job. The Sergeant Major agreed, but stated that the S4 office and the Post Engineer had a falling out and the Post Engineer had placed this last on his priority list of work to be accomplished on the Downs Barracks area.

The Sergeant Major now said that the 58th would do this. The Angel said they would, just as soon as his unit had finished the training they were now taking in shortening the time it took for his troops to make their target run, especially the ADM (Atomic Demolition Platoon). The Angel also said, that with the proper training and rerouting of access roads, they should be able to cut

15 minutes off of their target run. The Sergeant Major just did not hear the Angel and like a little boy who had been denied candy, stomped around in a childish anger. The Angel, in the presence of the Sergeant Major called the S3 (Operations and Training) officer and put the choice to him. The S3 said, "Target Run" and that was what the Angel did. However, when the Angel's troops returned from the target run, he had a squad from the 58th work on the garbage rack. The Sergeant Major considered this too little, too late.

When the Angel took over the 58th in the field at Hanau, Germany, he found that a large number of his non-high school graduates had been denied the right to study for and to be administered the high school level GED (General Education Development) test. It seemed that there had always been one reason or another that they could not take the test. The Angel checked this out with the Personnel Sergeant, who said that it was too much trouble, that most of them could not pass the test anyway. The Angel considered this extremely poor reasoning and said so to the Personnel Sergeant. He then stated that he could not get slots for them to take the test. The Personnel Sergeant also tried to argue that transportation was also a problem, getting the troops to V Corps in Frankfurt and returning them. The Angel said that his unit would furnish the transportation for any trooper in the first and provisional squadron who wanted to be administered the GED. The Personnel Sergeant then flatly stated that he would not have orders cut for them to take the test. The Angel then stated that if he would not get off his Air Force ass and the get the job done that he would do it for him. The term "Air Force ass" was because the Personnel Sergeant recently had been discharged from the Air Force and had reenlisted in the army. The Angel called a friend of his in the testing section at V Corps and made arrangements for his troopers to take the GED. He also used some of his college personnel to teach them the basics they would need to comprehend the test. He then trucked them to Frankfurt for the test. Most of the troopers passed, a small percentage would have to retake the test in time. This simple procedure lifted the morale of the unit to a new height. The troopers now knew that the Angel could and would go to bat for them. Because of this situation, the Personnel Sergeant now had a case of the ass for the Angel and this would come home to roost in time.

The way it came home to roost was very simple. The Personnel Sergeant stopped reporting a promotable slot for a 121.87 MOS (Military Occupation Specialty) as being vacant and at that time promotion was luck, being in the right place at the right time. Oh well, for the good of the troops it was worth it for the Angel.

Shortly after the new company commander reported into the unit he called the First Sergeant, the Angel, into his office and informed him that he was going to submit a request that the Angel be awarded the Soldier's Medal for the incident in the arms room during the CMMI and AGI inspection. A couple of days later he called the Angel into his office and told him that he could not submit the request because it would make the young officer of the soldier's platoon look bad for not taking action on the day the young trooper had gone crazy. Well, you win some, you lose some, and some get rained out. The Angel would just continue to march.

Subsequent to the CMMI and the AGI inspection, things slowed down to a routine, border duty, training and a high standard to maintain. Of course, there were small things that would happen anytime you get 280 young and vigorous men together 24 hours a day. Some things are just bound to happen. Some are humorous and some not so humorous.

In the 58th Engineers we had one enormous and muscle bound draftee from Memphis, Tennessee. This AFQT score was not high enough for him to re-up as a regular. This soldier was usually mild mannered and, because of his size and strength, no one messed with him. Therefore, the Angel was surprised when his phone rang one night about midnight and he was told that this soldier was running amuck on the third floor of the billets. He was turning over foot lockers and wall lockers and in general tearing things up. The Angel told the NCO who was in charge of quarters that his job was to see that the billets were maintained in good order. The Angel was surprised when the Charge of Quarters told him that he was afraid of the man.

The Angel said that he would be right over in a few minutes as his quarters were only about 100 yards from the billets. When the Angel arrived at the orderly room the CQ said that the soldier was still raising hell up on the third floor. The Angel then went to the A and R room (athletic and recreation room) and picked up a ball bat. He then proceeded to the third floor. He then ordered the soldier that was raising hell to get into his sack (bunk). The soldier stated that no one there could make him go to bed, whereas, the Angel swung the bat just over the soldier's head and put a large dent into a wall locker. The Angel then said the next one would be right over the bridge of his nose. The soldier was not too drunk or too dumb to reason and he knew the Angel would do as he said. The drafted soldier then said that his first shirt (The Angel) was the only man he respected in the unit and, if need be, he would go with him through hell. But right now he was getting into his sack as his first shirt had ordered. The ruckus was now over. The next morning, the Angel had him sign a "Statement of Charges," for those things he had destroyed the night before. The soldier caused no more turmoil in the unit and was an outstandingly well-behaved soldier until he was shipped back to the United States for discharge.

On another occasion, the Angel was called to report to the Provost Marshall's office as one of his men from the 58th was caught coming through the fence that surrounded Down's Barracks. The Angel asked the Provost Sergeant if the soldier was caught after curfew. He shook his head in the negative. The Angel then asked the soldier why he had not gone through the gate, for as he remembered, he had seen the soldier pick up a pass and sign out in the orderly room after duty on that day. The soldier broke into a big grin and said, "By golly, that is right, I did. I'm legitimate." He then told the Angel that he was so used to coming through the fence that he had forgotten he had a pass. They all had a hearty laugh and the Provost Sergeant released the soldier to the Angel.

Not all humorous things had to do with soldiers. On occasion, something funny or serious could originate with a dependent: either the wife or the child of a career soldier. One incident the Angel is especially cognizant of happened to his wife. His wife, a shy, good-looking girl from a farm in Wisconsin, was at her wit's end one day when the Angel came home after a routine duty day. She met the Angel at the door and said, "Angel, I think I'm in trouble."

This was her story. A couple of dependent children were playing in the quarter's garbage bin. The Angel's wife had told the youngsters not to play in the garbage bin because she had seen a two headed rat in the bin. In playing in the garbage one of the boys cut his finger on a used razor blade. He and the other boy ran home and told their mother that the one boy had been bitten by a two headed rat. This caused the mother to panic and she called the Provost Marshall, who in turn called the veterinary officer. When the MPs cordoned off the quarter's garbage bin and the soldiers from the veterinary office started spraying the area, the Angel's wife asked what was going on? When told, she realized it was her story that had started all this commotion. Therefore, she became scared. The Angel had a laugh and let the matter die of its own accord.

The Angel had a good working relationship with the Provost Sergeant and when one of his troopers did something out of the ordinary, the Provost Sergeant would ask the Angel first. Usually, between the two of them, they could settle whatever infraction came to the fore.

On one call, the Angel had to sign for one of his young NCOs, a trooper who had made Buck Sergeant on his first enlistment and was celebrating his promotion by eating the flowers in the Fulda City Park. He was down on his hands and knees grazing like a cow. It was good for a fine to cover the expense of the flowers and to satisfy the Burgermeister of Fulda.

A week or two later this soldier's friend, also a young Buck Sergeant, was caught paddling a flower pot down the Fulda River. The flower pot came from the end of one of the bridges across Fulda River.

Not all events were as humorous as the above things. Another young Buck Sergeant was living with his wife on the economy. He was anxious to soak in the culture of Germany and therefore, lived off post at his request. One night after his duty was finished, he was at home taking out the garbage when a gang of German young men, who were anti-American in feeling, beat and stabbed him violently and ruthlessly outside his apartment. This gang was never identified and that was probably a good thing. The Angel believes that members of the 58th would have taken vengeance against them, for the troopers of the 58th talked and would have carried out a process of retaliation against these hooligans.

Every winter would come a training maneuver called "Winter Tract." Elements of the Second Armored Division would take over the responsibilities of the 14th Armored Cavalry Regiment and of the 58th Engineers. It was a maneuver that the Angel looked forward to. However, there were trying times. On one occasion, the Angel was happy that he had accepted the tank commander from the First Squadron. A light mist was falling as the 14th and the 58th were closing on one of their bivouac areas; it was dark and the Angel would not allow the tanks to move or change positions without a ground guide. The Angel was acting as ground guide for the leading tank commander when they came to a down grade on the cobblestone street or road. There was a bank on each side of the road. The Angel did not realize that a film of moisture had formed over the cobblestone and frozen. The tank started sliding was out of control. The Angel tried to get out of the way by going up the bank, but they were icy also. The tank continued to slide toward him. Now the experience of the tank commander came into play. He dropped the dozer blade on the tank. It caused some maneuver damage, but probably saved the life of the Angel.

On changing from one bivouac order to another one morning during "Winter Track," the Angel briefed his troopers and informed them, that because of the icy conditions, not to stop the convoy on an upgrade, but stop so that the lead element should go four clicks (kilometers) beyond the top of the upgrade, thereby giving the last elements of the convoy plenty of space so they would not be stopped on an upgrade. This was because the ice would be difficult for the drivers and operators to keep their assigned vehicles from sliding into each other. Yes, you have probably guessed it, in charge of one element of the convoy was the officer who had failed to take action when the trooper went off of his nut in the arms room. Sure enough he tried to stop his serial of the convoy on a hill. The Platoon Sergeant, a well trained and self motivated NCO did not follow his request for stopping his serial on the hill, but did what the Angel had said in the briefing. When the second joker carried the issue to the CO, the CO called in the Platoon Sergeant and asked him why he had not gone along with the shave tail's request. The Platoon Sergeant told him that he had been told what to do by the Lieutenant and by the Angel and he sure as hell did not want the Angel mad at him. The CO said that he understood the situation and dismissed the Platoon Sergeant and in private came down rather hard on the Lieutenant.

About 90 days before his due date to return to the Continental United States the Angel received his orders for his assignment in the States. Yes, back to the land of the big PX. He was to be stationed as the career counselor at the Granite City Engineer Depot. It was a promotable slot. The Angel had been giving some thought to extending his tour in Europe. However, with his tiff with the Sergeant Major and the Personnel Sergeant, he knew his chances for promotion would probably not come until they both had rotated. With the plum of assignment he now had, he had better take it.

Then with about one month to go before normal rotation the Angel's orders were revoked and other orders were cut. The Angel had been out politicked again. Someone had slipped in and taken his plum assignment at the Granite City Engineer Depot and the Angel was now assigned to the Recruiting Main Station in Chicago. What a blow this was! Right then and there the Angel was giving himself two years to make Sergeant Major or retire.

The Angel chose to return to the states via surface transportation. He and his family returned on the USNS Darby. The return trip was like a vacation. The sons of the Angel were old enough to appreciate the trip.

When the Angel and his family arrived in New York, the first order of business was to pick up his automobile which had been shipped about a month before their departure from Germany. When they picked up their car, there was an area with the most aggressive auto salesman that the Angel had ever encountered. They would hang right on to your car. When they hung onto the Angel's car, he grabbed an arm of the salesman, accelerated to about 35 miles an hour and let the arm go. The last the Angel saw of the salesman he was rolling in the street. Perhaps he wouldn't be so aggressive to the returning soldiers from now on. Surely, he had been taught, and, the Angel hopes, learned a very good lesson.

The Angel was determined to make a vacation of the trip from New York to Chicago. Therefore, he took the northern route through Canada and returned to the States at Sault St. Marie, Michigan. At customs coming back into the States, the Angel had some trouble because of the German plates or Armed Forces license plates on the car. Finally, after a discussion, he was allowed to proceed. The trip continued until they arrived at his wife's parents' home in Nekoosa, Wisconsin. It was a good visit, but all good things must end so at the end of his delay in route time, the Angel reported into the RMS in Chicago.

On his interview he was told that he would be stationed in Chicago. The Angel informed the CO of the RMS that he was or at least did not intend to live in Chicago and have his two sons which were teenagers, attend school there. He reminded the Lieutenant Colonel in a polite manner that he was Airborne and

Special Forces qualified and that if necessary, he would ask for a reassignment to a parachute unit. The CO of the RMMS looked surprised, but did answer that he had a recruiting station open in Sterling, Illinois. However, this slot would not put the Angel in a promotable situation, and he would not be promoted until the centralized promotion system was on line and working. The Angel knew that this would be a very hard area to recruit in, as it was an area of outstanding farms and high paid jobs in the steel mill. He also knew and was told that the last half dozen recruiters in Sterling did not meet their quotas and had been reassigned out of recruiting. The Angel, always sure of himself, was sure he could produce. It would be difficult, but he could do it.

The Angel took the Sterling, Illinois Station, and moved his family to Rock Falls, Illinois, just across the Rock River from Sterling. It was difficult, but he met quota each and every month subsequent to his assignment.

Rock Falls had an outstanding high school and the boys of the Angel did extremely well there. They both blended well and were accepted as leaders in the high school. While in Rock Falls, it was the junior and senior years of the eldest boy, Mike and the freshman and sophomore years for the youngest, Pat.

During the second semester of Mike's junior year, he initiated the correspondence for appointment to the United State Military Academy at West Point, New York. It was an extremely happy day in the Angel's household when Mike's appointment (Presidential) came through and he was accepted as a cadet at West Point for the Class of 1971. Oh, happy day! How could you have it better, than to be paid to attain probably the best education in the country?

By this time, the Angel knew that he would probably not be promoted to Sergeant Major in the time space he had given himself a couple of years ago. So the thing to do now, was to start setting things up for the coming retirement. He had come into the military as a high school drop-out, back in 1943 and the military had been good to him. He had taken and passed the GED for high school, and the CLEP test for two years of college. He had taken several courses by extension from different universities. He had been an on-campus student at the University of Kansas and the University of Missouri. However, he still did not have a bachelor's degree. So, when he retired that would be the first order of business. Along about February or March of 1967 the Angel very reluctantly applied for retirement from the US Army on August first of that year. He did this with a very heavy heart and with 22 years, 8 months and 22 days of honorable service. He had practically been raised in the military. He had been Navy and Army and now he was ready for the challenge of life as a civilian. This transition would not be very difficult for the Angel had several years of assignments off-post and in a civilian community; and he had replaced himself with his oldest son entering the Academy at West Point in July of 1967.

As time drew near for the Angel's retirement things started cooking that would happen in the near future. Centralized promotions would be up and running within a year, and in October the military would receive the largest pay raise that it had ever had. The Angel considered withdrawing his retirement. Then after giving it good thought, he would not become a victim of a follower of the carrot on a stick. It would cost him a promotion and money, but what the hell, he knew that whatever he did he would wind up in the top 10 percent.

When Mike's enrollment date to report to the Military Academy rolled around, the Angel loaded the Volkswagen with those things he would need and drove him to West Point. The Angel's last night with his son until that Christmas was at the Thayer Hotel on the Academy grounds. The Angel was extremely proud of that boy, no not a boy, he was a man now. The next morning, the Angel walked with his son up the hill to the reporting area. He shook hands with him and told him not to let him down and allowed him to proceed through the courtal gates. On the other side of the gate, the Angel heard an upperclassman shout, "Drop that bag bean!" The Angel smiled for he knew that Mike was in good hands. By the end of the first day they had started to look like a military unit and not like a group of civilians who did not know the uniform of the day.

Now the Angel could start planning for his retirement which was less than a month away. He was contacted by Fort Sheridan, Illinois, regarding his retirement parade. In a line unit this would have been an honor, but at Fort Sheridan it was lumped into the regular routine, therefore, the Angel did not request a parade. The Angel did request that the troops be given that time as free time for a long duty-free weekend. Did they follow through with his request? He never found out, but doubts that the power to be allowed a duty-free Saturday morning. After all, he was 125 miles away from Fort Sheridan. The recruiters in his area of responsibility did give the Angel a very nice retirement party in Rockford, Illinois. They even rented a room for the Angel so that he would not have to drive back to Sterling, Illinois, all bent out of shape. Even the recruiters from the other services got in on the party. The Navy recruiter said that the Angel was the only person he knew that could sell refrigerators to the Eskimos. Of course, the comment was made in jest and good humor. Well that was it, the last hurrah! At 00.01 hours on August the first 1967, the Angel was now a member of the retired reserve. If recalled, it would be after the pregnant women and crippled men had been depleted!

THE UNIVERSITY YEARS

Prior to being retired from the US Army he had sought and gained admission to two different universities: one in Missouri and one in Wisconsin. He was accepted at both places for the autumn semester of 1967. The thing that tipped the scales toward Wisconsin was the fact that his father-in-law was ill with what would be diagnosed as cancer of the lungs. Therefore, the University of Wisconsin at Stevens Point was the one he would enter. The Angel had elected to strive for an undergrad degree in education.

After being a student in several military schools the Angel found the course work to be not nearly as challenging as the military schools had been. Therefore, he could carry a full load without any trouble. After all, he was not there to become a professional student, but to get a degree so he could become a productive teacher and civilian citizen.

Because of his age, 38, the students in his classes looked up to him for leadership. The Angel was more or less the link between teacher and student. The young students in many cases were afraid to approach their professor with a grievance of any kind fearing that it would affect their GPA (grade point average). The Angel was more than happy to intercede for the student if it was a true and not an imagined grievance on the part of the student. Most of the faculty mentors were fair; however, a few were completely egocentric, to the point of becoming mentally unstable. As in most colleges and universities there was then and still remains a tighter supervisory control over their teaching faculty.

The Angel having picked up excellent study habits while attending military schools breezed through the curriculum that would lead to his sought-after degree in education.

One thing that did bother the Angel somewhat was the fact that over the years he had completed about 90 semester hours in such places as the University of Kansas and the University of Missouri. When he entered the University of Wisconsin at Stevens Point they disallowed about 30 semester hours of credited courses work. They indicated that in some cases the work was not relevant to the degree the Angel was striving for, and in some areas they just said that it had been so long since the Angel had taken the course that he would have to retake it. After all, in American Military History the Angel had been making it since

1943. The instructors really became angry when, on some subject they were teaching, the Angel would inform them that it was not as they were teaching and that he knew, because he was there.

The Angel found out that he would have to do one semester of student teaching. After having taught in several military schools, it seemed rather silly to waste the time being a student teacher just to be certified by the State of Wisconsin. The Angel could understand why a person who had never taught any subject would be required to student teach, but one who had many hours and days or even years on the platform teaching, it was just to extract tuition money. However, even though it was a foolish thing, the Angel went along with the established procedure of the university.

The Angel was assigned to two schools in Wisconsin Rapids. Each school would have him for eight weeks. He did eight weeks at Mead School and eight weeks at Howe School. During the time that he was doing his student teaching, the principal at Mead Elementary School called the Angel into his office and asked him if he would consider teaching in the Wisconsin Rapids school system. The Angel indicated that he surely would, and the principal stated that he would ask the Superintendent of the system to hire him and assign him to Mead School. He later told the Angel that the superintendent had concurred with his request and that the contract would be forthcoming. The Angel filed this information in the back of his head and continued to teach after properly thanking the principal. It was just another 4.0 semester.

At the end of the student teaching semester, the Angel received his Bachelor of Science degree in Intermediate-Upper Elementary education. He also applied for and received his certification to teach from the Department of Public Instruction, State of Wisconsin. Again, Oh Happy Day! Now all he had to do was await the contract from the superintendent's office. He waited and waited, but no contract was forthcoming. The school year came to an end and still no contract from the Wisconsin Rapids school system. The Angel was being solicited by other school systems throughout the state to sign a contract with their school system. Finally, the Angel received an outstanding contract offer from the Elkhorn, Wisconsin, school system.

With this contract in hand, the Angel walked into the Wisconsin Rapids superintendent's office and very politely informed the superintendent that he wanted very much to teach in Wisconsin Rapids, but that they would have to beat the Elkhorn offer if they wanted him. They would have to draw up the contract that day for his signature. It was now or never with them. The superintendent said that the starting salary in Wisconsin Rapids was below what the Angel would start at in Elkhorn. The Angel let him know that if he could not meet or beat the salary stated on the Elkhorn contract that he would go to Elkhorn.

The superintendent excused himself saying that he would only be gone a minute, that he had something he had to check on. In a few minutes he returned with a contract in hand that gave the Angel five years of teaching in military schools. This brought the starting salary in Wisconsin Rapids over the salary that had been offered by Elkhorn. The Angel signed the contract and left the office with a copy of the contract in hand. The Angel did notice that his assignment would not be to Mead School, but to Children's Choice School; this did not bother the Angel as a sixth grade is a sixth grade anywhere. The actions and problems are in general the same for all 11 and 12 year olds.

Yes, the Angel was extremely happy and he considered blessed. He had an extremely good contract to teach and his younger son, Pat, had received his appointment to the United States Military Academy at West Point, New York. Pat had received his appointment in December of 1969 and would be entering the Class of 1973 at West Point in July of 1969. Did the Angel make the right move by retiring from the US Army back in 1967? Yes, it was definitely the right move. Everything was neatly falling into place. Deo Gratias (thanks to God), Deo Juvante (with God's help) and Deo Volente (God willing), everything was falling into its proper place and the Angel was an extremely happy and lucky individual. How could life be better?

THE TEACHING YEARS

During the summer, the Angel met the principal of Children's Choice School. He had an outstanding rapport with the gentleman and knew after the first time he met him that there would be no friction between them. He was a no-nonsense and well thought of type of individual. He had his ticket fully punched as an educator for he had been a teacher for many years longer than he had been a principal. Therefore, there were very few problems that he had not had a prior experience with. He was children-oriented and believed in teaching with a firm but fair and demanding philosophy toward education. The principal was a student of philology. He had never ceased in his study of literary texts in order to determine their authenticity, meaning, etc.

The first year of teaching sixth grade youngsters came easily to the Angel. However, there were a few things that transpired that first year. It was a time of the parents getting used to the Angel as a teacher and of course, the Angel had to get used to and get to know the parents.

To start with that first year the Angel had 37 students in a room designed for a maximum of 25. The Angel had to go down the rows of students sideways. A 12-year-old youngster in his or her fast grow period does not know where their hands or feet are on a daily basis. The youngster who yesterday could stretch without hitting someone or something will a day or two later hit someone or something. At 11 or 12 years of age, they just do not know where their body parts are on a day by day basis. This, of course, caused a problem on occasion because the youngster hit would strike back.

Then of course, any new teacher in the building will be tried, for the youngsters want to know just how far they can go to get by with an infraction of the school rules and regulations.

The Angel must admit that some of the mothers did not enjoy having a former "A" team commander in the "Green Beret" teaching their child. They figured that all "Green Beret" soldiers must be murderers. I guess they thought that the Angel was going to bowl down the hall using the students head as the bowling ball. However, the majority enjoyed the fact that their youngster had a man for a teacher. This was especially true by the fathers of the students.

On one occasion, during that first year of teaching, the Angel had a situation arise that called for discipline measures. Using a rubber band, a student shot a staple across the room that struck a young lady very close to an eye. When the Angel was correcting the situation the young man resorted to a stream of profanity directed toward the Angel. The profanity would have made a preacher blush. The Angel using a hands on procedure and, using just enough force to control the situation, sat the boy into his desk seat. The Angel then requested a meeting with the parents of the boy for after school that very day. The principal, the Angel and the parents of the boy were present in the school office that day after school. The Angel noticed that the parents of the boy were becoming very belligerent. The parents had the same belligerence that the boy had displayed that day. The father, at the urging of the mother, continued to say that anyone who put a hand on their son would have to expect to take a beating from him. The Angel, after hearing this at least a half dozen times and becoming more angry each time he heard it, finally said, "I've heard all of this I want to hear. I sat your boy down by using my hands to guide him into his seat and thereby stopping a bad situation that the boy had caused. Now, if you truly believe what you are saying over and over, well, just cut your dogs loose and we will have at it right here and now."

The mother and father stormed out of the room and the Angel never saw the father again. However, the mother did show up for student conferences. The Angel knew that this woman had attempted to stir ill-will against him, but had not succeeded. As time went on, the parents of the students in the sixth grade came to like and to trust him in the teaching of their children.

All problems did not have the stress factor that the above mentioned one had. Some were just downright funny.

Things were moving along rather well at Children's Choice School when the Angel received a letter from his youngest cadet son. Pat was coming along well, Beast Barracks was over and he was doing well as a plebe, or at least as well as could be expected of a plebe. In his letter he had one request. Pat wanted me to write to Mike, who was now an upperclassman or a cow, and to tell him not to come and visit him anymore that year. It was not that he disliked his brother, it was just that every time an upperclassman came into the plebe room all the plebes had to hit a brace and follow any lawful order the upperclassman may ask of them. Pat's peers had been pressuring him to get his brother to stop coming to visit him. The Angel dutifully followed Pat's instructions. It was another problem solved. Now Pat could continue to march without peer pressure.

During the first year of teaching in the Wisconsin school system, the Angel noticed some teacher resentment toward the system. The teachers, in general, considered themselves underpaid and overworked. They felt that the student teacher ratio was completely out of whack. This resentment continued during the year and was the main topic of conversation in the teacher's lounge during lunch period. Failure to work these issues out via teacher, administrator, committees or some manner, and the teachers' lack of input into the learning process as it existed in the Wisconsin Rapids school system brought about a teacher strike during the second year that the Angel was in the system. The strike lasted about two weeks and finally ended in a compromise situation with both sides accepting the compromise but neither side happy with the outcome of the strike.

The Angel, always one to get involved with the politics of any situation, was elected as President of the WREA (Wisconsin Rapids Education Association).

The Angel knew that there was a great amount of animosity remaining between the teacher organization and the school administration. With the help of some other outstanding and devoted teachers, the Angel was able to come up with a contract for the year that was acceptable to both sides.

It was during the third year that the Angel was in the system that the animosity between the two sides boiled over again and brought about another strike. It was no fun to walk the picket line at 30 to 35 degrees below zero just to get the message across to the public. The majority of the public was with the teachers; a small percentage could care less, they just wanted school to open; and a very small percentage were with the side of the administration. The Angel was in charge of the picket line at Children's Choice School and he never had a problem getting teachers to walk the picket line. Of course, to keep them warm and happy he always maintained a thermos that contained brandy, honey and very hot water. Like the Angel says, he had no trouble with volunteers to walk the picket line and they were happy; some would stay on for two or three shifts. One of the things that was accomplished was to bring the teachers closer together with a feeling of comradeship that had never existed in the school system prior to the strike. This strike ended via a court order and a fine. However, this was later overturned and the fine returned to most of those who had been in the area when the injunction was served. Because this tended to split the teachers to those who received the money and those who did not, it was decided to take this returned cash and to create a scholarship fund for students going to college and working for a degree in education. You see, the money was put to the very best of use. The teachers who held out to the very last at Children's Choice School were the Angel and the physical education teacher. Actually, the students did not miss time from the school year as the lost time was made up at the end of the year.

By now, the parents' esteem for the Angel was outstanding. They knew he was firm, fair and friendly. The youngsters enjoyed the stories he told and referred to him as the "Ole Story Teller." This was the carrot on the stick procedure. When all assignments were in on time, he would tell them a story. If one or two students were slow getting in their assignment work, peer pressure would bring them around. It worked like a charm. Actually, there was not a great deal of difference between being a First Sergeant and teaching a sixth grade. The Angel as the leader had to produce the incentive for self motivation with a soldier or the sixth grade student.

After a few years of teaching the old tried and true principal of the school finally tossed in the towel and retired. This was a true loss to the system for he was one of the last "old school" principals. He was respected by the teachers and parents alike. His replacement, a young man just out of school himself, just could not do the job. He was one of those floating three to five year administrators. A year of a gung ho attitude, one or two years to find him out and a year to get rid of him. Many of these are floating around in the school systems, going from place to place. They make it through life until retirement by not doing their job and in general, wind up better off than the devoted teacher who puts 30 to 40 years in the system. Certainly, there should be more teachers approached for positions in administration than presently exists. So much for preaching.

The Angel always enjoyed taking his class on a field trip. It is an outstanding way to study the personality of the youngsters. On one trip to the zoo and museum in Milwaukee, Wisconsin, the students had a great time and a good learning experience. On the way back to Wisconsin Rapids, we stopped at a McDonald's in Madison for the youngsters to eat. One boy kept asking the Angel when it was going to get dark. To the Angel, this was a red flag. On returning to the bus, the Angel noted that the boy had switched seats and was now sitting with a girl. The Angel took a seat directly behind them and waited. They were whispering in each other's ear.

The Angel very quietly reached around the seat and very gently found the boy's hand. He squeezed it gently and let it go. The boy sat up very straight and froze with a look straight ahead, for he thought it was the girl who had squeezed his hand. The next day at school, the Angel said to the boy that he must like this certain girl. The boy blushed bright red and then it dawned on him what had taken place. He stammered out, "Mr. Angel, that was you that squeezed my hand wasn't it?" The boy knew he had been had.

In the classroom the Angel knew that the attention span for a sixth grader is about 20 to maybe 25 minutes. Therefore, if the class had been working hard, about every 20 minutes or so the Angel would use a little comic relief to break the tension and allow them to start anew on their project. He might tell them a short story, sing to one of the young ladies, break into a dance or dance with one of the girls. Those things were very good tension breakers and would bring on blushing faces and laughter. The class enjoyed these antics and they did not take away, but enhanced the learning procedure.

One morning the Angel came into the building and the secretary stated that someone had been trying to reach me. She stated that she had four or five calls from the same person but when she asked to take a message, the caller would hang up. While he was standing there, the phone rang again and the secretary handed me the phone. The call was from the principal of Mead School welcoming the Angel to the Mead staff for the coming school year. It was all right by the Angel but he did not know why he had been assigned to Mead School. It must have been the sorry excuse he had for a principal at that time. Therefore, the Angel just continued to march. The change did not bother him for he knew he could teach anywhere and any subject. However, when the parents of the sixth graders for the current year and the parents of the fifth graders who would be coming to the Angel's classroom the coming year got together, the fur would fly. First, they asked the Angel if he wanted the change. He said that he was happy at Children's Choice School but that he could teach anywhere he was ordered to. The ladies then organized a group to march on the superintendent's office and find out why the change had come about. The end result was that the Angel remained at Children's Choice School. This was a great and wonderful feeling for the Angel, to have the parents of students demand that the Angel wouldn't be transferred to any other school in the district.

During recess and lunch periods, the Angel could usually be found on the school playground playing games with the youngsters. He sometimes wondered what it would be like if a member of his "A" team in Special Forces (Green Beret) would drive by and see him playing hop-scotch with the children from the kindergarten class or the first graders. After all, in Special Forces, the Angel had been known as "Mean Gene of the Green Machine." It was just a thought that would pass through the Angel's mind on occasion.

The third principal that the Angel served with was an "old timer" in the Wisconsin Rapids School system. He was a low-key type of individual that was always seeking the path of least pressure. He had been a teacher for many years before becoming a principal. Therefore, he knew the problems that existed over a period of time in the classroom. He was extremely easy to work with and in general, gave the teachers a free reign in their area of knowledge and training. However, if a teacher was called before the superintendent, he was not much help. It was his philosophy to take care of himself first and he did a very good job of doing just that.

The Angel learned very early in his teaching career to talk in complete sentences and be sure you were understood by your students. Early on, with such a class overload, the Angel insisted that the students keep their feet under their desk so the classroom aisles would be clear of any obstruction. One boy had a hard time doing this. As the Angel was teaching and using the aisles, he told the boy, in a stern voice, to "Get under the seat." After saying this, the Angel continued with his teaching. The class now broke into loud laughter. When the Angel looked around he found the reason for the laughter. The boy who had his feet in the aisle had followed the Angel's command to the nth degree. He was now sitting on the floor under his desk. The Angel had to laugh also. After all, you cannot be angry with a young man who follows the teacher's directions.

After serving with the principal who had been brought up to his position from within the district, we the teachers were used to his faculty meeting and other meetings that came about. If the teacher asked for guidance in something they wanted to do in the education procedure, this principal would say that he or she could do it, but if he was ever called before the superintendent, he would deny that he had allowed the change in teaching methods. When he retired, I suppose one would have to say that he was an extremely likeable gentleman who was somewhat lacking in areas of command. Here, one might just say that this gentleman was liked very much within the community.

Teachers have a way of having little points of enjoyment that keep them interested in what they are doing at the time. The last day of school every year was usually a lighthearted day of waiting around to check out for the year and taking care of small things just to remain occupied throughout the day. One of the teachers in the building would usually make a large bowl of punch to drink throughout the day. The Angel, always one to have fun, did on one occasion, bring in four bottles of vodka and on the sly, emptied them into the punch. He noticed that more trips were being made to the punch bowl that year. The teacher who made the punch was just glowing from the positive comments they made to her about how good her punch was. By noon of that day, they were an extremely happy group of teachers. Many of them asked the maker of the punch for her recipe for making the outstandingly good drink. However, the little game the Angel had played almost backfired on him.

Along late in the day, the local law enforcement officer stopped by to wish us a good summer and in general just to "bat the breeze." While there, he mentioned that he had just received a new Breathalyzer and would show us how it worked. Naturally, he picked the Angel to demonstrate. The Angel tried to get out of the situation but the officer insisted, so the Angel agreed. The officer said that he would demonstrate by having the Angel blow into the thing and then he would give him a drink of brandy and retake the test. The Angel blew into the thing and the meter read .05. The officer said that he just could not understand the reading. Without the intake of alcohol, it should read .00. He said that it was a good thing we had caught this error because now he would have to recalibrate the Breathalyzer. I am sure he did not have the slightest idea that the punch was spiked.

The last principal the Angel worked with was an import into the Wisconsin Rapids school system. Again, we had a principal that was an extremely likeable person, but on occasion, he did not practice what he preached. He indicated that he was a consensus type of principal that would operate on what the group considered proper. The truth was that as long as the consensus of opinion went his way, he was a consensus man. But if the group did not agree, his opinion took precedence. Therefore, there really was no need for a meeting and discussion—it was going to be his way in the end. We teachers understood the situation, so we would agree with him right off the bat and get the meeting over with in short order. The Angel liked and enjoyed the man very much, but as a true leader, he fell a little short.

That is, of course, if one defines a leader as "one who can take you through hell and make you feel happy you took the trip." The Angel must say here that many in education administration fell short in leadership ability when measured by the above yardstick for a leader.

The Angel was now approaching as much time in the teaching profession as he had served in the military. For some reason, his mind could not fathom putting more time in education than he had served in what he considered his prime profession. So, with 22 years of teaching, the Angel applied for retirement. After all, he had taught at Children's Choice School, in the same room, at the same desk, since 1969. For some reason, it just felt as if the Angel should be getting orders to go somewhere and those orders just would not come.

The ceremony for the Angel's retirement had three phases. First, the youngsters that the Angel was teaching and the students he had taught gave the Angel a retirement party that he will never forget. Along with the party, came a large pencil drawing of the Angel. It was all framed and bore the title of "The Ole Story Teller." Second, came a party that was thrown by his teaching peers. This made the Angel extremely happy—to be recognized by your peers is one of the greatest honors one can have bestowed on him. Third, came the party given by the Wisconsin Rapids education system where the school administrators presented the Angel with a plaque in recognition and appreciation for his service to the Wisconsin Rapids school system. It almost made the Angel withdraw his retirement request. However, once the Angel had made up his mind to do something, like retire, he would not backtrack. So, it was on to retirement, with a tear in his eye.

THE POST RETIREMENT YEARS

The Angel slipped into retirement very gracefully. Being fully retired gave him time to do the things that he always wanted to do, but not be pressured into trying to do them all at once and in short order. He could now take long walks by Lake Petenwell. He found a spot by the lake that no one came around. This became his "think spot." It was a place to formulate and carry out plans that he made. In short, it was his spot.

Prior to retirement, he had considered moving back to Missouri or northwest Arkansas. After all, he had entered the service a long time ago, in 1943, and except for visiting, had not been around Stanton, Sullivan or Franklin County since then. He found out that he now knew more people in the town's cemetery than he knew who were still alive. The town's honky-tonks had, a long time back closed, moved or burned down and those he knew did not at this time frequent the honky-tonks of today. It is said that one cannot go back and the Angel began to believe that saying.

The Angel, who at one time knew almost everyone in Franklin County, attended church one Sunday and out of a full congregation he found only three people that he knew. How sad he was at this time. Gradually, he came to realize that he would probably be better off if he remained in Wisconsin. He was sure this was what his wife wanted also. After all, he could always return to the Ozark Mountains for vacation.

The Angel also noticed that he could very easily tell if he met one of his ex-students at a concert, at the mall or at the library. Those who knew the Angel, but had not been a student of his, would address him by his first name but to the ex-students, it would be Mr. Angel.

One very humorous thing happened at the mall in Wisconsin Rapids. The Angel was soaking in the wisdom of the elders on the "old man's bench" while his wife shopped. During this time, about 20 young, beautiful ladies stopped and shared verbiage with the Angel—you know, time of day, what are you doing now, etc. After about 20 had come by and stopped to talk, one of the old men on the bench, with a confused look on his face, asked the Angel, "Just what kind of business are you in anyway?" He did not seem to believe the Angel when he said that they all had been his students while they were in the sixth grade.

The Angel is now completely retired. Even when called to the phone at home and asked if he would work as a substitute teacher if the system needed one, his answer was no. In fact, it was heavy on the no side. After all, retirement was so great that every day felt as if it was Sunday. It was an outstanding feeling not having to report to anyone but the Internal Revenue Service.

THE BEGINNING OF THE END

The Angel considered himself the luckiest man in the world. He had grown up wild and free as a boy. The Angel had entered the military underage, which allowed him to retire from the United States Army at an early age. He had truly enjoyed the military profession. However, even while in the service of his country, he had marched to his own drummer. The Angel had been in many a dangerous situation and had always come out on top of the heap.

Along the way, the Angel had picked up an education that caused him to earn a Master's degree in education and had attended several higher education systems. He had been fortunate that education came easy for him.

The Angel, along the road of life, had married a beautiful and completely desirable woman as his wife. His admiration for her would never wane. She was as much a part of the Angel as his right arm.

He had two extremely outstanding sons. Both had graduated from the United States Military Academy at West Point, New York. Both boys had a Master's degree from the University of Arkansas; one in Foreign Affairs and one in Industrial Systems Analysis. One son had retired as a regular army 20-year length of service retirement. The other son had completed eight years as a regular army officer, had given up his regular commission for a reserve commission and had completed enough time to qualify for a retirement income at age 60.

Both sons have outstanding families. Each had two girls and one boy. All of the grandchildren are good looking and intelligent. They are the pride and joy of the Angel.

The Angel is proud of the fact that he had been able to teach in Children's Choice School in Wisconsin Rapids for 22 years. He can truly say he enjoyed and liked every youngster he had the opportunity to teach. The Angel's breast swells with pride every time he hears of a student that he taught who is doing well in life. He likes to think that he played a small part in their success. The Angel also enjoyed the rapport he had with the parents of his students. With the exception of one or two old soreheads along the way, the parents were great.

Yes, it has been an exciting and wonderful way to pass through life. If the Angel was to live it all over again, there would not be many changes. The Angel wants the reader to know:

THAT THE END IS NOT YET!!

As the author gets closer and closer to that time when he receives his last formation on earth and is greeted by the great commander above, he will depart with this poem in mind. The author of this poem is unknown.

"Fiddlers' Green"

Half way down the trail to hell,
In a shady meadow green,
Are the souls of all dead troopers
    camped
Near a good old-time canteen,
And this eternal resting place
Is known as fiddlers' green.

Marching past, straight through to hell,
The infantry are seen,
Accompanied by the engineers,
    Artillery and marine,
For none but the shades of
    Cavalrymen
Dismount at fiddlers' green.

Though some go curving down the trail
To seek a warmer scene,
No trooper ever gets to hell
Ere he's emptied his canteen
And so rides back to drink again
With friends at fiddlers' green.

And so when man and horse go down
Beneath a saber keen,
Or in a roaring charge of fierce melee
You stop a bullet clean,
And the hostiles come to get your scalp,
Just empty your canteen,
And put your pistol to your head
And go to fiddlers' green.

Author unknown

213

ORDER FORM

Please send me a copy of this book, *Under Age Angel*.

Name _____

Address _____

City/State/Zip _____

Send _____ copies at $20.00 each

Sales Tax
Please add $1.10 tax for books shipped to Wisconsin addresses.

UPS Shipping
Please add $3.50 for the first book and $1.00 for each additional book.

Payment
Please send total amount in check or money order to:

James E. Richardson
1611 Apple Street
Wisconsin Rapids, WI 54494

....

ORDER FORM

Please send me a copy of this book, *Under Age Angel*.

Name _____

Address _____

City/State/Zip _____

Send _____ copies at $20.00 each

Sales Tax
Please add $1.10 tax for books shipped to Wisconsin addresses.

UPS Shipping
Please add $3.50 for the first book and $1.00 for each additional book.

Payment
Please send total amount in check or money order to:

James E. Richardson
1611 Apple Street
Wisconsin Rapids, WI 54494

ORDER FORM

Please send me a copy of this book, *Under Age Angel*.

Name _____

Address _____

City/State/Zip _____

Send _____ copies at $20.00 each

Sales Tax
Please add $1.10 tax for books shipped to Wisconsin addresses.

UPS Shipping
Please add $3.50 for the first book and $1.00 for each additional book.

Payment
Please send total amount in check or money order to:

**James E. Richardson
1611 Apple Street
Wisconsin Rapids, WI 54494**

···

ORDER FORM

Please send me a copy of this book, *Under Age Angel*.

Name _____

Address _____

City/State/Zip _____

Send _____ copies at $20.00 each

Sales Tax
Please add $1.10 tax for books shipped to Wisconsin addresses.

UPS Shipping
Please add $3.50 for the first book and $1.00 for each additional book.

Payment
Please send total amount in check or money order to:

**James E. Richardson
1611 Apple Street
Wisconsin Rapids, WI 54494**